China in World History

The
New
Oxford
World
History

China in World History

Paul S. Ropp

OXFORD
UNIVERSITY PRESS

2010

OXFORD
UNIVERSITY PRESS

Oxford University Press, Inc., publishes works that further
Oxford University's objective of excellence
in research, scholarship, and education.

Oxford   New York
Auckland   Cape Town   Dar es Salaam   Hong Kong   Karachi
Kuala Lumpur   Madrid   Melbourne   Mexico City   Nairobi
New Delhi   Shanghai   Taipei   Toronto

With offices in
Argentina   Austria   Brazil   Chile   Czech Republic   France   Greece
Guatemala   Hungary   Italy   Japan   Poland   Portugal   Singapore
South Korea   Switzerland   Thailand   Turkey   Ukraine   Vietnam

Copyright © 2010 by Oxford University Press, Inc.

Published by Oxford University Press, Inc.
198 Madison Avenue, New York, NY 10016

www.oup.com

Library of Congress Cataloging-in-Publication Data
Ropp, Paul S., 1944–
China in world history / Paul Ropp.
p.   cm.
Includes bibliographical references and index.
ISBN 978-0-19-517073-3; ISBN 978-0-19-538195-5 (pbk.)
1. China--History.   2. China—Civilization.
3. China--Civilization—Foreign influences.   I. Title.
DS735.R67 2010
951—dc22
2009051140

3 5 7 9 8 6 4 2

Printed in the United States of America
on acid-free paper

Frontispiece: Qing dynasty incense burner, stoneware with iron wash and glazes.
Freer Gallery of Art, Smithsonian Institution, Washington, D.C.:
Gift of Charles Lang Freer, F1900.57a-b

For CJ, Simone, and Silas

Contents

Editors' Preface

This book is part of the New Oxford World History, an innovative series that offers readers an informed, lively, and up-to-date history of the world and its people that represents a significant change from the "old" world history. Only a few years ago, world history generally amounted to a history of the West—Europe and the United States—with small amounts of information from the rest of the world. Some versions of the old world history drew attention to every part of the world *except* Europe and the United States. Readers of that kind of world history could get the impression that somehow the rest of the world was made up of exotic people who had strange customs and spoke difficult languages. Still another kind of "old" world history presented the story of areas or peoples of the world by focusing primarily on the achievements of great civilizations. One learned of great buildings, influential world religions, and mighty rulers but little of ordinary people or more general economic and social patterns. Interactions among the world's peoples were often described from only one perspective.

This series tells world history differently. First, it is comprehensive, covering all countries and regions of the world and investigating the total human experience—even those of so-called peoples without histories living far from the great civilizations. "New" world historians thus share in common an interest in all of human history, even going back millions of years before there were written human records. A few "new" world histories even extend their focus to the entire universe, a "big history" perspective that dramatically shifts the beginning of the story back to the Big Bang. Some see the "new" global framework of world history today as viewing the world from the vantage point of the Moon, as one scholar put it. We agree. But we also want to take a close-up view, analyzing and reconstructing the significant experiences of all of humanity.

This is not to say that everything that has happened everywhere and in all time periods can be recovered or is worth knowing, but that there is much to be gained by considering both the separate and interrelated stories of different societies and cultures. Making these connections is still another crucial ingredient of the "new" world history. It emphasizes connectedness and interactions of all kinds—cultural, economic, political, religious, and social—involving peoples, places, and processes. It makes comparisons and finds similarities. Emphasizing both the comparisons and interactions is critical to developing a global framework that can deepen and broaden historical understanding, whether the focus is on a specific country or region or on the whole world.

The rise of the new world history as a discipline comes at an opportune time. The interest in world history in schools and among the general public is vast. We travel to one another's nations, converse and work with people around the world, and are changed by global events. War and peace affect populations worldwide as do economic conditions and the state of our environment, communications, and health and medicine. The New Oxford World History presents local histories in a global context and gives an overview of world events seen through the eyes of ordinary people. This combination of the local and the global further defines the new world history. Understanding the workings of global and local conditions in the past gives us tools for examining our own world and for envisioning the interconnected future that is in the making.

Bonnie G. Smith
Anand Yang

Preface

My purpose in this book is to narrate the long history of China within the larger context of world history. At each step along the way, I will try to address these questions: How has the development of Chinese civilization compared with contemporaneous civilizations elsewhere in the world? What has China shared with other civilizations, and what are the unique or distinctive traits of Chinese civilization? What is the history of China's relations with cultures and peoples beyond its borders? How have foreign peoples—merchants, diplomats, missionaries, and soldiers—affected the development of Chinese civilization? What have been the most important changes and continuities in China's long history?

Today we think of China as the world's oldest continuous civilization. An identifiable and sophisticated Chinese culture emerged by 1500 BCE and has shown remarkable continuity in its language, cultural values, and social and political organization over the past three and a half millennia. A major question in the study of China is how such remarkable linguistic, political, and cultural continuity could be maintained for so long over such a large area. Why was China, alone among the early human civilizations, able to sustain political, cultural, and linguistic unity and continuity over an entire subcontinent through a period of three thousand years without the benefit of modern industrial technology?

Jared Diamond has noted that all the great civilizations except China's have been melting pots of many divergent peoples, languages, and cultures. And he insightfully adds that China began its early history as "an ancient melting pot."[1] That is, the area that defines China today began with a multiplicity of peoples, languages, cultures, and ethnicities, which, beginning in the second millennium BCE, came to be conquered, dominated, absorbed, marginalized, or pushed away by the Han Chinese people, who around 1500 BCE formed a sophisticated civilization with Chinese writing, bronze technology, an efficient and productive agriculture supporting large walled cities and towns, and powerful armies with crossbows, bronze spears, and horse-drawn chariots.

The distinctive patterns of Chinese social, economic, and cultural life have been profoundly influenced by the geographical setting of the East

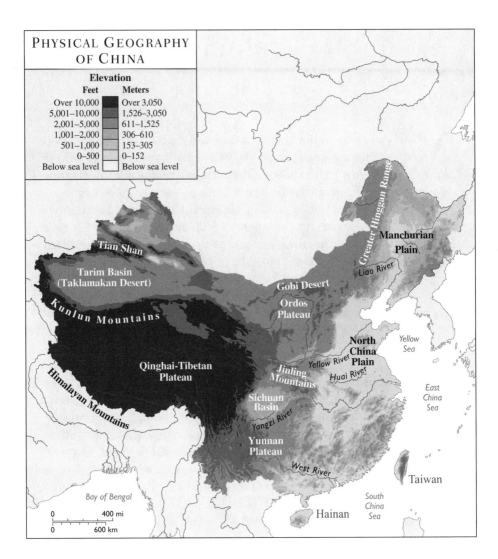

Eurasian subcontinent, which seems a logical starting point for this survey. For much of China's history, Chinese rule only included the eastern half of today's People's Republic of China (excluding much of Manchuria in the northeast, Mongolia in the north, Xinjiang in the northwest, and the Qinghai-Tibetan plateau in the west and southwest).

The eastern Eurasian subcontinent forms a kind of checkerboard of mountain ranges running north to south and east to west, surrounded by steppe lands, deserts, and mountains. To the north of China are the forested steppe lands of Siberia in the far north, the forested mountains of Manchuria in the northeast, and the arid flat grasslands of Mongolia in the north. To the west lie the barren stretches of the Gobi and Takla Makan deserts, and to the southwest the Qinghai-Tibetan plateau, with the world's highest mountain peaks. To the east the long coastline, with few natural deep harbors, has provided another natural barrier against potential external threats for much of the past three millennia. These peripheral regions of ocean, arid steppes, deserts, and mountains were natural barriers that helped the Chinese maintain relative political and cultural continuity over three millennia.

The geographical setting of China helped facilitate political unity by limiting external threats from beyond China's borders and by allowing greater ease of communication and transportation within China proper than with the outside world. Throughout China's history, the peripheral areas have been relatively poor and sparsely populated. Until recently, for example, only 5 percent of the People's Republic of China's population lived in these regions. Yet, as will become clear below, these peripheral regions have also been steady conduits of products, customs, and peoples into the Chinese political and cultural realm. Thus, geography has deeply influenced both the remarkable continuity and the profound changes in Chinese life over the past 3,000 years.

Within China proper, or what we might call Inner China, two great river systems—the Yellow River in the north, the Yangzi River in central China—wind their way from west to east, draining water from the Himalayan range and from the other mountains that separate the rivers into the Pacific Ocean. Both rivers have been key factors in the development of Chinese civilization.

The Yellow River of north China is so called because it carries enormous quantities of yellowish silt, the fine-grained loess soil that covers most of the north China plain. Blown eastward from the Gobi Desert over many millennia, and also deposited far and wide by frequent flooding, this "Yellow Earth" (sometimes a metaphor for China itself) covers some parts of north China to a depth of 80 meters (280 feet). Its natural fertility helped facilitate the early development of agriculture and the growing of wheat and millet along the Yellow River around 5000 BCE. Because North China is relatively dry (the Himalayas cutting it off from the monsoon rains of South and Southeast Asia), the Yellow River has remained too shallow in many places to serve as an effective shipping route. In the semiarid climate of North China, the Yellow River has been a key source of water for settled agriculture over the past four thousand years.

In central China, the Yangzi River carries far more water than the Yellow River and provides a major transportation and shipping artery through the center of the country. Abundant rainfall and subtropical temperatures in the Yangzi River valley make rice cultivation and double cropping possible. The same rainfall typically leaches fertility out of the soil in the Yangzi valley, but with the abundant application of human and animal wastes, and with the long growing season and abundant rainfall, the southern lower Yangzi valley has been the most prosperous part of China in the last thousand years. In the upper Yangzi, the Sichuan basin provides fertile and flat rice paddies watered with abundant rainfall and irrigation from many smaller tributaries of the Yangzi.

A third river system, the West River in the far south of today's China, also flows from the Himalayas to the Pacific, but it drains a much smaller area and has fewer tributaries than the Yangzi River. The far south of China, with its rugged mountains, thick tropical rain forests, and accompanying tropical diseases, was fully incorporated into the Chinese state only in the last thousand years. This region is also the home of the largest number of non-Chinese peoples, hill tribes, and ethnic minorities, many of whom originated farther to the north but were pushed southward by the expanding Han Chinese settlers, especially in the last millennium. The West River delta regions in southeastern China enjoy abundant rainfall and a year-long growing season that allows three crops a year. The four major centers of Chinese population today are the eastern plains and deltas of the three great river systems and the Sichuan basin in southwest China.

When looking at China in the context of world history, several distinctive Chinese traits stand out. Since the early emergence of civilization along the Yellow River, Chinese agriculture has been the most labor intensive and the most productive in the world. Wet rice production, for example, is extremely labor intensive and also extremely efficient in the numbers of people it can sustain per acre of paddy land. Thus, the very nature of Chinese agriculture provides a strong impetus for population growth. Throughout most of its history China has been one of the most densely populated areas on earth.

Some have argued that the labor demands of irrigation and water management have conditioned the Chinese to be a collective-minded rather than an individualistic people. Karl Wittfogel famously argued that this "hydraulic society" produced a unique form of "Oriental despotism," in which the needs of the ruler and the collective always took precedence over the needs and rights of the individual.[2] While most scholars today reject any simplistic geographic determinism, it is undeniable that the Chinese have long shown a keen interest, and great skill, in organizing people for specialized tasks on a large scale, whether for wet rice cultivation, bronze or pottery making, or the building of roads, dams, canals, and defensive walls.

Another strong continuity in Chinese civilization has been a respect for ancestors and an emphasis on family life organized in a patriarchal fashion, that is, with descent traced through the male line, the senior male assuming authority over everyone else, and males alone inheriting property. Royal tombs from as early as 1200 BCE reveal that ancestor worship was a key social practice at least among the political and social elite. When Confucius in the fifth century BCE praised filial piety as the foundation of all moral virtues, he was affirming values that were already centuries old.

A final distinctive trait that has been evident throughout the last four millennia in China is a tendency toward what I might call an optimistic humanism. Chinese thinkers have generally seen the universe as a friendly place and human beings as capable of steady moral improvement if not perfection. They have also generally seen all of human life and the entire cosmos as one interrelated whole where every single entity is ultimately related to every other entity. This holistic worldview is evident in most Chinese approaches to ethics, cosmology, society, government, economics, medicine, and history.

Cultural continuity will thus be a major theme in the history that follows. But cultural continuity is only one side of the coin in China's long history. Change is the other equally important factor. We should keep in mind, for example, that the geographical parameters of today's China did not take shape until the eighteenth century, less than 250 years ago. China's geographical boundaries throughout its history were constantly shifting, sometimes expanding and sometimes contracting. And contrary to the popular stereotype of China as isolated and unaffected by the outside world, China was frequently influenced in profound ways by the peoples and cultures beyond its borders, whether by armed nomads to the north and west, Arab traders traveling by the Silk Route or by sea from the Middle East, Indian traders and Buddhist missionaries from South Asia, non-Chinese peoples including Koreans and Japanese in the Northeast, Vietnamese in the Southeast, Tibetans in the Southwest, and hundreds of hill tribes in what today is south and southwest China.

I cannot give a detailed picture of every phase of Chinese history in this short book, but I will try to cover the essential developments in each period, with special attention to the ways the Chinese people lived and viewed their world. I will also try to situate these developments within the context of world history, noting parallel or contrasting developments elsewhere, and paying particular attention to Chinese contacts and interactions with other peoples and places. The sorry history of imperialism in modern times has made the Chinese (and the rest of us, too) more self-consciously nationalistic about their (and our) country and its past. As Victor Mair has noted, modern nationalism and narrow academic specializations everywhere have led historians today to downplay international, interethnic, and intercontinental contacts and influences, especially in earlier times.[3] The popular assumption of Chinese (and many Western) historians has been that China developed its unique form of civilization without many outside influences or contributions. I will challenge this assumption directly. I believe it is no denigration of Chinese genius or ingenuity to note how often the Chinese have borrowed institutions, inventions, products, and procedures from non-Chinese outsiders, sometimes willingly and sometimes reluctantly or by force, but all the while adapting them all to Chinese purposes.

China in World History

CHAPTER I

The Formative Age: Beginnings to Third Century BCE

In the 1920s, at a village called Zhoukoudian, twenty-seven miles southwest of Beijing, a team of Chinese and Swedish archeologists ignored the occasional gunfire of warlord armies competing for control of north China and patiently excavated a cave at a place the peasants called "Chicken Bone Hill" because of the many small bones in the hill's red clay soil. Their work was amply rewarded with one of the richest discoveries (beginning with a single tooth in 1921) of the remains of one of our earliest human ancestors, known to the world as Peking Man. These early human ancestors occupied the cave at Zhoukoudian from roughly 400,000 years ago up until 200,000 years ago. About five feet tall, Peking Man (and Woman) hunted and cooked wild animals, used sharpened stone tools, and had a brain capacity about halfway between that of great apes and modern human beings. Peking Man's primitive existence, half a million years ago, is a vivid reminder to us that human civilization has taken a very long time to develop.

Somewhere between 10,000 and 8,000 years ago, people in what today is north and central China began to develop settled agriculture, paralleling similar developments in Mesopotamia and parts of Africa and South America. Through domesticating animals and growing their own food, especially millet (a dry land cereal grain) in the middle Yellow River valley of the north and rice (which requires wet fields) in the Yangzi River valley to the south, people began to evolve more populous and complex societies. The climate during this era was warmer and moister than it is today, which no doubt contributed in helping people first discover the miracle of growing their own food.

By 5000 to 4000 BCE, a number of Neolithic settlements were scattered throughout what we call China today. Two of the best documented of these, from around 3000 BCE, are known as the Yangshao, or painted pottery culture, in the northwest and the Longshan, or black pottery culture, which developed at about the same time and extended from the northeast down the coast all the way to today's Vietnam. The Longshan people made beautiful tools and ceremonial objects of jade, a very hard mineral that can only be shaped with abrasive use of sand and metal drills requiring a great deal of time and energy. Because of its hardness and its lustrous green beauty, jade has been seen as a precious stone in China from the late Neolithic up to the present day.

Out of these Neolithic cultures organized in villages there eventually arose, between 2000 and 1500 BCE, more highly developed societies in which people specialized in different kinds of productive occupations. Farmers produced enough food to support a non-agricultural population that included artisans who produced non-agricultural goods, administrators who collected taxes and set rules and regulations for society, and soldiers who defended or expanded the territory under the government's control.

In contrast to many other societies, the early Chinese accepted the world and human existence as facts of life that needed no supernatural explanation or divine creator. They assumed the world was a friendly place, and they credited advancements in civilization to human beings, not to gods or divinities. This optimistic humanism became one of the distinctive aspects of Chinese thought and culture up to modern times. It stands in sharp contrast to the ancient Greek fascination with tragedies, to the jealous tribal God of Judaism, Christianity, and Islam, and to the elaborate metaphysical speculations of Indian mystics.

Among the most important cultural heroes in China's earliest historical records were three "sage-kings," Yao, Shun, and Yu, who were known particularly for their virtue and their loving concern for the welfare of their subjects. Yao passed his throne on to Shun rather than his own son because Shun was clearly superior to all others in his devotion to the public welfare. Shun, in turn, chose as his successor an engineer, Yu, who tamed the floods of China's major rivers. In this early conception of the state, rulers were seen as analogous to parents, and the state was seen as the family writ large. Having established prosperity by taming China's rivers, Yu passed on his political authority to his own son, thus beginning what came to be known in the historical record as the Xia dynasty, traditionally dated 2200–1750 BCE. Around 1750, the Xia was overtaken by rulers of the Shang, which remained in power for about seven hundred years.

There probably was some regional power around 2000 BCE known as the Xia, but it has not yet been verified by the archeological record. In the 1930s, archeologists proved the historicity of the Shang dynasty by discovering its capital through an unlikely coincidence. During a malaria epidemic in 1899, drugstores in and around Beijing did a lively business selling "dragon bones," believed to cure the illness when ground up and served in a soup. One day a scholar of ancient Chinese culture was stunned to see on one of these dragon bones a very early form of Chinese writing. His discovery eventually led archeologists to begin excavations at Anyang, a source of these bones in the north central province of Henan. There they uncovered the tombs of the last thirteen kings of the Shang dynasty.

"Dragon bones" were in fact the flat undersides of turtle shells and the shoulder blades of cattle. The ancient writing on them came from the practice of divination or the consultation of ancestral spirits by the rulers of the Shang dynasty. Shang diviners first drilled a hole into the bone and posed a yes-or-no question to an ancestral spirit. When they inserted a red-hot bronze rod into the drilled hole, the intense heat made cracks in the bone. The diviners (Shang kings and their shaman-like advisors) then interpreted the configuration of the cracks to answer the question. Artisans then carved on the cracked bone the date, the name of the diviner, the spirit consulted, the question, and the answer provided. In this curious way, "dragon bone soup," whether it cured malaria or not, led scholars to discover Shang oracle bones, providing a unique window on early Bronze Age China.

Anyang, it turned out, was the Shang capital at the height of its power (around 1300–1000 BCE). In 1950, an earlier Shang capital, with similar archaeological findings, was discovered in Zhengzhou, directly south of Anyang. Today we have more than 100,000 oracle bones from Shang sites, and scholars have deciphered roughly 2,000 characters (also called ideograms), or about half of the known total. These are the earliest known examples of Chinese writing. In addition to oracle bones, the Shang also produced large numbers of bronze vessels of remarkable artistic quality that were used in sacrifices to the dead.

Bronze technology marks the birth of Chinese civilization. An alloy of copper and tin with a small amount of lead, bronze requires first the location, mining, and refining of the appropriate metal ores, followed by the smelting of the three metals in exact proportions at very high temperatures (over 1,000 degrees Centigrade). In contrast to the Mesopotamians, who produced small quantities of forged or hammered bronze perhaps five centuries before China, Shang bronze makers mined abundant deposits of copper and tin ores to cast molten bronze in huge quantities and in highly sophisticated designs.

Bronze technology was a hallmark of both the Shang and (its successor) the Zhou societies, and some vessels were inscribed with

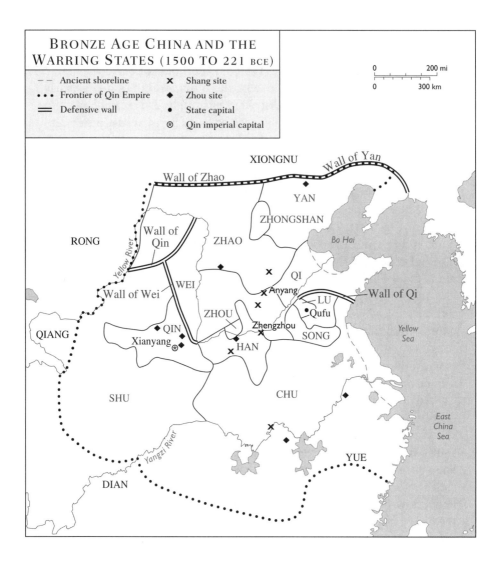

information about their sacrificial purposes. The technology involved a complex sequence of carving a negative model of the outside of the vessel, putting it, in several pieces, around a clay core (which outlined the inner surface of the vessel), and then pouring hot molten bronze between the inner core and the outer piece molds. Once the molten bronze cooled, the piece molds were removed, and the result was a bright, luminous vessel that was then smoothed and polished. Many items were made of bronze, including hair ornaments, weapons such as daggers and spears, and horse harness fittings, but the most common early bronze objects were sacrificial vessels (for wine and food) used to pay one's respects to the noble deceased ancestors of the Shang (and Zhou) kings, or to commemorate military victories or the appointment and installation of vassals and officials of the royal family.

The most lavish tomb findings from Anyang to date are from the tomb of Lady Hao (Fu Hao), one of sixty-four consorts (or wives) of the Shang king Wu Ding (reign ca. 1215–1190 BCE).[1] Whereas most other Shang tombs were at least partially looted long before

This bronze zun, or ritual wine vessel, in the shape of two rams is from the thirteenth or twelfth century BCE. Such cast bronze vessels, used by royal families primarily in sacrifices to ancestral spirits, required the large-scale mining of copper, tin, and lead, smelting the ores at 1000 degrees centigrade, and the design of complex negative molds in clay. The Trustees of The British Museum, British Museum, London, Great Britain / Art Resource, NY

This Shang oracle bone inscription explains that the diviner asked if Lady Hao's childbearing would be good if it came on a certain day. The result, also recorded on the bone, was that her childbearing, in the end, "was not good," as she gave birth to a girl. From the collections of the Institute of History and Philology at the Academia Sinica, Republic of China

the twentieth century, Lady Hao's tomb, though smaller than many, was discovered completely intact in 1976, yielding 3 ivory carvings, 468 bronzes (weighing about 3,500 pounds and requiring 11 tons of ore to produce), 500 bone hairpins, 590 jade objects (from sources far beyond Shang control), and nearly 7,000 cowry shells (from the sea coast), which were used as money. From oracle bone and bronze inscriptions, we know that Lady Hao was King Wu Ding's favorite consort and that she led Shang troops into battle and performed oracle bone divinations herself.

Shang bronzes and oracle bones reveal the Shang as a very hierarchical society in which some were slaves and servants at the bottom, many were illiterate farmers, menial laborers and craftsmen, and a few were privileged aristocrats who lived and died amid great wealth and splendor. The elite in this society paid careful attention to the care of dead ancestors, on the assumption that kings who were powerful in life were even more powerful in death. Thus, survivors filled the graves with bronze sacrificial vessels, and kings were accompanied in death by their servants, slaves, mistresses, and animals such as pigs and dogs, all sacrificed to join them in their large and lavish tombs. Most of the human victims buried in Shang tombs were military captives. When Shang military officers in horse-driven chariots led a few thousand foot soldiers into battles with hostile neighbors, they often returned with captives who then became slaves or were killed and buried with high-ranking members of the Shang nobility. Some royal tombs contain chariots and horses that were also sacrificed to accompany the deceased.

While the Shang was only one of several advanced societies in the Yellow and Yangzi River valleys with enough agricultural surpluses to support an elite ruling class and artisans who crafted sophisticated weapons and ceremonial bronze and jade artifacts, only the Shang produced Chinese writing. Written Chinese is both a powerful and efficient means of communication. Because spoken Chinese has only about 400 distinct syllables (in contrast to about 1,200 in English), many Chinese words are homophones that sound alike but have distinct meanings. Written Chinese allows for these homophones by creating a unique character for every word. Characters are not just arbitrary lines; some are pictographs, such as *mu* 木, for tree, or *nü* 女, for woman (derived from the archaic pictograph suggesting a kneeling figure, 女). There are also ideographs suggesting concepts such as one 一, two 二, three 三, up 上, and down 下.

And many Chinese characters are made up of compound components such as 好 a woman and child, meaning good, or 安 a woman under a roof, meaning peace. In addition, many characters have a phonetic component that indicates pronunciation and another component, called the radical, that signifies meaning. The following characters are each pronounced *ma* and include the component 馬, which means horse. Adding a mouth radical 口 creates the particle 嗎, which has a function similar to that of a question mark at the end of a sentence; with a woman radical 女, it becomes the character for mother 媽; and a jade radical 玉 makes the character for a kind of quartz 瑪.

Because this written language is so powerfully symbolic, it is adaptable enough to accommodate spoken dialects that are mutually unintelligible, even to accommodate different languages altogether. Native speakers from south China, for example, pronounced Chinese characters so differently from northerners that the two typically could not communicate in their spoken dialects, but they both wrote and read the same characters, so they could communicate easily in writing. Thus, written Chinese, rooted in the Shang dynasty, has been a powerful unifying force throughout the long political history of China, helping to unite north and south, east and west, in one political system. Eventually, Japan, Korea, and Vietnam all adopted Chinese characters into their written language, even though their spoken languages were completely unrelated to spoken Chinese.

Shang rulers were deeply concerned with ancestor worship, another custom with a very long history in China. The kings and their divination specialists or advisors conceived the afterlife as a mirror image of the hierarchical society they had organized in this life, and they saw their own dead ancestors as ranked in a hierarchy of power after death, with more distant ancestors being more powerful. Shang kings and diviners appealed to a "Lord on High" (Shangdi) whom they saw as the most powerful spirit of all, able to control rain, thunder, wind, and to harm or protect the Shang state and society. They addressed oracle bone inquiries and made frequent sacrifices to deceased ancestral spirits, the only intermediaries who could communicate directly with the Lord on High. The deceased ancestors depended on the living for respect, wealth, food, and drink, and in return for these the deceased conferred blessings on their living descendants. These rituals sometimes took dramatic form, as a young person would channel the spirit of an ancestor, drink much sacrificial wine (millet ale), eat lavish food, and thus inspired, report directly to the living from the world of the dead.

The Shang ruling house controlled several walled city-states with its own troops and ruled a much larger area indirectly through its allied vassals and soldiers. These allies recognized Shang power as supreme and were allowed to administer their own territory while supplying the Shang center with annual tribute payments in goods, crops, or military aid. The extent of Shang political power is not entirely clear, but archaeological finds have demonstrated that sophisticated bronze technology was spread far and wide across much of what we know as China today. An elegant six-foot high bronze statue of a man contemporaneous with the Shang was discovered in 1986 in Sichuan (near Chengdu), far beyond any direct Shang influence. This site in Sichuan contains jades, extraordinary bronze masks, and axes of many kinds, all just as sophisticated as anything found at Anyang, but without any evidence of writing.

Shang contacts with other cultures ranged far beyond the Yellow River valley. Hundreds of preserved corpses or mummies of an identifiably Caucasian people were recently discovered in the Takla Makan Desert of Xinjiang Province in China's far west. These tall people (men up to six feet tall) with round eyes, large noses, light skin, and light (including blond and red) hair date from 2000 to 500 BCE and clearly indicate that Caucasian people lived in Central Asia even before the Shang dynasty. The graves of these mummies, well preserved in the dry desert air of the Tarim Basin, contain plaid textiles resembling those of Celtic Europe. These people, unknown to the modern world even twenty years ago, seem to have ridden horses and used horse-drawn chariots.

They might help explain how the chariot came to China, as it appears in the Shang archeological record suddenly in its fully developed form around 1200 BCE. China's first wheeled vehicle, the chariot, was introduced to the Shang polity from the Caucasus where it was developed several centuries earlier. Domesticated horses probably came to the Shang from the Mongolian steppe, and the military use of the chariot required skilled artisans to build the chariot, and skilled horse trainers and charioteers who were probably non-Chinese originally. The chariot provided military leaders and archers with unprecedented speed and mobility.

Around 1045 BCE, a former Shang vassal from the west, the Zhou people, invaded and conquered the Shang capital. The Zhou worshiped *tian,* or Heaven (literally the sky) which refers not to a particular place but to the whole cosmos as a benevolent force that helps right prevail in human affairs. Portraying the last Shang kings as oppressive, immoral, and irresponsible, Zhou scribes argued that Heaven therefore blessed the Zhou conquest and bestowed on Zhou leaders the right to take over Shang territories and rule in their place. This was the origin of the Mandate of Heaven (*tianming*), the notion that Heaven aids a virtuous ruler and grants him the right to rule over his people, a concept still popular in Chinese political culture today.

There is far more written documentation on the Zhou period than on any earlier era. Zhou texts credit three men in particular with the military and political success of the early Zhou state: King Wen, King Wu, and the Duke of Zhou. They praise King Wen (the Cultured King) for his blueprint for the Zhou conquest and for creating the Zhou ideal of the compassionate ruler concerned for the people's welfare. They laud King Wu (the Martial King) for presiding over the defeat of the Shang forces and establishing Zhou power in the Yellow River valley. And they praise the Duke of Zhou, the brother of King Wu, for taking over as regent for his young nephew, King Cheng, when King Wu died prematurely. While the Duke of Zhou was suppressing several rebellions against Zhou rule, he spelled out for the first time the idea of the

Mandate of Heaven, and he acted only in the interests of King Wu and his son, and never tried to seize power for himself. More than any other official, the Duke of Zhou was the special model of heroic government service later held up by Confucius and his followers.

While the Zhou texts described the Shang as a large state ruling "all under Heaven," so as to claim similar status for the early Zhou, it is clear that both the Shang and Zhou were actually regional powers among a variety of competitors. We might call them "soft states,"[2] with permeable boundaries and loose alliances with many different peoples, and with alliances based more on gifts and ritual exchanges than on taxes or formal lines of authority. Yet, whatever the degree of idealization in early Zhou sources, their very abundance and the reverence surrounding them have assured that the cultural values associated with Kings Wen and Wu and the Duke of Zhou were central to the ideals that came to dominate Chinese political culture for more than 2,000 years.

In many aspects of culture and technology, the Zhou had already assimilated much from the Shang by the time of the conquest, including the use of chariot warfare, writing, and bronze. Like the Shang, the Zhou rulers presided over a sharply hierarchical society, and established a decentralized political system in which regional overlords and vassals (usually relatives by blood or marriage) ruled outer territories on behalf of the Zhou kings and received Zhou protection in return for regular contributions of crops, money, and soldiers to the Zhou court.

In some ways, the Zhou made significant advances over the Shang. Human and animal sacrifices gradually disappeared, and written texts in the Zhou became much longer and more sophisticated than any surviving writing from the Shang. Consultation of oracle bones gave way to a more sophisticated system of divination based on an ancient text called the *Book of Changes* (*I Ching* or *Yijing*). As with the tortoise shell diviners, one approached the *Book of Changes* with a question already in mind. This type of divination incorporated a whole philosophy of change in human affairs and in the cosmos, assuming that change is inevitable in all situations of life, that change occurs according to unchanging principles, and that human beings have freedom to act, but only within the constraints of particular given situations and contexts. The *Book of Changes* is not simply about maximizing one's power, wealth, or influence; it urges ethical behavior in every situation on the assumption that moral behavior brings good results and immoral behavior will only hurt others and oneself. The Chinese have long seen the work as one of the most profound in their tradition.

While most of our documentation from the Zhou reflects the life of the elite, some poetry in the *Book of Songs*, a revered collection of 305 Zhou poems, illustrates the hopes and fears of the common people as well as the concerns of the court. This folk song, for example, reflects youthful love in conflict with parental authority, a theme that runs through much of Chinese literature.

> I beg of you, Zhongzi,
> Do not climb into our homestead,
> Do not break the willows we have planted.
> Not that I mind about the willows,
> But I am afraid of my father and mother.
> Zhongzi I dearly love;
> But of what my father and mother say
> Indeed I am afraid.[3]

In 770 BCE the Zhou capital of Hao was conquered by two former Zhou vassals, who in alliance with several tribal peoples rebelled and killed the Zhou king. Those of his courtiers who escaped the city reestablished a new Zhou capital city near today's Luoyang, several hundred miles to the east. Thus, we call the period from 1045 to 770 BCE the Western Zhou period, when Zhou rule was supreme through much of north China. The period from 770 to 256 BCE we know as the Eastern Zhou, which is further subdivided into the Spring and Autumn period and the Warring States period, named after two histories of the era. *The Spring and Autumn Annals* and its detailed commentary, *The Zuozhuan* (The Zuo Tradition), report the declining effectiveness of Zhou rule during these years, as former Zhou vassals in outlying areas became more and more independent. Similarly, *The Intrigues of the Warring States*, a collection of (often fictionalized) anecdotes, describes interstate conflict and competition from 403 to 221 BCE, giving that period the apt name of the Warring States, when the Zhou court held power only in a tiny enclave surrounded by larger states including Chu to the south, Wei to the north, and Qin to the west. The Zhou realm was finally extinguished entirely by the powerful Qin in 256 BCE.

During the turmoil of the Warring States period, independent states mobilized large numbers of commoners to build walls, dams, dikes, and irrigation canals and by these means to increase agricultural productivity dramatically (growing millet, wheat, soybeans, and rice) in order to support standing armies of up to several hundred thousand. Iron gradually came into general use, permitting the development of more lethal weapons, and eventually (by the third century BCE) rulers began drafting thousands of able-bodied peasants as foot soldiers who replaced the old Shang and early Zhou forms of warfare led by aristocrats in chariots. Old chivalrous codes of warfare, in which one state would not attack another during a period of mourning, or until its enemy had troops in place, gave way to a much more ruthless style of battle with no holds barred. In the chilling opening words of the ancient classic *The Art of War* attributed to Sunzi (which probably dates from the mid-fourth century BCE and is still read today in military academies and business schools), "Warfare is the greatest affair of the state, the basis of life and death, the Way (Dao) to survival or extinction. It must be thoroughly pondered and analyzed."[4]

As local lords became increasingly independent and Zhou kings lost their aura of authority and power, more states began to use laws and contractual agreements (instead of marriage and kinship alliances) to keep peace and order, and a multistate system gradually emerged. With ever greater investments in warfare, rulers began to recruit soldiers and officials on the basis of their skill and organizational abilities rather than their noble birth. In the intense competition for resources and military power, many rulers and officials gradually lost faith in the old religious beliefs of the Shang and early Zhou. It became increasingly clear that a state's capacity to mobilize armed, disciplined, and well-fed warriors determined the outcome of battles far more than any ancestral spirits.

There were at least 148 small states in the eighth century BCE, but by about 400 BCE only seven major states remained, along with several small ones that managed to survive by allying with powerful neighbors or playing their larger neighbors against each other. During this time, every state sought out the best political and military advice it could find, and everyone understood that the surviving states were engaged in a lethal competition for control of ever larger areas.

In the Chinese Warring States environment of change, uncertainty, and increasing insecurity, a variety of Chinese thinkers traveled among the competing states and debated the central questions of the day: What is most important in life? What makes a human being? How should humans live in families and communities? What is the cause of social, political, and military strife and unrest? How should human society be organized? Who has political authority and why? And perhaps most important, at least for many kings or would-be kings, how can I conquer the world? In striving to answer these and other questions, the thinkers of the late Zhou period presided over one of the most creative eras in all of Chinese history, commonly known as the period of the Hundred Schools of Thought.

By far the most successful and influential school of thought during the Warring States period was the Legalist School (*fajia*). Legalist doctrines were developed in several different states over several centuries, and Legalists both guided and responded to many of the technological and organizational innovations of the period. In the ambitious western state of Qin, rulers abolished serfdom (where peasants were bound to the land and owned by a lord) and assigned land directly to peasant families, whom they taxed, taking a percentage of their crops. They drafted peasants as soldiers; promoted soldiers and officials on the basis of merit rather than birth; and enacted strict laws with harsh punishments on the theory that the harsher the punishment, the less it would have to be used. The Legalist rulers of Qin organized their entire state toward agricultural production, increasing trade, and the mobilization of all economic resources in the service of war.

Born in 551 BCE, Kongzi, whom we know as Confucius,[5] deplored these changes and called upon rulers to return to the beliefs and practices of the early Zhou. Confucius reflected some of the changing attitudes of the day as well, such as the growing emphasis on competence rather than birth in choosing officials. He was essentially a private teacher and accepted students from all social backgrounds. Agnostic about the existence of ghosts and spirits, he saw religious rituals and ancestral sacrifices as needed by the living, to express respect and gratitude for their dead forefathers. He made no claims to have any supernatural powers and modestly said that he only loved to study the wisdom of the ancients so that he could pass on the best of his civilization's heritage to future generations. He also had a sense of humor, remarking at one point, "The fact remains that I have never seen a man who loved virtue as much as sex."[6]

Confucius hoped to convince rulers to adopt his idealistic vision of benevolent rule based on early Zhou rituals and reverence for ancestors. He argued that the most basic human quality is our capacity to empathize with each other, a quality suggested by the virtue of *ren*, variously translated as humanity, benevolence, kindness, or reciprocity.[7] All people have the capacity for kindness, he asserted, but it needs to be nurtured and encouraged through education, ritual, and the emulation of virtuous models (including one's parents, teachers, and great moral leaders of the past). He wisely noted that people learn most not from reading books but from watching and emulating those around them. And he argued that in the proper hierarchical society, those in the lower positions learn how to behave from those above them. Thus, the most important quality for a king to have was virtue so that his subjects would naturally be inspired to serve him loyally and virtuously. Like Jesus five hundred years later, Confucius believed that virtue was powerful and contagious, but in the war-torn era of his time, he had difficulty persuading any ruler to implement his teachings. He never rose very high in any government and died in 479 BCE, feeling himself a failure.

More than a century after Confucius, Mengzi, known to the West as Mencius,[8] expanded on the optimistic idealism of Confucius by proclaiming unequivocally that human nature was good and that morality and ritual were more effective than any amount of brute force in motivating people to behave properly. Mencius was more of a storyteller than Confucius, and his collected sayings helped to popularize the values of Confucius through clever dialogues, colorful anecdotes, and short parables. To demonstrate the goodness of human nature, he argued that any person, upon seeing a child about to fall into a well, would automatically respond by trying to save the child, not through any ulterior motive but simply because humans naturally hate to see a child suffer. Mencius was more influential in his own time than Confucius had been, and he served as an advisor to two major states. He justified the steep social hierarchies of the day by saying it was right and just that those who work with their heads rule over those who work with their hands. Yet he also admonished kings and princes that the common people were more important than their leaders.

He interpreted the Mandate of Heaven as the natural working out of politics in which rulers who care for the people consequently win their support, whereas those who offend the people or exploit them will lose their support and fail. The Mandate of Heaven gives a king the right to rule, but, he reminded kings, quoting an earlier text, "Heaven sees with the eyes of its people. Heaven hears with the ears of its people."[9] The king's first duty is to attend to the welfare of the people. Mencius's unfettered idealism helped keep the Confucian tradition alive even as it continued to lose ground to the Legalist trends of the Warring States period.

In contrast to the idealistic Mencius, Xunzi, a slightly later follower of Confucius, actually served as a government administrator. He accepted many of the changes of the Warring States period and tried to make the ideals of Confucius relevant to the times. In contrast to the short declarations of Confucius and the dialogues and parables of Mencius, Xunzi wrote full-blown essays on self-improvement, government regulations, military affairs, rites and rituals, music, human nature, and

Heaven. Xunzi understood how much the state was changing in his own time, and he embraced the development of a complex bureaucracy of officials promoted and demoted on the basis of their job performance. He had seen enough of Warring States behavior to argue, against Mencius, that human nature is evil, in that people are inherently selfish. But Xunzi rightly regarded himself as a follower of Confucius. While recognizing the necessity and power of law and state authority enforced with a highly organized bureaucracy, Xunzi also saw Confucian rituals and early Zhou texts as effective guides to proper human behavior. He argued, as Confucius and Mencius had, that filial piety, one's love and respect for one's parents, was the most fundamental foundation for all other moral teachings and behavior.

At the forefront of the secular and rationalistic tendencies of his own time (at least among the elite), Xunzi gave a completely naturalistic interpretation of nature and its workings. When there were droughts, floods, or hurricanes, these were just the natural arbitrary workings of nature in Xunzi's view, not the supernatural intervention of Heaven or any divine being. The true omen or portent that signified the loss of the Mandate of Heaven was not a natural disaster but the state's failed response to it. Thus, while Xunzi accepted the large bureaucratic state based on the rule of law, he also argued forcefully that such a state could be guided most humanely and most effectively by the values of Confucius and Mencius.

While Legalists were steadily building up the lethal powers of the state and Confucians were urging the restoration of early Zhou idealism and the use of ritual in both families and governments, others were attacking both Legalists and Confucians from other angles. One group assembled around Mozi, a thinker who lived sometime between Confucius and Mencius and who argued that Confucians were wasteful in their emphasis on rituals, music, and ceremonies in honor of the dead. Mozi and his followers argued that rulers owed the people not elaborate ceremonies to awe them but the basic necessities of food, clothing, and shelter. The school's most original teaching was its call for "universal love," in which every adult bore equal responsibility for every child. The Mohists also made interesting developments in logic and the study of optics and motion (in part for the purposes of defensive warfare), but they failed to inspire followers for more than a few generations, and their call for universal love seemed puzzling and impractical to most Chinese.

A more long-lasting challenge to the Confucian and Legalist visions of society came from a group of thinkers we now know as Daoists, or the School of the Dao. Dao (Tao in some translations) means literally the Way, and it was used by Confucians and others to mean the way one should live, or the way rulers should govern. For Sunzi it meant the way of warfare. However in two enigmatic early Chinese texts, the *Daodejing* (or *Tao Te Ching*—The Classic of the Way and Its Power) and the *Book of Zhuangzi*, the concept of *dao* has cosmic implications and includes such meanings as the first cause of all things, the totality of the universe, the laws of nature and all creation, and whatever is unchanging and everlasting. To make matters more complicated, the *Daodejing* begins with the admonition "The Way (Dao) that can be told is not the constant Way; The name that can be named is not the constant name."[10] So this Way is the mysterious source of all things that can't be captured in words. Yet the *Daodejing* goes on to use 5,000 words to say a number of things about the Way in its eighty-one sections (some in poetic form and some in prose).

Attributed to the philosopher Laozi (who may or may not have existed), the *Daodejing* has long been beloved as a great work of literature by Chinese of every persuasion. In mystical poetry and cryptic prose, the author extols the Dao, harmony, and what is natural, and gives concrete advice on individual survival in a dangerous age and even military advice to would-be rulers.

The earliest known version of this work was found in 1993 in a tomb at Guodian, Hubei Province, dating from about 300 BCE. This text, the *Guodian Laozi*, consisted of seventy-one bamboo slips in three bundles, which included material from thirty-one of the eighty-one sections in today's *Daodejing*. Also in the tomb were more than six hundred other bamboo slips containing writings we would mostly associate with the Confucian school of thought, suggesting that the Confucian and Daoist schools of thought were not necessarily oppositional in their early evolution. The Guodian texts are quite representative of the overall gist of the later *Daodejing*, but not so explicitly anti-Confucian or anti-Mencian as later versions of the text. These findings lend credence to the view that the *Daodejing* was an anthology compiled by several anonymous hands over a century or more.

The general tone of the *Daodejing* is that rulers should not try to build a powerful state because the main principle of change in the universe is the reversal of opposites (unceasing alteration of *yin* and *yang*, as seen in the phases of the moon, the alteration of the seasons, and the endless cycles of human life and death). To become powerful is to guarantee one's fall. To remain weak and inconspicuous is to increase one's chances of survival. Nothing is softer or more yielding than water, or harder than rock, the author notes, but over time water erodes and triumphs over rock.

A second Daoist work, the *Book of Zhuangzi*, is a prose collection attributed to a philosopher of the same name (literally Master Zhuang, the polite name for Zhuang Zhou), who also may or may not have existed. The *Book of Zhuangzi* is the most original and inventive book in all of Chinese thought and literature. Full of satirical and whimsical flights of fancy, the philosopher Zhuangzi appears to challenge all assumptions of the Confucians and Legalists and all other schools of thought as well. Zhuangzi mocks with cynicism both the serious moral declarations of Confucian philosophers and the state-building strategies of the Legalists. One saying often attributed to Zhuangzi, probably erroneously but tellingly nevertheless, captures well his cynicism toward politics and still applies in surprising ways today: "This one steals a buckle and he is executed, that one steals a country and he becomes its ruler."[11]

According to the *Book of Zhuangzi*, all the philosophers of the Hundred Schools period were arguing over insignificant matters arbitrarily chosen to try to prove their cleverness, to gain favor with the powerful, or to win prestige in a shortsighted quest for fame and fortune. Zhuangzi told a story about a frog who lived in a well that he believed was the most beautiful and spacious place on earth. Yet when he invited the Giant Turtle of the Eastern Sea to join him, the turtle could not get even one foot into the frog's small well. For Zhuangzi, all the Warring States philosophers were frogs in their own little wells. They did not realize that the universe was a vast and wonderful place, and that humans were just one tiny aspect of reality and not very consequential alongside the sun, moon, and stars. He attacked everyone's values and arguments, but with such style, wit, and imagination that his book has been a favorite among educated Chinese down to the present day.

While Confucians lamented the decline of early Zhou ideals and early Zhou power and Daoists attacked Confucians and Legalists as self-righteous meddlers in people's lives, the Legalists proceeded to promote the changes that would end the Warring States period. The book that synthesized a variety of Legalist teachings into one systematic doctrine was the *Book of Han Feizi*, a chilling set of calculations of raw power, traditionally attributed to Han Feizi (Master Han Fei), a prince of the small state of Han in the third century BCE.

In contrast to most thinkers of the day who saw wisdom in the study of the past, Han Feizi argued that the past was dead, buried, and irrelevant to the needs of the present. Human nature is evil, he declared with confidence, and the only things that motivate people are promises of pleasure and threats of pain. Laws should govern everything, and there should be no exceptions. The ruler can trust no one, not even his wife and children, perhaps especially his wife and children, because they might have the most to gain by plotting against him. Rulers should be aloof, remain mysterious in the eyes of all people, and never let their own thoughts and feelings be known to others. Officials are mere tools of the ruler in the efficient organization of the state and the army, and they should be promoted and demoted solely on the basis of their effectiveness in carrying out their assigned duties. If an official failed in his duty or exceeded his duty, he should be punished equally in either case, because any "extraordinary service" was likely nothing more than a bald attempt to curry favor with the ruler.

In some ways, the *Book of Han Feizi* only summarized what was already happening in the Warring States period, but it spelled out more clearly than any other source how to organize a political, economic, and military machine devoted entirely to building the power of the state and its king. Its insights have proven remarkably prophetic (1,800 years before Machiavelli developed similar ideas in *The Prince*) in describing much of the functioning of the nation state in modern times.

In the dangerous era of the Warring States, political knowledge was both precious and dangerous, as illustrated by the historian Sima Qian, who told the following story. When Han Feizi visited the state of Qin, Prime Minister Li Si recognized his brilliance and had him imprisoned and forced him to drink poison, because he feared that if the King of Qin conferred with the Han prince, Li Si's own position might be threatened. In the end, in Sima Qian's view, Han Feizi's sad fate demonstrated the same sad truths he preached. If power was all that mattered, it was to be expected that the most brilliant Legalist thinker of all time might be killed by a rival in the name and the game of power.

Although the Legalists triumphed in wiping out all rivals to the Qin state in 221 BCE, their triumph resulted in a sophisticated imperial state system that ultimately ensured the survival of texts from most of the schools of thought in the Hundred Schools period. The rich ferment of ideas in the Warring States period was not as clearly divided into "schools" as later divisions between Confucians and Daoists and Legalists would suggest. For example, the writings found in Warring States tombs have consistently been eclectic, representing many strands of thought including Legalist, Daoist, and Confucian. The Confucian Xunzi once taught the Legalists Han Feizi and Li Si, and even strict

Legalists accepted the importance of rituals to legitimize state power. The Daoists, who satirized power-seekers and attacked the reliance on words to convey truth, used highly erudite words to make their case precisely to the power-seekers of the elite.

China was not alone in experiencing unprecedented levels of change and uncertainty during the early Warring States period (roughly 600–400 BCE). Great thinkers around the world responded to profound changes under way in their societies, including expanded trade in goods and ideas, the decline of earlier social and political structures, and the increasing reliance of states on iron weapons and standing armies. The writings of Confucian, Daoist, and Legalist thinkers and Mozi in China, the Hebrew prophets in Mesopotamia, the great Vedic scriptures of the *Upanishads* and the teachings of the Buddha and Mahavira (the founder of the Jain religion) in India, and Plato and Aristotle in Greece all subjected their societies' common beliefs and customs to the cold scrutiny of reason and challenged political leaders to pay more attention to the welfare of the common people. Despite contrasts in their approaches and ideas, they respectively laid the intellectual foundations for great new empires in Persia, India, China, Greece, and Rome.

Compared with these other societies, early China seems striking in the following ways: the strong emphasis on the family as the basis of civilization; the tendency to see the state as an extension of the family; the desire and ability to build a large-scale centralized bureaucratic state; and the emphasis on ancestor worship and belief in the wisdom of the past as a guide to the present and future (though the Legalists dissented on this point). Perhaps the two most distinctive aspects setting early China apart from ancient Mesopotamia, Greece, and India were (1) the assumption, at least among the literate elite, that the world's creation was simply given and self-perpetuating, not dependent on a divine power far above human beings, and (2) the tendency to see all things on Earth and in the cosmos as closely interrelated. In the Chinese view, the meaning of life could only be grasped by human beings through their own efforts and reflections on their own past.

CHAPTER 2

The First Empires:
Qin (221–206 BCE) and
Han (206 BCE–220 CE)

The Qin, like the Zhou before it, grew powerful on the Western fringe of what was then considered the developed world.
Whereas the central states were surrounded by potential and
real threats, the Qin had more freedom to develop its power uncontested
by strong neighbors. Another consequence of its relatively "backward"
status was that the Qin court did not have a wealthy and entrenched
nobility to contend with; thus it was much quicker to centralize power
than were its rivals. The Qin kings were much rougher types than the
aristocratic rulers of the other states. One Qin king reportedly died
from overexertion in a weight-lifting contest, an activity unimaginable
in a court fashioned in the Confucian mold.

The great buildup of Qin power began in earnest in 361 BCE with
the arrival in the capital of Lord Shang, a young nobleman defector from
the state of Wei. A shrewd and ambitious politician, Lord Shang quickly
gained the confidence of the Qin king and began to institute a series of
reforms to increase the power of the king and the reach and efficiency
of the central government. Lord Shang abolished hereditary feudal
ranks and made all ranks and titles dependent upon job performance
in warfare and government administration. He oversaw the institution
of strict laws, which were carved in stone and circulated to all parts of
the kingdom. Punishments for infractions included cutting off the nose
or feet, death by boiling in a cauldron, tearing apart by chariots tied to
the limbs, slicing in half, and burying alive. The Legalists argued that
these severe punishments were necessary to deter any and all breaking
of the law. Peasants were now free to buy and sell land and were taxed
a low enough percentage of their produce so as to encourage them to
increase production. Lord Shang was killed in 338 BCE, but by then the
Qin state made up nearly 30 percent of the territory and population of
the Warring States and was much wealthier than any of its rivals. As a
result, it took less than 120 years for the Qin to mobilize its growing

economic resources in the great task of conquering and pacifying all of the Warring States.

The men most responsible for this monumental task were King Zheng, who ascended to the Qin throne as a mere boy of thirteen in 246 BCE, and his chief minister, Li Si, who had worked as a lowly clerk in the southern state of Chu and who came to the Qin state just about the same time that King Zheng rose to power. For the first few years of King Zheng's reign, the real power behind the throne was the prime minister of Qin, Lü Buwei, whom Confucian historians later charged with being the actual father of (the therefore illegitimate) King Zheng. We will probably never know the truth of this story because the records of the Qin dynasty have been compiled and recorded for many centuries by Confucian historians who had many reasons for hating the Qin regime and all associated with it. Nevertheless, it is clear that Li Si ingratiated himself with Lü Buwei and King Zheng by sharing their ambition and clearly outlining ways to steadily bolster their power. King Zheng assumed power in his own right at age twenty-two in 237 BCE; just two years later, Lü was forced to drink poison. Thereafter, Li Si became Commandant of Justice, overseeing the internal administration of the strict Qin laws in all areas under Qin control. For the next fifteen years, King Zheng and his civil and military advisors presided over the rapid military conquest and political takeover of all the other Warring States.

In quick succession, Qin occupied the state of Han immediately to its east in 230, defeated Zhao on its northeast border in 228, and defeated Wei (to the south of Zhao) in 226. One year later, Qin conquered the largest rival state, Chu, which had controlled the entire Yangzi River valley all the way from the southwest border of Qin to the Pacific Ocean. The state of Yan in the far northeast fell to Qin in 222, and last but not least, the small state of Qi, just to the south of Yan, fell in 221, bringing to an end the era of the Warring States. Thus, in the space of a decade King Zheng, Li Si, and a small circle of close advisors to the king presided over the conquest of what they saw as the entire civilized world.

Once the last state, Qi, had fallen into Qin hands, King Zheng adopted a new and elevated title, Qin Shi Huangdi, the First Emperor of Qin (literally the First Sovereign Lord of Qin). Within a few years, Li Si was promoted to the position of chancellor, the highest and most powerful civilian post under the emperor. As chancellor, Li Si was the mastermind of the unification process in a stunning series of changes imposed on all the former states. The aristocratic families of all the states were forced to move to the Qin capital of Xianyang, where new palaces were built for them and they were far removed from their former power bases and kept under close surveillance. All the former currencies of the states, and their standards of weights and measures, were replaced by Qin currency and Qin standards. The states had evolved different styles of writing Chinese over the centuries, and these styles were also replaced by the Qin "small seal" style of writing. Axle lengths of chariots and carts, which had also differed from state to state, were now regularized so that roads throughout this new empire would be accessible to one size of chariot and cart. More than 4,000 miles of imperial highways were built to facilitate transportation throughout the empire. This level of state centralization and standardization was not achieved in Europe until 2,000 years later. Hundreds of thousands of conscript laborers built a Grand Canal from south to north China and unified parts of earlier state walls into one Great Wall[1] extending 4,000 miles along the northern and western borders of the empire. Qin Shi Huangdi took numerous inspection tours throughout the empire and had inscriptions carved in stone to commemorate his visits and his achievements.

Against officials who argued for the establishment of decentralized rule after the Zhou pattern (with imperial princes and allies independently ruling outlying territories), Li Si prevailed in establishing a centralized state, dividing the entire Qin kingdom into thirty-six large administrative units called commanderies (*jun*), and subdividing each commandery into several counties (*xian*). Each commandery and each county were presided over by a civil official, a military official, and an inspector official, each reporting directly to the court or central government. The Qin administrators divided the entire population of all the former states into small groups of five and ten families and made each group collectively responsible for the behavior of everyone in the group. If anyone in the group committed a crime, all would be held responsible and punished equally unless they reported the crime themselves. Thus the entire population was mobilized in the task of law enforcement.

The Qin success was breathtaking in its scope and in the speed of its accomplishment, but it was also highly dependent on a very few extremely capable and hardworking men at the center of power, most especially Li Si and Qin Shi Huangdi. As the emperor became increasingly obsessed with seeking immortality for himself, he also became increasingly paranoid about avoiding death and seeing to his own protection after death. He had his lavish tomb built over a period of more than a decade and positioned armies of terra cotta warriors around it for protection in the afterlife. Peasants digging a well in the 1970s

These life-sized (6 to 6 1/2 feet high) terra cotta warriors, in battle formation adjacent to the tomb of the First Qin Emperor in Shaanxi province, were intended to protect the emperor's tomb in the afterlife. In three pits near the tomb, archaeologists have discovered 8,000 warriors, 130 chariots with 520 horses, plus 150 cavalry horses, all made of terra cotta, most of which have not yet been excavated. Photo by Brad Stern

discovered the head of such a warrior, and this has led Chinese archaeologists to one of the most spectacular discoveries of the twentieth century, more than 7,000 life-sized terra cotta warriors in full battle formation, with row upon row of infantry, bowmen, and spear carriers, commanded by officers in four-horse chariots. The sight of this excavation outside the old Qin capital (near today's Xi'an) offers a truly awesome glimpse into the long-lost power of the Qin state in the age of its great conquests.

Confucian historians have long claimed that the First Emperor buried alive some 460 Confucian scholars who criticized his rule in 212 BCE and one year later burned all non-Legalist works the government could collect. Today, historians have cast serious doubt on these stories and have shown that many of the stone inscriptions left by the First Emperor and his court paid utmost attention to questions of court rituals and music, all derived from earlier Zhou understandings that we now identify as Confucian. So the Qin should be seen more as synthesizing rather than destroying many of the trends and traditions of the Zhou era.

New tomb finds from the Qin period suggest that the laws were enforced conscientiously with relative equality, fairness and with some flexibility. It is also clear that the First Qin Emperor, for all his paranoia and egomania, was a very capable and tireless monarch who worked extremely hard in reading hundreds of memorials daily from every part of the empire. Moreover, from today's perspective we can see that the Qin dynasty, for all its excesses, accomplished something truly monumental in creating the centralized bureaucratic empire that became the institutional model for all subsequent Chinese dynasties up until the early twentieth century. If the Qin didn't last as long as the popular slogan of longevity that was chanted to the emperor ("10,000 years!"), it did establish a workable pattern of government that has been one of the longest lived in human history.

The Qin state was built for warfare, but once it defeated all rival states, its harsh conscription methods no longer served a useful purpose. After Qin Shi Huangdi died in 211 BCE, Qin rule rapidly disintegrated, beginning with mutinies by conscripted laborers who were treated so harshly that they had little to lose by openly rebelling. Their rebellion quickly spread to the Qin military. As civil war erupted, many former noble families hoped that some kind of decentralized feudal rule could be reestablished to allow them to return to their home areas and reassert the privileged positions they had enjoyed before the Qin conquest. The two major contenders to succeed the Qin were Xiang Yu, a brilliant aristocratic general, and Liu Bang, an equally brilliant but low-born general of peasant background. Xiang Yu seemed a more likely emperor, and he promised to do just what the former noble families hoped, to restore the former kingdoms in a feudal-style federation of semi-independent states. But Xiang Yu was overconfident and stubborn enough to underestimate the strategic advantages that Liu Bang enjoyed, having occupied the strongholds of the fallen Qin dynasty. Liu was also a shrewd judge of character, and he rallied a group of loyal generals who led their troops to fight courageously and effectively in his cause. Thus, in 202 BCE, Liu Bang's army decisively defeated Xiang Yu's forces. Xiang Yu narrowly avoided capture and, with only twenty-eight of his loyal troops remaining at his side, committed suicide to prevent the disgrace of surrender to his enemy.

Liu Bang had proclaimed himself king of the Han state already in 206 BCE, and in 202 BCE he took the title of emperor. He proceeded to call on the same religious rituals Qin Shi Huangdi had invoked to assure the world of the moral and political legitimacy of his new empire. Liu Bang was one of only two emperors in all of Chinese history to rise from humble peasant background to ascend the dragon throne. He established his capital at the northwestern city of Chang'an (Eternal Peace), very near the old Qin capital, and kept many of the governing institutions established by the Qin, but declared several amnesties, freeing many of the victims of the harsh penalties of Qin law. Liu Bang kept about one-third of the empire, in one hundred commanderies in the west, under his own direct administration while parceling out two-thirds of the empire in the east as semi-independent kingdoms to his brothers, sons, and most trusted generals. This rather informal style of early Han rule notwithstanding, the old indirect feudal rule of the early Zhou period was gone forever. As the founding generation passed from the scene, Han emperors gradually abolished the kingdoms and brought most of the empire under the direct control of the central government.

Liu Bang died in 195 BCE and left his fifteen-year-old son on the throne, in part because of his confidence in the young man's mother, the formidable Empress Lü. When her son died in 188 BCE, she placed an infant on the throne so she could hold power herself, and when that young emperor died, she replaced him with another infant, so she basically held power herself from 188 to her death in 180. Empress Lü was a ruthless woman who has long been condemned by Confucian historians as usurping power from the Liu founding family, killing the rightful heirs to the throne, and placing many of her own relatives in powerful positions, but she was also a competent ruler who provided stable leadership at a time when the Han dynasty came under significant military threat from a nomadic people, the Xiongnu, on its northwestern frontier. Once Empress Lü died, many of her relatives were killed or dismissed from office, and power was restored to the Liu family. She was cited ever after by Confucian historians as evidence of the dangers of powerful women in the imperial palace.

The most significant threat to the Han dynasty in its early years came from the Xiongnu nomads of central Asia who united under a charismatic leader, Modun, at about the same time as the Qin unification of the Warring States. By unifying and extending a network of northern walls, the Qin and early Han rulers attempted to push the Xiongnu off their traditional grazing lands and expand the agricultural base of the Chinese state. But as Modun united more and more nomadic tribes under his own control, he frequently led successful raids inside the Chinese walls. Chinese troops could seldom match the nomads' mobility and shooting accuracy from horseback. The early Han court

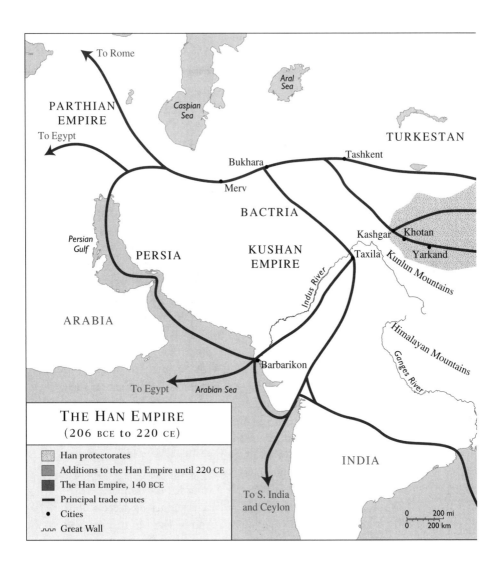

To Rome

Aral Sea

PARTHIAN
EMPIRE

Caspian
Sea

To Egypt

TURKESTAN

Tashkent

Bukhara

Merv

BACTRIA

Kashgar Khotan

Persian
Gulf

PERSIA

KUSHAN
EMPIRE

Taxila Yarkand

Kunlun Mountains

Indus River

ARABIA

Himalayan Mountains

Ganges River

Barbarikon

To Egypt

Arabian Sea

THE HAN EMPIRE
(206 BCE to 220 CE)

INDIA

Han protectorates
Additions to the Han Empire until 220 CE
The Han Empire, 140 BCE
Principal trade routes
Cities
Great Wall

To S. India
and Ceylon

0   200 mi
0   200 km

pursued a policy of "peace and kinship" (*heqin*), attempting to avoid war with the Xiongnu by sending lavish gifts of silk, gold, and grain and offering Xiongnu leaders Han princesses in marriage.

In their treaties with the Xiongnu, the Han recognized the nomadic state as its equal (despite the internal court rhetoric of universal imperial sovereignty). During the early Han, the dynasty functioned more as a tributary vassal of the Xiongnu Empire rather than vice versa. But unlike the Han dynasty, the Xiongnu Empire remained a loose

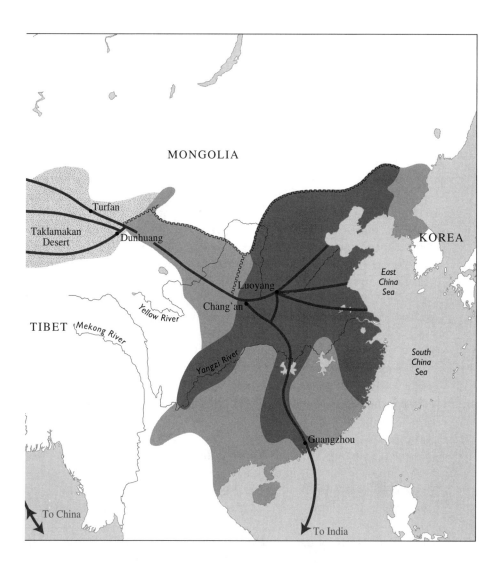

confederation of tribes, not a tightly centralized state, so no peace treaty could be enforced along the entire northern frontier. To the Chinese, frequent Xiongnu raids were simply evidence of nomadic treachery and dishonesty.

In 145 BCE, a young ambitious emperor, Han Wudi (the Martial Emperor), took the throne. He was to reign for fifty years, putting his stamp on the institutions of the Han dynasty as no other Han emperor. He greatly strengthened the army, launched a massive horse-breeding campaign, and in 134 BCE began a series of military campaigns against the Xiongnu nomads, ultimately pushing them far back into central Asia and away from the Han centers of wealth and power. His successors discontinued Han Wudi's aggressive approach, but they successfully maintained a chain of guarded defensive watchtowers far into central Asia, and they refused to send tribute, thus depriving the Xiongnu court of its main source of booty. The Xiongnu gradually splintered into several groups, including one that allied with the Han and settled inside the Chinese walls.

Han relations with the Xiongnu were to have profound consequences for Han relations with the outside world and for Chinese-nomad relations in subsequent ages. Even as the Han Chinese came to define their empire and their civilization in self-conscious contrast with the "barbarian" nomads on their borders, they also absorbed many aspects of that nomadic culture into the Chinese identity. Chinese methods of warfare were profoundly shaped by nomadic horsemanship and archery. Several Han emperors became very fond of nomadic dress, food, music, and dance, and such attractions spread to many in the Han social elite as well.

Under the protection of Chinese forces in its western hinterlands, trade flourished along a whole network of routes through central Asia that became known collectively in the nineteenth century as the Silk Roads. Some of the silks and precious metals the Chinese gave to the Xiongnu as gifts or bribes eventually found their way, through many intermediary hands, to Afghanistan, India, Persia, and eventually Rome. Han Chinese, especially in the elite, developed a strong fascination with "exotic" goods from beyond the western borders of the empire. They imported many things from Central Asia, including carpets, clothing, musical instruments, elixirs that promised immortality, new types of fruits and dairy products, and white facial powder, dubbed "barbarian powder," which adorned the faces of aristocratic Han women and can still be seen today worn by Japanese Geisha.[2]

Parthian merchants frequently served as middlemen in the East-West trade of the Han era, and Indian and Chinese merchants also developed a growing seaborne trade southward from the southernmost Chinese port city of Guangzhou, through the Southeast Asian lands of Malaya, Sumatra, and Burma, and across the Indian Ocean to Ceylon and India. By the late Han period, much of the Chinese silk that made its way to Rome traveled by sea through many intermediate hands past India and on to the Mediterranean. In turn, by the late Han, Indian merchants and Buddhist monks carrying their scriptures, artworks, images, and other religious accoutrements such as incense, made their way to China by both land and sea.

Han Wudi was the most consequential Han emperor for a number of other reasons besides his economic and military success. He greatly strengthened the power of the emperor by eliminating threats to the throne from imperial in-laws, eunuchs, and Confucian scholar-advisors. He raised state revenues very substantially by establishing central-government-run monopolies on the production of salt, iron, copper, bronze, and alcohol. Although he acted like a Legalist emperor in many ways, he also narrowed the curriculum of the state academy to teach prospective officials by focusing on the doctrines of the Confucian school, and he did more than any other emperor to establish Confucianism as a state-sponsored doctrine. He removed some regional overlords, curtailed the power and influence of many aristocratic families, recruited officials from humble backgrounds, and instituted examinations for officials in the Confucian classics.

From the reign of Han Wudi onward, Chinese emperors came to be seen not only as the military commander-in-chief but also as the cultural leader of the empire and its foremost patron of the arts and scholarship. It was especially on this basis that the emperor demanded and received the support, loyalty, and service of China's educated elite. Thus emperorship came to be identified with the arts and values of Chinese civilization, in self-conscious contrast with (and despite constant borrowing from) the nomadic cultures on China's borders.

The most influential scholar of the Han era, in subsequent periods if not in his own time, was Sima Qian, a court historian under Han Wudi. When Sima defended a Han general unfairly accused of treason, he was sentenced to death or castration for the crime of insulting the emperor. Everyone expected Sima Qian to take his own life, as castration was seen as the ultimate humiliation, which would send one to the underworld in a maimed condition. He agonized over his decision, and in the end he decided to accept the pain and humiliation of castration and to live on in order to complete his beloved history, as he later explained in a letter to his friend Ren An:

> When I have completed this work, I shall deposit it in the Mountain of Fame, so that it can be handed down to men who will understand it, and penetrate to the villages and great cities. Then, although I should suffer death from ten thousand cuts, what regrets should I have?[3]

All the dynastic histories from the Han dynasty up to the twentieth century have been modeled after Sima Qian's *Records of the Grand*

Historian. He climbed the Mountain of Fame to a greater height than he could have imagined, and he represents to this day the faith of Chinese scholars that their honest writings can in fact outlive the monarchs and power-holders they might criticize and condemn.

The most influential Han dynasty scholar in shaping the Confucian philosophical tradition was Dong Zhongshu (ca. 175–105 BCE) who resigned his low official position (because Han Wudi ignored him) and devoted himself to teaching others. Dong Zhongshu saw the emperor as the Son of Heaven and an intermediary between Heaven and Earth. If the emperor was virtuous, he argued, the result would be harmony between Heaven and Earth. Dong took earlier *yin-yang* theories (that change occurs as a result of complementary opposites interacting) and five-phase theories (that all changes operate by sequential laws whereby water gives way to earth, earth gives way to wood, wood gives way to metal, metal gives way to fire, and fire gives way to water) and incorporated them into a comprehensive Confucian framework. He included aspects of Daoism (the emperor rules from above by nonaction) and Legalism (the emperor is a semidivine lawgiver on whom the harmony and welfare of the whole world depends) in an overall Confucian imperial ideology that would survive into the twentieth century.

Despite Emperor Han Wudi's undisputed accomplishments, at the time of his death he left the government hard pressed to pay for the many initiatives he had begun. As large landholders found ways to avoid paying taxes, Han dynasty society became increasingly divided between rich aristocratic landholders and poor tenants, slaves, and landless vagabonds. In an attempt to address the problem of large nontaxed estates, the imperial regent Wang Mang seized power and declared the Xin (New) Dynasty in 9 CE. He rationalized his seizure of power with the Zhou-dynasty concept of the Mandate of Heaven that justified rebellion against an unjust ruler. He tried to abolish slavery, seize the property of large landholders, and redistribute land to the restless poor. But his measures only roused the opposition of the most powerful elements in society, and a tremendous Yellow River flood in 11 CE helped inspire open and widespread revolt against Wang Mang's rule.

Wang was killed in 23 CE, and forces loyal to the Liu ruling family of the Han restored the dynasty two years later. The new emperor, Guangwu, claimed Heaven's Mandate for the Liu family, following the precedent of Wang Mang, and established the cult of Heaven (*tian*) as the primary imperial cult, which soon eclipsed in importance the imperial ancestral cult of the early Han. The Mandate of Heaven was to remain the moral and political rationale for all subsequent dynasties.

Guangwu also moved the Han capital several hundred kilometers east of the destroyed Chang'an to the city of Luoyang. Thus the period from 25 to 220 CE is known as the Later Han or Eastern Han.

Despite the political upheavals of the Wang Mang usurpation and the relocation of the capital to Luoyang, the Han dynasty remained strong and expansive for another century of economic prosperity and cultural creativity. Luoyang became the second largest city in the world (after Rome), and Han political control extended from Korea in the northeast to the foothills of the Himalayan mountains in the southwest, and from Vietnam in the southeast to the Silk Roads oasis towns of central Asia in the northwest.

Han society was highly stratified, especially by modern standards, but it was also more fluid than most preindustrial societies. No families outside the imperial household could guarantee their high social position by heredity alone. In the Confucian view, scholar-officials ranked highest in the social hierarchy, followed by peasants and artisans (the productive backbone of society), followed by merchants at the bottom (seen by Confucians as nonproductive exploiters of the labors of others). In reality, merchants often became quite wealthy, and when they did they saw to it that their sons or grandsons received the classical education that would allow them entrance into the highest status group of scholar-officials.

For most of its history, the Han government achieved a workable balance between central control and local autonomy. Officials were recruited through a system of recommendation by people already working in the government, but all officials were required to study the texts of Confucianism. Through government sponsorship, and the writings of such scholars as Sima Qian and Dong Zhongshu, Confucian values came to permeate the attitudes and lives of the educated elite, and to some (limited) extent, to seep down to the lower levels of society including illiterate peasants. At one point as many as 30,000 young men studied the Confucian classics in the Imperial Academy at the capital. Education in the Han was further facilitated by the invention of paper around 100 CE. This made the dissemination of writings much more efficient than the earlier method of writing on narrow strips of bamboo. The Han government also had many Confucian works carved in stone, which was seen as the appropriate way to preserve the sacred writings of the past. Young scholars came from all over the empire to make stone rubbings of these writings or to copy them by hand and thereby disseminate them more widely. Much of what we know today about China before the Han comes from the conscientious and meticulous efforts of Han scholars.

The relative peace and stability of the Han dynasty over several centuries produced a population of some sixty million people, an extensive market economy that linked different regions into an integrated whole, and a degree of prosperity that had seldom been seen in the world before that time. Because the Han elite tended to bury their dead in elaborate tombs, some of the most spectacular archeological discoveries in the twentieth century have been made through the excavations of Han tombs. Tombs often included miniature models of homes, household goods, servants, entertainers, and official retinues in formal procession, giving us intimate glimpses into Chinese ways of life and death in Han times.

One of the most famous excavations of a Han-era tomb came in the 1960s in Mawangdui, a small village outside Changsha in Hunan Province. This was the tomb of Li Cang, a high official of a regional king who had been an early supporter of the Han founder Liu Bang. Li Cang's own tomb was badly damaged, but the adjoining tombs of his wife, Lady Dai, and their son, were well preserved. Lady Dai's tomb included 154 lacquer boxes, trays, cups and bowls, 51 ceramics, 48 bamboo cases of textiles and other household goods, and 40 baskets of clay replicas of gold and bronze coins. Much to the amazement of the archaeologists involved, they discovered Lady Dai's corpse so well preserved, in four interlocking coffins and wrapped in twenty layers of silk, that her flesh was soft and her muscles were still elastic. Her stomach contained more than a hundred melon seeds, a 2,000-year-old testimony to her last meal. On the top of the innermost coffin lay a beautiful painted silk funeral banner, which has become one of the most studied archeological finds of the last half century.

Scholars are still debating the many possible symbolic meanings of the banner, a task made more difficult by the wide variety of practices and beliefs about the dead expressed in Han writings. Some tombs included passports to the underworld for the deceased, to document their possessions and prevent mistreatment from the underworld bureaucracy. Others include "tomb-quelling texts" designed to ward off evil from the newly deceased and to enforce the strict separation of the living and the dead. Yet other Han documents speak of cultivating long life or attaining immortality by transcending the normal confines of biological death. There was clearly a concern among the Han Chinese that if a person was wrongly killed or a deceased person was not properly cared for, the person's spirit might escape the tomb and seek vengeance on the wrong-doers. Such a belief, along with the Confucian admonition to treat one's ancestors with utmost respect whether dead or alive, helps explain why so many tombs of the Han elite were filled with household and luxury goods.

In addition to elaborate tombs for the dead,[4] in the later Han period some members of the elite began building large aboveground shrines to their dead ancestors. These served as public gathering places for ancestral sacrifices. The largest and most complete of these shrines from the Han was dedicated to Wu Liang, a man who had refused to accept appointment in an officialdom he saw as corrupt. The walls of his shrine were decorated with stone carvings that aimed to depict the entire history of the world, from the deep mythological past right up to the present and from the most mundane details of daily life to the heavenly realm of the immortals. A popular deity in Han times was the Queen Mother of the West, who presided over the *yin* realm of the immortals on Kunlun Mountain, where the golden peaches of immortality ripened only once every 3,000 years.[5] Her less revered counterpart, the King Father of the East, presided over the *yang* realm of the immortals.

The wall carvings of the Wu Liang Shrine depict a wide variety of people, including ancient kings, filial sons and virtuous men, wise ministers, famous assassins, and eminent women. Among the latter were women who exemplified the highest Confucian virtues of self-sacrifice for the sake of morality. One was a beautiful Zhou dynasty widow, Gaoxing, of the state of Liang, who was so determined to remain a chaste widow that she cut off her own nose to discourage any men from seeking her hand in marriage. Another was the Virtuous Aunt of Liang, who intended to save her brother's son from a fire but in the excitement of the moment picked up and saved her own son instead. Discovering her mistake, she was so chagrined that she ran back into the flames to her death, claiming that she could not face the shame of having saved her own son instead of her brother's.

Although most written historical records from the Han period focus on men to the exclusion of women, the most famous female scholar in all of Chinese history lived in the Han dynasty. This was Ban Zhao, whose father, Ban Biao, had vowed to continue the great history of China that Sima Qian had begun. When Ban Biao died prematurely, his son Ban Gu, Ban Zhao's brother, took up the challenge and completed the *Book of Han*, the official history of the Han dynasty. Ban Gu's twin brother achieved equal prominence as a military general and conqueror of many formerly independent kingdoms in Central Asia. Despite her subordinate position as a woman, Ban Zhao matched the accomplishments of her brothers. Married to a prominent official who died as a young man, she devoted herself to raising her one son and to a life of study and writing.

使者
奉金者
梁高行

Extremely beautiful and pursued by many suitors after her husband's death, the Widow Gaoxing of the state of Liang responds to a marriage proposal by cutting off her own nose, thereby discouraging all marriage proposals and preserving her widow chastity. This ink rubbing was made from one of many wall carvings depicting historical scenes and commemorating virtuous behavior in the ancestral offering shrine for the Wu family erected in front of Wu Liang's grave in 171 BCE. Feng Yupeng and Feng Yunyuan, *Jinshi Suo* (An index to bronzes and stone carvings), 1821

She wrote many poems, helped her brother Ban Gu complete his Han dynastic history, and wrote *Precepts for My Daughters*, the most famous instruction booklet for women in all of Chinese culture.

Since most ethical and philosophical works were written for men, Ban Zhao decided to write ethical instructions specifically for women. She admonished women to exhibit three qualities or virtues: to act with modesty, deference, and respect; to be diligent and hardworking; and to serve their in-laws and carry out the ancestral sacrifices with reverence and dignity. Thus she could assure a good reputation for herself and her family. But, she concluded, "if you fail in any of these three things, there will be no good name to be spread, and divorce and dishonor will be unavoidable!"[6] Her advice was particularly relevant to elite members of her own class, which included all the women of the court, where intrigue and power struggles were very common. Ban Zhao knew the sad fate of powerful empresses who tried to exercise power themselves and ended up being killed along with their closest relatives. In this light, her *Precepts for My Daughters* can be read as an effective manual of survival for women in a dangerous and male-dominated environment.

Ban Zhao's precepts reflect elite ideals but not necessarily the social realities of the Han era. We know that many imperial wives in the Han period were very aggressive in asserting their power. The emphasis on filial piety in Han Confucianism made it hard for most emperors to ignore the desires of their mothers, even after the emperor reached adulthood or middle age. Consequently, empress dowagers often found ways to dominate the Han court, especially late in the dynasty's history. Many dynasties in China were eventually weakened and destroyed by lethal power struggles among four competing groups: empress dowagers and their families, Confucian officials in the imperial bureaucracy, military commanders, and court eunuchs.

In the later Han, the two most powerful groups around the throne were the imperial eunuchs and the families of empresses. Eunuchs were a unique class of people in imperial China. As castrated males, they were scorned, yet as the personal servants of the emperor, they could at times become his closest personal friends and advisors, giving them more power than any other group of people. Eunuchs often came from very humble backgrounds. Why else would they agree to undergo castration (a serious risk to life itself in an age before modern surgery)? Eunuchs were given the duty of managing palace life so as to ensure that any children born in the palace would be legitimate descendants of the emperor and not the product of illicit liaisons between imperial women and lowly servants. Since eunuchs had no descendants of their own, they had fewer temptations to build up their own personal wealth, but the lure of wealth and power was still seductive; and the number of eunuchs tended to grow over time in each dynasty.

In the later Han, there were thousands of eunuchs, and they became so powerful that they were granted the right to adopt heirs of their own. In 124 CE, court eunuchs managed to place an infant on the throne so they could control state affairs in his name. In 159 CE, they helped an emperor execute the entire family of the powerful mother of his predecessor. The eunuchs led a series of purges in 166 and 169 in which they killed or exiled thousands of officials from the civil bureaucracy.

All of this turmoil at the court only intensified the weakness of the Han central government, as military leaders in outlying regions paid less and less attention to their "superiors" in the capital, and wealthy families found more and more ways to avoid taxation. Two structural changes in the Eastern Han proved fatal to the dynasty. The court ended the practice of peasant conscription (partly out of fear of armed peasant rebellions) and relied instead on professional armies made up of voluntary recruits, convicts, and non-Chinese nomads resettled within the walled frontiers. These professional soldiers easily formed long-term allegiances to their personal commanders rather than to the Han court. Thus, when trouble erupted in any one area, armies were as likely to join in the unrest as to support the court's attempts at suppression.

With the central government in complete disarray, it lost the capacity to provide effective relief in times of natural disaster. In 184, a rebellion broke out among the followers of a Daoist religious cult, the Yellow Turbans, which marked the beginning of the end for the Han dynasty. The country dissolved into civil war, as numerous generals declared their independence from the Han and aspired to establish their own new dynastic rule. They proved incapable of doing so, and what had been the Han dynasty split up into three rival kingdoms, each led by a former general or warlord.

The Han dynasty officially came to an end in 220 CE, but its legacy was to reach all the way to the twentieth century. Having lasted more than four centuries, the Han formed the imperial pattern of legalist institutions rationalized by Confucian ideology that was to inspire every subsequent dynasty until the last (the Qing) fell in 1911. At its height, the Han court ruled an empire of about two and a half million square miles (about 70 percent of the contemporary United States) with sixty million people under its direct control. The Han is often compared to the Roman Empire, as both existed at the same time and were near equals in size. Han China was relatively land-locked and almost exclusively agricultural, in contrast to the Roman Empire (known to the Chinese as the Da Qin or Great Qin Empire) with its many trading routes on the Mediterranean Sea. And Han China was much more culturally uniform, with its single written language, its Confucian ideology, and its shared elite culture. The Han government and army were more tightly controlled by one family and its civil officials than was the case in the Roman Empire. And finally, although the Han capital of Luoyang fell almost two centuries before the sack of Rome, in contrast to the irrevocable breakup of the Roman Empire, the Han pattern of one vast unified land-based empire was to be repeated again and again in China into the twentieth century.

CHAPTER 3

The Era of
Division (220–589)

When the last Han emperor was killed in 220, there were three powerful warlord families who each hoped to restore order quickly and establish a new and long-lived empire in its place. In the north, the Cao family of Han officials steadily gained power for themselves, and in 220 they proclaimed a new dynasty, the Wei. In the southwest (today's Sichuan) Liu Bei, a distant relative of the Han ruling family, proclaimed the Shu Han dynasty (Shu being the name then for that region), which he saw as the rightful successor to the great Han; and in the lower Yangzi River valley Sun Quan, another powerful general, proclaimed the Wu dynasty.

These three rivals were later immortalized in one of China's greatest novels, *The Romance of the Three Kingdoms*, which weaves together many historical tales and popular stories to portray the third century CE as a time of great military heroism and bravery, as well as treachery and betrayal. All Chinese in modern times, from primary school children to illiterate peasants and artisans, are familiar with the great heroes of *The Romance of the Three Kingdoms*. There is a subtle irony in this novel as well, for it shows that the virtuous do not always win power over their rivals, and it suggests that the Mandate of Heaven will likely go to the cleverest general with the strongest battalions rather than the wisest or most moral leader. *The Romance of the Three Kingdoms* may be the second most important book, after the *Analects* of Confucius, for an understanding of Chinese culture.[1]

Despite the bravery, strength, and treachery of the warlords of the Three Kingdoms era, none of them came close to conquering all of the former Han dynastic territories. Instead they only managed to destroy the old Han order. In 263 the Wei forces defeated the Shu Han in the southwest, but only two years later a former Wei general removed the Wei emperor and proclaimed the Jin dynasty. In 280, the Jin defeated the Wu state in the Yangzi valley of central China, thus briefly unifying the empire under central control. But the Jin was itself short-lived, as mounted Xiongnu tribesmen, with improved efficiency through the recent invention of the stirrup, laid waste to the Jin capital, Luoyang, in 311. For more than a century thereafter, north China was torn by incessant warfare among competing groups, including many non-Chinese nomadic tribesmen who originally came from areas north and west of China proper.

The earlier distinction between Han Chinese and non-Han "barbarians" broke down entirely during this period of rapid change. Some nomadic groups had lived within the Great Wall for decades, and the roles they played, whether as allies or opponents of the Han dynasty, were of ever-increasing importance in the political control and organization of the Yellow River valley. Many of these groups learned the Chinese language, intermarried with Chinese, and adopted Chinese modes of dress and diet, while remaining self-consciously loyal to some of their own tribal ways. The very definition of "Chinese" greatly expanded during this era to incorporate many non-Han peoples as well as their material cultures and social customs. In the process, many Han Chinese also embraced in varying degrees formerly "barbarian" ways, including their tastes in food, fashions, music, and art. Far from differentiating Han from non-Han cultures, the term "barbarian" came to be applied by many different groups to their rivals. North and south evolved in different ways, but both could now claim to be "civilized Chinese," and both could aspire to recapture the old Han ideal of one all-encompassing centralized empire.

To flee the bloodshed and chaos in north China following the Han dynasty collapse, more than two million people, including many of the north's wealthiest families, fled to the Yangzi River valley, where they attempted, with little success, to set up an effective central government with a military strong enough to reunify the country. In both the north and the south, society became increasingly stratified as wealthy families organized their own private armies for protection, and landless peasants fled to these wealthy estates to work as serfs and indentured servants in return for food and protection against marauding armies. A succession of weak dynasties were established at Jiankang (what is today Nanjing) on the Yangzi River, but no political ruler was able to establish a secure tax base with a stable and strong central government.

During the Han period, perhaps only 10 percent of the population lived as far south as the Yangzi River valley. After the Han, large-scale migration to the south would transform the Yangzi valley into China's most prosperous region. The wealthy families who fled southward beginning around 200 took with them thousands of farm laborers and mobilized them to drain swamps and build level paddy fields surrounded by earthen dikes. This made possible the flooding and draining of rice fields with precision, which allowed the south, with more abundant rainfall and the many streams and tributaries of the Yangzi River, to become China's richest rice-producing region. The many rivers and tributaries in central and south China made transportation more efficient and long-distance trade more feasible than in the north.

In addition, wealthy families in the Yangzi Valley, sometimes with government subsidies, could afford the long-term investment required for mulberry trees, necessary for the production of silk. Silk worms are so tiny at hatching that there are 700,000 in a pound. In five weeks, these worms will eat twelve tons of mulberry leaves and will themselves grow to a combined weight of five tons. Each worm, about four or five inches long at maturity, then spins a cocoon of a silk thread about one mile in length and as fine as a spider's web. The production of silk is incredibly labor intensive, as each cocoon must be carefully softened in scalding water and unwound onto a spool. Several of these fine threads are spun together to make a strong silk thread, which is only then ready to weave into cloth. The five tons of silk cocoons will, after painstaking processing, produce only about 150 pounds of finished silk cloth.

In this era of political division and internal weakness, long-distance trade flourished as never before, and silk was a major driving force in this development. Merchants brought gold, silver, and luxury goods— such as textiles from Persia and pearls, ivory, incense, and coral from South and Southeast Asia—to trade for the coveted Chinese silks, as well as bronze objects and lacquerware. Guangzhou on the far southeast coast became a thriving center of international trade, and by the early sixth century, the capital of the Southern Liang dynasty, Jiankang, on the Yangzi River in central China, was the largest and most luxurious city in the world, with a population of one million.

In contrast to northern cities, which were divided by the government into discrete rectangular administrative units to confine markets to particular areas, Jiankang had markets scattered throughout the city so that commerce permeated urban life. The Yangzi and its many tributaries afforded the economical movement of goods to and from the southwestern interior and in the other direction, to the eastern coast. Consequently, Jiankang was a major center of trading networks that extended westward as far as Sichuan and Tibet and eastward down the southeast China coast to Southeast and South Asia. From there, with the help of Indian and Muslim traders, Chinese goods found their way westward as far as Syria and Rome.[2] As a result of all these profound economic changes, the reconstructed empire that ended the era of division in 589 was a far more prosperous country with a far more developed economy than anything that existed in Han times.

During the era of division, China was also greatly transformed in terms of art, culture, and religion. When the Han dynasty collapsed, so did the faith that many scholars and officials had had in the Confucian doctrines that justified and rationalized the Han order. As Confucianism appeared incapable of sustaining order, many people naturally began to turn to other philosophies and religions.

By the end of the Han, Daoism had been transformed in some areas into a mass religion, largely made up of peasants led by faith healers who promised that the destruction of the Han dynasty would usher in a golden age of peace and prosperity under Daoist leadership. One such Daoist visionary, the leader of the Yellow Turban rebellion, inspired 360,000 of his followers to rise up against the Han in 184, but this movement was quickly wiped out by Han forces. Another Daoist sect, the Celestial Masters, flourished for almost a century in southwest China and avoided suppression by dispersing into remote areas, retreating from political and military battles, and concentrating on their religious practices of warding off demons and illnesses. The Celestial Masters sect has survived as a major branch of the Daoist religion down to the present day. It maintains a popular following, especially in Taiwan, and practices rituals for burial and for the living to facilitate cosmic harmony, purification, and healing.

In intellectual circles, many scholars and officials began to question the state-sponsored Confucian doctrines of the Han and to explore anew the old Daoist teachings of the *Daodejing* and the *Book of Zhuangzi*. These thinkers did not necessarily abandon the ideals of Confucius, but they often pointed out how frequently rulers in the post-Han world paid lip service to Confucian ideals while practicing ruthless and immoral policies.

In the third century CE, the most famous intellectual critics of the age came to be known as the Seven Sages of the Bamboo Grove. Named after the meeting place where they supposedly gathered to drink wine, play music, and write poetry, they also argued about abstract nonpolitical issues such as the nature of reality, or being and nonbeing, in a form of dialogue called "pure talk." Although there is no hard evidence that these men actually knew each other in their lifetimes, stories of their meetings spread far and wide and helped to define a new ideal of cultivated literati (or scholar-artists) who sought fulfillment not in political engagement but in the private pursuits of pleasure and the arts.

One of the Seven Sages was Ji Kang, a brilliant poet, lute player, and alchemist who experimented with the transformation of metals in search of drugs to promote long life. Ji Kang attacked official life as both boring and immoral. He said he preferred to avoid the hypocrisies of the court and to enjoy instead the freedoms of private life and the beauties of nature far from the pressures of high politics. When a friend of his accepted an official position and wrote to Ji Kang to suggest that he might do likewise, he replied with a blistering attack on officialdom. He concluded his letter: "All I want now is to remain in my old hut, bring up my children and grandchildren, take a stroll from time to time with old friends, drink a glass of wine, and play a melody on my lute. That is the sum of my ambition."[3] His letter found its way into the hands of the Duke of Jin, who had hired Ji Kang's friend, and the duke was so offended by its implicit attack on official circles that he sentenced Ji Kang to death in 262. Three thousand of his students and followers signed a petition to the duke asking him to pardon Ji Kang, but to no avail. From prison Ji Kang wrote of his desire to survive but also made clear his contempt for his persecutors. On his way to the gallows, he watched the lengthening shadows of the sun and played a mournful tune on his lute.

Another leader of this group was Ji Kang's good friend Ruan Ji, who wrote haunting poems that extolled the beauties of nature, called for naturalness and spontaneity over sterile rituals, and satirized the immoral behavior of many Confucian scholars in his own time. When he was chastised by someone for walking in public with his own sister-in-law (because men and women were not to be seen together in public even if they were closely related), he replied, "Surely you don't mean to suggest that the rules of [Confucian] propriety apply to me!"[4] Another of the Seven Sages, Liu Ling, once appeared stark naked at the door of his home to greet some visitors. Seeing the shocked look on their faces, he explained, "Heaven and earth are my dwelling and this room is my pants. Who asked you gentlemen to come inside my pants? And where's the harm anyway?"[5]

In such a dangerous age, when rulers fought constant wars and frequently executed officials and citizens even for minor offenses, many began to question the Confucian principle that a good man's first duty was to serve the state.[6] The trends of nonconformity, withdrawal from government service, and new interest in the values of the early Daoist philosophers and the later Daoist religious movements all helped provide fertile soil for the rise of Buddhism in China. The arrival of Buddhism was easily the most momentous of all the changes during the long period of division.

Compared with most world religions, the original teachings of the Buddha are unique in that he performed no miracles, believed in no supernatural god or creator, and depended on no deity or divine revelations as the basis of his teachings. He simply claimed to have insight into the nature of the human condition and ways to improve it. Born an Indian prince—Siddhartha of the Gautama clan—the Buddha lived, interestingly enough, at about the same time as Confucius. India was already an old civilization with a very rich tradition of Hindu scriptures and teachings about the need to transcend or move beyond the physical world to the world of pure spirit. Raised in luxury and married to a beautiful princess who had borne him a son, Siddhartha turned his back on all that at age twenty-nine, when he vowed to embark on a religious search for enlightenment; in particular, he wished to solve the riddle of human suffering. He studied with a variety of Hindu teachers and sages for a period of six years. At age thirty-five, while meditating under a Bo tree in the northern Indian state of Bihar, he had a sense of great awakening (Buddha means "awakened one") and felt that he finally understood the causes and the cure for human suffering. In his first sermon after this, he summarized his new insights, which have come to be known in Buddhism as the Four Noble Truths. The first is that *dukkha*—a Sanskrit term meaning suffering, pain, imperfection, or anguish—is unavoidable in human life. The second is that *dukkha* has an identifiable cause: human desire or craving. We desire to escape pain and never to be separated from our loved ones, but pain in life and separation through death are unavoidable. The third noble truth is that we can end our suffering if we understand and accept our own impermanence and eliminate our many desires for life to be different from the way it is. The forth noble truth is that the way to achieve this acceptance and this end of suffering is to follow a moral, compassionate life of spiritual discipline, meditation, and concentration.

In addition to these teachings, Buddhists shared the common Indian assumptions of the time: that all human beings are spirits reborn again and again into a succession of physical bodies, working toward enlightenment over a period of many lifetimes. Rebirth is governed by laws of karma, whereby every act has consequences equal to the act. Good actions have good consequences in this life or the next incarnation, and bad actions likewise have bad consequences.

The Buddha's teachings were sufficiently general and varied that different people emphasized different aspects of his thought, and by the time Buddhist missionaries carried their religion to China, it was a very complex religion with many different schools and branches. In Theravada Buddhism, which thrived in India and spread especially in Southeast Asia, the Buddhist path of self-discipline was seen as so strict and difficult that only monks and nuns could hope to reach enlightenment. In Tantric Buddhism, which developed particularly in Tibet, the emphasis was on elaborate prayers and rituals to ward off evil spirits. In Mahayana Buddhism, which became most popular in China, laypeople could also hope for enlightenment, in part through faith in the power of the Buddha and his many bodhisattva disciples. (A bodhisattva is one who has attained sufficient spiritual insight to reach nirvana, but who remains in the world to help relieve the suffering of others.) Despite the nontheistic teachings of the Buddha, some schools of Buddhism developed an array of deities that people could appeal to for protection and assistance in this life or the next.

There were many obstacles to the growth of Buddhism in China. Chinese thought centered very much on this world and on family obligations, whereas Indian philosophy was very abstractly metaphysical, seeing multiple worlds beyond the concrete physical world. The languages of the Buddhist texts, Sanskrit and Pali, were completely unrelated to Chinese, making translation of basic Buddhist concepts quite difficult. The most serious contradiction between Buddhist practice and Chinese values was that the highest level of religious devotion in Buddhism was to shave one's head and become a monk or a nun. This was seen as a serious violation of Confucian filial piety, because one's first filial obligation was to have children, who in turn would worship one's parents' spirits after one's own death.

Buddhist missionaries and early Chinese converts used the ideas of reincarnation and the laws of karma to justify monastic life as a performance of filial piety: by becoming a monk or a nun, one could win merits for one's ancestors in the afterlife and thereby contribute toward one's parents' rebirth at a higher level of spiritual development or at a higher socioeconomic level. Similarly, by contributing money for the construction of Buddhist temples, monasteries, or works of art, one could earn karmic merits for oneself and one's family members both in this life and the next.

Despite the many obstacles to the spread of Buddhism in China, many other factors made China ripe for the transplanting and growth of this Indian religion. The translation itself of Indian terms into Chinese made many Buddhist concepts seem familiar to the Chinese. The Buddhist terms for teaching (*dharma*), enlightenment (*bodhi*), and *yoga* were all translated into Chinese as *dao*, the way, making these concepts seem almost Chinese. The highly abstract Indian term *nirvana* was rendered into Chinese as the familiar negative term *wu*, as in *wuwei*, or nonaction, meaning emptiness. The Indian term for morality, *sila*, was rendered in Chinese as *xiaoxun*, or filial piety, making Indian morality appear to be very Chinese and very compatible with Confucianism.

Many Chinese after the fall of the Han were in search of some alternative to Confucianism, and Buddhism met a number of different needs in the traumatized society of the time. Some of the eccentric followers of Daoism after the fall of the Han had emphasized the need for emotional detachment in order to deal with the profound uncertainties of the age. To many Chinese, Buddhism seemed to be a variation on this Daoist theme of having few desires and finding contentment in small pleasures. As some intellectuals turned against Confucian doctrines and undertook abstract debates on the nature of being and nonbeing, they were strongly attracted to the rich intellectual tradition of metaphysical speculation in Indian Buddhism. And some missionaries and early Chinese Buddhist converts were very adept at presenting Buddhism in terms familiar to Confucians and Daoists alike.

The greatest translator of Buddhist texts into Chinese was Kumarajiva (344–413), a half-Indian monk who lived in the oasis town of Kucha in what is today Xinjiang Province. Kumarajiva's Indian father had come to Central Asia to study Buddhism, and when Kumarajiva was seven, his mother, a native Kuchean princess, decided she wanted to become a nun. When her husband objected, she refused to eat; after six days he relented, and she and her son entered the Buddhist clergy. The young Kumarajiva was brilliant at languages, and he and his mother traveled to Kashmir, where he studied with one of the great Buddhist teachers. Later, back in Central Asia, he studied both Theravada and Mahayana doctrines and became convinced of the superiority of the Mahayana teachings. When a Chinese warlord in the region captured him and held him captive for a number of years to prevent his spreading his doctrines more widely, he quickly became fluent in Chinese. In 401, a regional Chinese ruler heard of his brilliance, defeated the general who had held Kumarajiva captive, brought him to the city of Chang'an, and set him to work supervising as many as a thousand monks in translating the major Buddhist scriptures into Chinese. The results were spectacularly successful. From 402 until his death in 413, Kumarajiva oversaw the accurate translation of more Buddhist scriptures into Chinese than any other translator ever.

Buddhist followers and Buddhist institutions seemed well designed to meet a variety of social and political needs in China. In south China, where civil wars were frequent and banditry was widespread in the countryside, walled Buddhist monasteries offered protection and the promise of food and safety to otherwise destitute people. Buddhists built inns along roadways offering meals and lodging to travelers. They also opened pawnshops where poor people could deposit items of value in order to secure loans that were often essential to keep families fed or secure seed for a spring planting in hard times.

In north China, important political factors contributed to the rise of Buddhism. The Chinese saw the invading nomadic tribes who competed for the control of the Yellow River valley as uncivilized and uncultured. These invaders were drawn to Buddhism precisely because it was not Chinese and offered them a "high culture" and sophisticated religion of their own. In the early fourth century, a tribe called the Tuoba—part of the Xianbei, a larger group of nomads—occupied parts of northwest China. They began to learn Chinese, to intermarry with Chinese, to use Chinese advisors, and to implement Chinese-style political organization. In 386, they proclaimed the Northern Wei dynasty in the Chinese style. Establishing a permanent capital at Pingcheng (in today's northern Shanxi Province), the Wei rulers adopted a Chinese-style law code and began taxing Chinese peasants under their control. By 430, the Northern Wei was the largest and strongest government in China, extending over the entire drainage area of the Yellow River.

From 425 to 494, the Northern Wei emperors and their court (with private backing from officials, monks and nuns, and private families as well) sponsored the carving of thousands of Buddhist statues in a group of sandstone cliffs and caves at a place called Yungang (near their capital of Pingcheng and close to today's Datong in Shanxi). These caves contain five massive sculptures of the Buddha (from twenty-six to sixty feet high) that may have been modeled on the first five emperors of the Northern Wei dynasty. Much of the work was completed in a few years of very hectic activity, from 483 to 490, perhaps at the suggestion of a monk as to how the court could express its repentance of an earlier attempt to suppress Buddhist practices. In this short span of time, the walls of fifty-three main caves were filled with more than 50,000 carvings. This was a massive undertaking that employed hundreds of skilled craftsmen, who worked as slaves of the state. A donor's list found at Yungang is inscribed with the names of 120 donors.

In 494, the Northern Wei rulers moved their capital southward to Luoyang, which they rebuilt into a flourishing city on the ruins of the former Eastern Han capital. At a place called Longmen, ten miles outside of Luoyang, they commissioned artists to carve out another monumental set of caves with fine limestone walls. Subsequent rulers of the Tang dynasty continued to sponsor the creation of Buddhist sculptures at Longmen for about four hundred years.

This large Buddha from the Northern Wei dynasty (460–493 CE), in Cave number 20 at Yungang, near modern Datong (Shanxi Province), is now exposed to the elements because of the collapse of the cave. The formerly nomadic Tuoba Wei rulers of the Northern Wei sponsored the creation of thousands of elaborately carved Buddhist figures at Yungang to demonstrate their religious devotion and cultural sophistication. Photo by Paul Ropp

In addition to these caves associated with emperors and would-be emperors, numerous other Buddhist works of art were created during the period of division that have survived to the present day. In the far northwestern village of Dunhuang (in today's Gansu Province) archaeologists in the twentieth century discovered another set of caves adorned with Buddhist carvings sponsored by a large monastery there, along with a whole library of Buddhist scriptures produced over several centuries starting in the fourth century CE. About eight hundred miles to the west of Dunhuang, near Kucha, where Kumarajiva lived as a child, another group of caves at the small town of Kizil shows the popularity of Buddhism in Central Asia (near today's Kyrgyzstan) starting in the fourth century CE. These caves are notable for the vivid multicolored paintings, in Indian style, that adorn their walls. One of the paintings at Kizil illustrates the close connection between merchants and the spread of Buddhism in China, as it shows the Buddha lighting the way for a traveling merchant. Interregional trade was essential to the rise of Buddhism in China, for merchants often brought missionaries along with them on their travels and paid their expenses so they could devote their time and attention to spreading word of the religion.

Despite all of this growing interest in Buddhism, Confucian doctrines did not die out or lose their appeal for those who still dreamed of reuniting the north and the south of China into one large empire. The same Northern Wei rulers who sponsored the creation of Buddhist art works at Yungang and Longmen also devoted time and attention to promoting Confucian social and political values and to building a strong centralized bureaucratic state with a stable tax base. In 465, Empress Dowager Feng rose to a powerful position upon the death of the emperor, her husband. She dominated the new emperor, her young son, and after his death in 476 controlled the Northern Wei court as the regent for her young step-grandson. Until her death in 490, she controlled the court, and she undertook a sweeping set of reforms that transformed the semitribal organization of the Xianbei court into a full-blown Chinese-style bureaucratic government. She promoted more Chinese officials into influential governmental positions, and she increased the building of Buddhist monasteries.

These massive guardians from the central Fengxian Temple at the Longmen Buddhist grottoes near today's Luoyang protect the nearby image of a sitting female Buddha said to be modeled on Tang Empress Wu. After the Northern Wei rulers moved their capital to Luoyang in 493 CE, they sponsored more carvings of Buddhist statues in these cliffs at Longmen, and the carving continued through the Tang era for the next 400 years, culminating in these naturalistic and graceful sculptures. Photo by Paul Ropp

The most far-reaching of Feng's reforms was the institution of the "equal-field system." Under this system, all land belonged to the state, but the state in turn assigned every family twenty *mu* (a *mu* is one-third acre) of land permanently for the cultivation of mulberry and other trees. In addition, every family was given lifetime control over forty *mu* of farm land for every able-bodied man in the family (including slaves) and thirty *mu* for every ox the family possessed. Only officials' families could own more land than these standard allotments. In exchange for these generous allotments of land, every family was obliged to pay annual taxes on the land they farmed. This system was designed to ensure that all available land was occupied by taxpaying farmers and that no one could accumulate unlimited land holdings without being taxed. It remained a viable taxation system into the eighth century.

Empress Dowager Feng's step-grandson, the Xiaowen Emperor, continued her policies, and when he moved the Northern Wei capital in 494 from Pingcheng to Luoyang, he began a further series of reforms to continue the process of promoting Chinese cultural and political values. The ruling family took a Chinese surname, Yuan, and the emperor had the early Confucian text *The Classic of Filial Piety* translated into the language of the Xianbei. A major motivation behind the Xiaowen Emperor's various reforms was to curb the power of the military establishment in the Northern Wei system, and this alarmed several generals so much that they rose in rebellion against him in 496. He managed to suppress the rebellion, but he died in 499, and the Northern Wei quickly declined in a spiral of plots and power struggles between Xianbei generals, Chinese officials, and child emperors and their regents at the court. In 524 Xianbei troops rebelled against Luoyang, and those sent to suppress the rebellion turned against each other. Luoyang was sacked, and the Northern Wei collapsed in 534. Several generals proclaimed short-lived "dynasties," including the Northern Qi dynasty (552–77) and the Northern Zhou dynasty (557–81). In 581, a Xianbei general with a Chinese name, Yang Jian, usurped power from the Zhou and declared his own dynasty, the Sui. Taking the Chinese reign title of Sui Wendi (the cultured emperor), he was in a very few years able to send his armies successfully into south China and to reunify the north and south in 589 for the first time in three and a half centuries.

The long period of disunion from 220 to 589 was a time of extraordinary political change that witnessed the ethnic and cultural hybridization of Han Chinese and non-Han nomadic peoples and institutions in north China, and the full incorporation of the Yangzi River valley under Han Chinese control for the first time in the south. During this time,

Daoism flourished as a philosophy and religion. Buddhism became the dominant religion in north and south China alike and in turn gave rise to the first sophisticated development of Chinese sculpture and the creation of the magnificent Buddhist caves of Yungang, Longmen, and Dunhuang. According to historical records from the time, by the late fifth century there were nearly 6,500 Buddhist temples and more than 77,000 monks and nuns in north China. And in the early sixth century, there were reported to be more than 2,800 Buddhist temples and more than 83,000 monks and nuns in the south.

In the same years, the literati developed a new ideal of the artist-recluse who is free from the obligations and headaches of officialdom. Poets broke away from the early Confucian idea that poetry's main purpose was the teaching of moral lessons and instead began to emphasize the overriding importance of spontaneity, creativity, and the expression of authentic emotion in poetry. These new artistic ideals helped inspire creative new developments in poetry, painting, and calligraphy. It is no coincidence that writers of this time created the first Chinese literary anthologies based on the idea of literature as artistic creation and not simply moralistic preaching. Fiction writing also developed new approaches as Buddhist missionaries discovered that suspenseful stories were more successful than moralistic instructions in spreading their message.

All these changes meant that China in 589 was a very different civilization from what it had been in the Han dynasty. China was now a much wealthier, more urbanized, and more commercialized country than in Han times. As a result of the growing prosperity, international trade, and cultural creativity of the three and a half centuries following the fall of the Han, the succeeding Sui-Tang period was to be one of the most vibrant and rich cultural eras in all of Chinese history.

CHAPTER 4

Reunified Empires: Sui (581–618) and Tang (618–907)

During the long three and a half centuries of disunion after the fall of the Han dynasty, the weak southern regimes were dominated by powerful aristocratic families who saw themselves as the true guardians and protectors of Chinese civilization. They looked down on the more powerful northern governments of the Wei and its successors as only half-civilized barbarians, unlearned in the ways of Confucianism and ignorant of proper etiquette, rituals, and social hierarchies. It particularly disturbed the southerners that women were far more outspoken and independent in the nomadic cultures of the north than in the aristocratic Confucian families of the south. The northern rulers, in turn, looked upon the southern political regimes as effete, snobbish, and pretentious. These differences and prejudices meant that any serious effort to reunify China into one integrated empire faced a cultural challenge as great as the military challenge.

The man who succeeded in reunifying the north and south was Yang Jian, born in 541 to a mixed nomadic-Chinese family with a Chinese surname. A powerful military official under the Northern Zhou, Yang inherited his father's title as the Duke of Sui in 568. He was a courageous and competent military leader who saw no contradiction between his devout faith in Buddhism and his military way of life. Yang Jian's wife was from a very prominent, partly Chinese and partly Xiongnu family. She was eventually to function nearly as a co-emperor with her husband. Upon their marriage, when he was sixteen and she was thirteen, Yang Jian promised never to take a concubine, and his wife soon became his constant companion and closest advisor.

In his rise to power, Yang Jian was both capable and lucky. He was capable enough to recruit the most able military generals and civilian officials to his cause, and lucky enough to have as his first enemies the incompetent relatives and retainers of the corrupt court of the Northern

Zhou. By 589, forces loyal to Yang Jian had eliminated all remnants of the Northern Zhou ruling elite, including fifty-nine princes and their families. That same year they overwhelmed Jiankang, the capital of the southern kingdom of Chen, and conquered the Yangzi River valley, bringing north and south under one central government, the Sui dynasty, for the first time since the fall of the Han in 220.

To set up a successful dynasty over both north and south was anything but simple. In three decades that were as dramatic as the Qin conquest of the Warring States, the Sui armies and civil government brought to China a much higher degree of military unity and political integration than the country had ever known before. Yang Jian took the reign title Wendi, "the cultured emperor," suggesting that he well understood that cultural factors were as important as military ones in unifying north and south. In addition to his efficient armies, he had capable ministers who justified his every move in terms of the Confucian classics and the beliefs and practices of Daoism and Buddhism. They described in detail the sins of both the Northern Zhou regime and the southern rulers of Jiankang and promised to bring peace, stability, and prosperity to the land with the assistance of Heaven's Mandate.

Sui Wendi implemented the equal-field system of the Northern Wei dynasty throughout the empire. Every able-bodied male owed the state one month of labor per year, and the Sui now mobilized millions of laborers to reunite and reconstruct the Great Wall on the northern and western borders. Even more important for the future of the empire, they drafted hundreds of thousands more to construct the Grand Canal, first linking the city of Yangzhou south of the Yangzi River with Luoyang and eventually extending farther southward to Hangzhou and northeast to a point near today's Beijing. The finished canal, extending twelve hundred miles, was forty paces wide and deep enough to accommodate boats carrying five hundred to eight hundred tons. The Grand Canal ensured the steady flow of taxes paid in grain from the prosperous south to the seat of government in the more arid north.

Sui Wendi also ordered the building of a grand new capital at Chang'an on the site of the Western Han capital. The city was laid out in a rectangular grid, with the imperial palace at the center of the northern side. The remainder of the U-shaped city was divided into 108 wards, 106 for residences and two for markets to be conducted under strict government supervision. The entire city was surrounded by a five-meter-high wall of pounded earth that extended almost six miles from east to west and more than five miles from north to south. Although Chang'an remained a relatively empty walled expanse during Wendi's

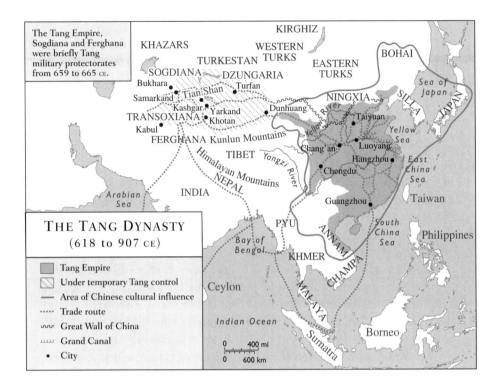

THE TANG DYNASTY
(618 to 907 CE)

- ▨ Tang Empire
- ▨ Under temporary Tang control
- — Area of Chinese cultural influence
- ⋯⋯ Trade route
- ∿∿ Great Wall of China
- ⊔⊔ Grand Canal
- • City

lifetime, it was to become within a century the largest and greatest city in the world.

Yang Jian's wife died in 602, after which he felt increasingly vulnerable and alone, and he himself fell ill and died in 604. His successor was their second son, Yang Guang, whom his mother had favored over his brothers in part because he appeared to her as more devoutly Buddhist and less sexually promiscuous. It is thus ironic that Yang Guang, who was given the reign title Sui Yangdi, was eventually portrayed by Confucian historians as the polar opposite of his father, a "bad last emperor" who quickly and wastefully lost the Mandate of Heaven. The reality is more complicated than this, to be sure, but it is undeniable that the Sui dynasty collapsed within a decade after Yangdi took power.

When a massive land and sea military expedition against the kingdom of Koguryo (in the northern part of today's Korea) failed in 612, Yangdi could not accept defeat and cut his losses. Instead, he mounted two more massive attacks on Koguryo in 613 and 614, and both were equally disastrous. These futile battles required excessive tax increases, lost much popular support for the dynasty, and revealed the growing weakness of the Sui court. A northern nomadic tribe that had been a Sui ally before the Korean invasions now turned against Sui forces and nearly captured the emperor himself in 615. Civil war soon erupted as many Sui commanders saw no more advantage in following orders from a monarch so prone to hopeless wars as Sui Yangdi.

In 617, Li Yuan, one of the major military commanders in north China (and a first cousin of Sui Yangdi), led his troops in revolt against the Sui, quickly capturing the capital city of Chang'an. Within six months of his initial act of rebellion, Li Yuan proclaimed a new dynasty, the Tang, and moved quickly against several rival armies in the north. His forces captured the secondary Sui capital of Luoyang in 621 and took the major cities of the Yangzi River valley by 624. In 626, Li Yuan's ambitious son Li Shimin imprisoned his father, killed two of his brothers, including the heir apparent, and seized the throne himself, taking the title Tang Taizong. By 628, all remnants of internal resistance to the Tang forces were eliminated, but Tang Taizong still had to contend with powerful nomads, the Khitans, and Eastern Turks on the northern and northwestern borders of the empire. Through a combination of military successes and strategic alliances with the Turks, Tang Taizong won for himself the title Great Khan, thus facilitating the joint Chinese-Turkish pacification of the Central Asian cities and oasis towns of the Silk Roads, extending Tang hegemony as far west as Kabul, Kashgar, and Samarkand by the mid-seventh century.

Tang Taizong ruled from 626 to 649. He succeeded where Sui Yangdi failed, in establishing his dynastic rule over a greater area than the Han had enjoyed and in putting the new dynasty on a firm foundation. Much like the Han before it, the Tang maintained the institutions put in place by their predecessors and used them more flexibly and effectively. To curb the power of the aristocratic families of the south, the Sui rulers had forced leading southern families to move to the capital city of Chang'an in the north. The Sui had instituted a new "rule of avoidance" (continued by the Tang), which stipulated that no official could serve the government in his own home district. This effectively ensured that local elites could not use their government positions to the advantage of their own families. The equal-field system, first implemented by the Wei in the north and by the Sui in the south, was also maintained by the Tang. And the Tang court mobilized and maintained the same two kinds of armies used by the Sui—both self-supporting soldier-farmers who served as militiamen in times of need and full-time professional soldiers.

Tang Taizong was ruthless in his seizure of the throne, but he was also a shrewd judge of character in appointing competent and loyal officials. Equally important, he was able to encourage, accept, and learn from their criticisms. He pacified the border regions of the empire from Korea and Manchuria in the northeast and across the long northern borders from the Tarim Basin to the edge of Persia in Central Asia. He also pacified the southern borders from Annam (precursor of today's Vietnam) in the southeast to Tibet in the southwest. These military victories were solidified by strategic alliances that helped neutralize potential hostile forces. The Tang rulers managed to create the world's largest empire at that time. This was possible because the strong central government in the early Tang enjoyed a solid tax base and the increasingly prosperous Yangzi River valley was now tied closely through the Grand Canal to the capital in the north.

Determined to impose his strong will on the entire empire, Tang Taizong issued a comprehensive legal code in 653, which was revised and reissued every fifteen years. The Tang Code is the oldest surviving complete legal code from China. Following Qin and Han precedents, the Code specifies a series of general principles and, in five hundred articles, a remarkably detailed list of crimes with stipulated punishments. The Code was to be applied universally, but in deference to Confucian ideas about social hierarchies, punishments differed according to the social status and rank of the offender. Penalties ranged from ten strokes with a light stick or whip to one hundred blows from a heavy stick (which could be fatal), from a few years to a lifetime of penal servitude, and from exile to the borderlands to execution. In keeping with Confucian values, a father would not be punished for beating his son, but a son who struck his father would be in serious trouble. The Tang Code became the legal model for all subsequent dynasties from Tang times into the twentieth century.

In the early twentieth century, a dramatic archeological find gave scholars an intimate glimpse of the ways that Tang power extended to the remote corners of the empire. At Dunhuang (where the Silk Roads began), a sealed-up cave was discovered containing hundreds of documents surviving from their creation in Tang times. Many of the documents were Buddhist scriptures, but because paper was scarce, the scriptures were often copied on the backs of any paper the scribes could find, including contracts, loan agreements, bills of sale for slaves or land, notices of divorce, adoption or family division, and so on. In addition, the many government documents found at Dunhuang demonstrate how, even in that remote town, the Tang government regulated prices in local markets and kept meticulous track of land deeds, sales, and transfers in carrying out the equal-field system of land allotments to all commoners.

The Tang was the most cosmopolitan of all Chinese dynasties. The Li family founders (like the Yang family founders of the Sui) had long intermarried with the Xianbei and other nomadic tribes of the north and west. The peace and prosperity of the Tang, the foreign roots of its court, and the security its forces provided through Central Asia made the Tang a period of unprecedented international trade. The Silk Roads flourished in the Tang as never before or since, and so did a flourishing trade on the east coast with Arab merchant seamen from south and Southeast Asia. The Tang capital, Chang'an, was one of the world's great global crossroads. All types of religious groups were to be found there, including Indian, Japanese, Korean, and Tibetan Buddhists, Persian priests, Nestorian Christians, Zoroastrians, and merchants from many parts of the globe, especially Turks, Uighurs, and Sogdians, as well as Jews, Arabs, and Indians. There were dance troupes from Tashkent and musicians from Korea and Southeast Asia, and the most popular music in Chang'an was Central Asian.[1]

Inspired by an intense enthusiasm for all things Buddhist, Sino-Indian trade thrived in the early Tang as never before. In the seventh and eighth centuries, forty Indian tribute missions visited the Tang court, carrying gifts to the emperor and thereby securing the right to trade such items as pearls, turmeric, precious Buddhist relics (bones of Buddhist saints believed to have special curative powers), incense, incense burners, and other Buddhist paraphernalia, all in exchange for Chinese silks, porcelains, and other products, including hides, peaches, and camphor. Chinese pilgrims and merchants in turn went to India to propagate Daoist doctrines among the Indians or to seek Buddhist scriptures, Ayurvedic medical information, or Indian longevity drugs.

The Tang is known as the greatest age of Buddhism in Chinese history. The Sui and Tang ruling houses both claimed their leaders were bodhisattvas devoted to the spread of the religion, and both dynasties patronized Buddhism with lavish gifts of land and tax exemptions for temples and monasteries. Both ruling houses continued the monumental Buddhist sculptures on the limestone cliffs and in the caves of Longmen outside of Luoyang. Because it had become popular, albeit in different forms, among both the highly educated elite and the illiterate masses, Buddhism was very useful to the Sui and Tang rulers in appealing to all social classes.

During Tang Taizong's reign, one of the great Chinese Buddhist pilgrims of all time, the monk Xuanzang, made a seventeen-year trip across the Central Asian deserts and Himalayan mountain range to India and back, securing precious Buddhist scriptures and giving the Chinese their clearest understanding yet of a number of important Buddhist schools. Xuanzang's pilgrimage was later immortalized in one of the masterworks of Chinese fiction, *Journey to the West* (also known as *Monkey*, the title of Arthur Waley's abridged but very effective translation). This sixteenth-century novel combines folklore, poetry, and imaginative tales in a gentle, comic satire of Chinese government, society, and religion. *Journey to the West* is one of China's most famous novels, and the comic adventures of Xuanzang have been popularized for centuries in innumerable operas and plays and, today, in animated cartoons and television serials.

By the eighth century, Buddhism was well integrated into almost every aspect of Chinese life; it had become a thoroughly Chinese religion with its own major schools, doctrines, and emphases. At Dunhuang, where the Silk Roads began, some thirteen monasteries housed nearly one-tenth of the entire area's population. Starting in the Northern Wei and continuing through Tang times, Buddhist artisans created the Caves of a Thousand Buddhas at Dunhuang, leaving five hundred cave temples with plastered walls filled with sculptures and paintings.

Among the unlettered masses, Pure Land Buddhism promised the faithful that one sincere appeal to Amitabha Buddha (the Buddha of Infinite Light) would guarantee one's eventual rebirth in the Pure Land of the Western Paradise where Amitabha presided. The upper classes were more drawn to the school of Tiantai Buddhism, named after the Tiantai Mountains where its sixth-century founder, Zhiyi, lived and wrote. With typical Chinese concern for universality and order, Zhiyi developed a systematic theory incorporating every known school of Buddhist doctrine and practice into one complex whole, on the grounds that every school had a valid, if different, meaning and purpose.

The most popular Buddhist movement among the educated elite came to be the Chan School (known in the West as Zen, after the Japanese pronunciation of Chan which means meditation). Chan Buddhism was introduced into China in the sixth century by the eccentric Indian monk Bodhidharma (which means the teaching of enlightenment). All people, he asserted, have the Buddha-nature within themselves, and the only effective way to fully realize their Buddha-nature is through meditation. The Chan school grew rapidly in China, and in many ways it combined elements of philosophical Daoism with Buddhism. Chan temples were usually built in beautiful mountain settings, with magnificent gardens where the peacefulness of nature was an aid to meditation. Chan masters following Bodhidharma emphasized that "the Dao lies in chopping wood and carrying water," meaning that the truth of religious life lay not in ritual, expensive icons, or works of art but in the common tasks of daily life. With its emphasis on spontaneity and the love of nature, Chan Buddhism helped to inspire much great poetry and painting in China from Tang times onward.

The economic consequences of Buddhism were at least as great as the religious and artistic consequences. Buddhist monasteries engaged in many economic activities, including sophisticated fund-raising, moneylending, and the running of pawnshops, flour mills, oil presses, and some of the world's first hotels, where travelers could find a hot meal and warm bed for a modest fee. Buddhism also stimulated a thriving market for religious icons and other paraphernalia, and Buddhist pilgrimages and festivals stimulated what became a vibrant tourist industry. Auctions, savings accounts with compound interest, and the sale of equities and bonds all originated with the entrepreneurship of Buddhist temples and monasteries.[2]

If the prevalence of Buddhism was one major indication of foreign influence in Tang times, another was the relatively powerful position of women. In the nomadic societies of the north, women rode on horseback as much as men, and when men were away tending livestock on far-flung pasturelands, women naturally supervised the running of their households. In Tang paintings, one can see robust, even chubby, women with rosy cheeks and full figures that evoke western European Renaissance depictions of female beauty, except that the Chinese women are fully clothed. We also see paintings of elite women riding horseback and even playing polo.

Given the relatively high status of women in Tang high society, it is not mere coincidence that the most powerful woman in all of Chinese history was Empress Wu of the Tang (her given name was Zhao, and she is most popularly known as Wu Zetian). She entered the imperial palace in about 640 to become one of Tang Taizong's concubines when she was only thirteen. When he died in 649, all of his concubines were to shave their heads and enter a Buddhist nunnery, but Wu Zhao managed to escape that fate and was soon back in the palace as a low-ranking concubine of the young Emperor Gaozong.

By the end of 652, Wu Zhao had borne the emperor a son and was promoted to a higher rank in the imperial harem. Within a few years, Emperor Gaozong deposed Empress Wang and replaced her with Empress Wu. Wu Zhao's critics claim that she first framed Empress Wang for the murder of her own (Wu Zhao's) daughter and then framed her again for the attempted murder of her husband, the emperor. In any case, Wu Zhao became empress in 656, and after Gaozong suffered the first of many strokes in 660, she began to dominate all the decisions of his court.

Empress Wu recruited a group of scholars to act as her personal advisors, and in 666 she and her palace ladies helped preside over special imperial sacrifices to Heaven, an unprecedented degree of female involvement in court sacrifices. In 674, the emperor and empress adopted new titles—Heavenly Sovereign and Heavenly Empress—implying their coequal positions in ruling the empire. When opposition to these moves

In this modern copy of an eighth-century painting, a Tang court lady with painted "moth eyebrows" and flowered headdress plays with her pet dog. Court paintings from the middle to late Tang portray women as full-bodied and physically active, in contrast to thinner, more frail and sedentary models of feminine beauty from the Song and later periods. Bildarchiv Preussischer Kulturbesitz / Art Resource, NY

surfaced in the court, she dealt with opponents ruthlessly, sending many to death, including two of her own sons. When Emperor Gaozong died in 683, Wu Zhao's seventeen-year-old son became Emperor Zhongzong, and as the empress dowager, she was in virtual control of the government. When the young emperor challenged his mother's authority within six weeks of assuming the throne, she had him replaced by his younger brother, Emperor Ruizong, whom she locked in a separate palace away from the decision-makers of the state.

After quickly suppressing an open rebellion by a number of imperial princes, Wu Zhao assumed power directly in 690, declaring that the Mandate of Heaven had passed to her own new Zhou dynasty.

Her Zhou dynasty lasted for fifteen years, until she was over eighty, in ill health, and very weak. She was finally forced to abdicate power back to her son Zhongzong in 705, and she died a few months later. Despite the terrible stories of her sexual escapades and the many cruel punishments she dealt out to her political foes, even her critics have had to admit that she was a more competent ruler than many of the men who have occupied the dragon throne. She brought new and much needed talent into the government by promoting the use of examinations to recruit officials, and she strengthened the power of the Tang monarchy by removing from power some of the more entrenched families in the Tang aristocracy. The main lesson male Confucian historians have drawn from Empress Wu's momentous career is that male rulers should never forget the terrible powers of a beautiful woman to manipulate weak men and destroy the "natural" social order in which women are supposed to serve men and not vice versa. Despite her being regarded as such a negative example, her tomb was placed beside that of the emperor Gaozong, where it can still be visited today.

The Tang was officially restored in 705, but the court was torn with factional power struggles until 712, when Empress Wu's grandson, Xuanzong, assumed the throne and brought much needed stability to the government. Xuanzong's long reign, from 712 until 756, marked both the high point of Tang power and Tang culture as well as the dramatic beginning of a long and torturous period of decline. In the early years of his reign, Xuanzong seemed to embody all the virtues of a great Chinese emperor, a philosopher-king who was both a conscientious administrator and a brilliant intellectual. Xuanzong's court became the center of high culture in the mid-Tang. He established schools and libraries, presided over elaborate and beautiful state ceremonies, and patronized poets and artists, all without forgetting his duties in setting fair taxes, keeping government expenses under control, and maintaining social order and peace on the borders.

Unfortunately, amid all the court ceremonies, intellectual discussions and lavish entertainments in Xuanzong's court, it became easy not to notice several danger signs on the horizon. A further added distraction for Xuanzong was that in his later years he fell deeply in love with a beautiful concubine, Yang Guifei ("Precious Consort Yang"), so much so that he began to grant her relatives all sorts of privileges and powers while ignoring the growing problems facing his government. The emperor would do anything to please his young concubine, who shared his love of poetry, painting, music, and dance. She became infatuated with An Lushan, a non-Chinese (Turkish-Sogdian) general who commanded a large army in the vicinity of today's Beijing. She helped An Lushan gain control of 160,000 troops, the largest armed force under one commander in the empire. The growing weakness of the dynasty was dramatically revealed in 751, when Tang armies suffered simultaneous crushing defeats in the southwest (today's Yunnan), in the far western outposts of Central Asia, and along the northeast borders with Korea.

To make matters worse, Xuanzong's longtime prime minister, who had effectively controlled the government for at least a decade, died in 752, inspiring new tensions among various factions in the capital. The many relatives of Yang Guifei had risen to great power and influence at the court because of her ties with the emperor, and they now began to fear An Lushan's power and to plot against him. When the emperor summoned him to attend a wedding at the capital in 755, An Lushan suspected a trap and refused to comply.

Four months later, the general led his troops in an open rebellion, and they quickly occupied the "eastern capital" of Luoyang where he proclaimed himself emperor. By July of 756, the rebel forces approached the capital of Chang'an, and Emperor Xuanzong and his "precious consort" Yang Guifei were forced to flee the city for their lives. With a few troops they headed south, but forty miles outside the city on the second day of the journey, the troops mutinied and refused to go any further unless the emperor agreed to have Yang Guifei killed. With some justification, they blamed her and her family for An Lushan's rebellion and this perilous retreat now forced upon them. The emperor tearfully ordered his chief eunuch to strangle his beautiful concubine, and the sad imperial procession continued its journey southward and out of danger.

An Lushan was assassinated by one of his own men in 757, and his troops split into two factions and began fighting among themselves. The Tang court, now under the leadership of Xuanzong's son, Emperor

Suzong, mobilized an army bolstered with mercenary soldiers, mostly Arabs and Uighurs from Central Asia. By the middle of 757, these Tang forces were able to recapture Chang'an. Even so, remnant rebel forces were not entirely eliminated until 763, when the last rebel general committed suicide. The price of peace was to grant a general amnesty for those who had joined the rebellion and to hand over some districts to the very generals who had rebelled there.

The An Lushan Rebellion signified the end of the Tang's domination of their neighbors. Many peasants fled from the areas of fighting, and the tax rolls were reduced by two-thirds, leaving the state treasuries depleted and the equal-field system in tatters. Local military commanders became increasingly independent and reluctant to send their tax revenues to the central government or to follow orders from the capital. Tibet was a powerful empire of its own in the eighth century, and Tibetan forces invaded and looted Chang'an in the fall of 763 and continued to do so periodically for years thereafter. This became a typical pattern of the late Tang. Nomadic troops along the northern and western frontiers began to charge the Chinese extortionate prices for the horses China needed for its own defense. They sometimes took ransom payments in exchange for not invading, and when that failed, they felt increasingly free to raid Chinese cities with little fear of reprisal.

Despite the long, slow decline of Tang political and military power, Tang society and the economy continued to flourish. As the tax system was eroded by the wars of the mid-eighth century, the government turned to a tax on salt to bolster its revenues. Other trade was left largely untaxed, and consequently, trade grew rapidly, especially internal trade and the sea trade with South and Southeast Asia. In the late Tang, Central Asian nomadic groups were increasingly free to raid the Silk Roads caravans laden with Chinese silks or porcelains headed west or those headed toward China with jewels, spices, horses, or textiles. Yet Sino-Indian trade continued to thrive with the growth of sea-based commerce from China's southeast coast around the Southeast Asian archipelago, past Burma and on to India. The southern port of Guangzhou was filled with Indian, Persian, Javanese, Malay, Cham, Khmer, and Arab merchants who brought fragrant tropical woods, medicines, spices, and incense to China in exchange for silk, porcelain, and even slaves.[3] As a result of this thriving trade, black pepper from India became a common part of the Chinese diet in Tang times, and many Chinese came to use the spices of South and Southeast Asia—including cloves, aloeswood, benzoin, saffron, and sandalwood—either as food condiments or in medical prescriptions.

The flourishing sea-based trade with India and Southeast Asia brought increasing prosperity to central and south China in the eighth and ninth centuries. By 742 the government census showed that half of the population (of perhaps sixty million) now lived in the southern half of the country. The Grand Canal helped to integrate the commercial economy within China proper and gave the Tang government in Chang'an and Luoyang access to the growing wealth of the south, primarily in the form of grain and silk. Tea also became a major item of internal trade. Produced first in the far southwest, its use spread throughout China, and by the mid-Tang it had become the national drink of choice. Because it required boiled water, the use of tea had major public health benefits as well and contributed to the rapid population growth of the Tang and subsequent periods.

Over the course of the Tang, Buddhist monasteries had become significant centers of wealth, with large holdings of tax-exempt land and many magnificent treasures of religious art. An estimated 260,000 monks and nuns and 100,000 slaves lived on these tax-free lands. In 845, Emperor Wuzong ordered the confiscation of most Buddhist temples and shrines, leaving one temple in each prefecture, and four in each of the two main capitals (Chang'an and Luoyang). Each surviving temple could have thirty monks or nuns, and everyone else was forced to return to lay life without any support from the religious establishment. The emperor ordered the bronze bells and images from the closed temples melted down into coins, the iron statues melted and converted into agricultural implements, and all precious gold, silver, and jade objects turned over to the Bureau of Public Revenue. Emperor Wuzong died in 846, and his successor ended the suppression, but in one short year much Buddhist wealth had been confiscated by the state, and Buddhism would never again be quite as powerful as it had been in the early and middle Tang.

By 860 the Tang dynasty was clearly in decline, as regional military commanders became increasingly independent of the central government and bandits roamed freely across the countryside. The largest rebellion was led by Huang Chao, an examination failure and unemployed scholar, whose forces captured and looted the southern port of Guangzhou in 879 before moving directly on the capital of Chang'an in 881. His forces were brutal and poorly disciplined, and he was defeated and driven out of the capital in 883. Huang Chao had revealed the great weakness of the government, inviting by example many others to follow his lead. The dynasty officially collapsed in 907, but it had lost all semblance of control at least three decades before that.

Despite its inglorious end, the Tang period as a whole has long been regarded as one of the truly great ages in Chinese history. By 700, Chang'an was the largest city in the world, with nearly two million people. It served as a magnet for merchants, diplomats, and religious pilgrims from all over Asia. In its political organization, economic prosperity and cultural sophistication, the Tang dynasty in the early eighth century was the world's greatest empire. In contrast to Europe, where Justinian in the sixth century and Charlemagne in 800 had tried but failed to match the size and scope of the Roman Empire, Tang China easily surpassed the great Han dynasty in its size, degree of central control, prosperity, and cultural sophistication. In varying degrees, Japan, Korea, and Vietnam all drew direct inspiration from the Tang Empire, including its capital city, its Confucian political philosophy, its schools of Buddhism, its art and architecture, its medical traditions, and its classical Chinese language. In 640, eight thousand Koreans were in Chang'an trying to absorb as much of China's culture as they could. Japan in the eighth century reformed its government and built its permanent capital in Kyoto, directly modeled on the example of Chang'an.

The one art form most identified with the Tang dynasty is poetry, which is seen in Chinese culture as the most honest and revealing way to express one's true feelings. At dinners and banquets the hosts and guests exchanged clever poems on the occasion. Men traded flirtatious poems with educated prostitutes or courtesans as part of the "courting" process, which might or might not result in a "sale." People recorded their daily activities in poems, wrote letters in poems, described great historic events or scenes of natural beauty in poems, and commemorated their departures from friends with tearful poems.

The Complete Poems of the Tang Dynasty, a compilation made in the early eighteenth century, contains 48,900 poems from 2,200 Tang poets. Ever since Tang times, all educated Chinese have been expected to be able to write, read, and appreciate poetry. Every young man who studied for the civil service examinations first learned poetry by memorizing *Three Hundred Tang Poems,* a book that includes samples from all the great Tang poets.

Most critics have agreed that the two greatest poets in Chinese history were the Tang poets Li Bo and Du Fu, who are sometimes seen as the *yin* and *yang* of Chinese poetry, or the Daoist and Confucian sides of the Chinese psyche. Such labels are oversimplified, but they capture something of the contrast between these two great men. Li Bo deliberately cultivated the self-image of a carefree genius who dashed off brilliant poems without any effort at all. He casually broke all the rules of poetry, considering them too constraining for his unbridled inspiration. He liked to give the impression that he cared nothing about fame and official rank and that he would just as soon throw his brilliant poems into a rushing stream as copy them into a notebook for posterity. Li Bo could use poems in the Confucian way, to criticize social ills and injustices, but he was more likely to celebrate the beauties of nature and the fun of drinking with his friends. More than with any other Chinese poet of any time, Li Bo's poetry celebrated his own unique self.

In contrast to Li Bo, Du Fu served in several positions as a conscientious Confucian official, and he was a careful craftsman in poetry, never violating the proper poetic form. He was the most versatile Chinese poet ever. He could be profoundly erudite, highly political, or critical of corruption and inequality, as well as light, playful, deeply compassionate, or intensely personal. Du Fu demonstrated the full range of his humanity in his poems, writing fondly of his wife and his children, his friends, and his daily routine.

Other Tang poets have also been immortalized in Chinese culture. Bo Juyi, for example, was one of the most popular poets during his own time, the late eighth and early ninth century, and on into the present. He wrote in a simple and direct style that made his poems popular with everyone, not just the highly educated. His "Song of Everlasting Sorrow" described the tragedy of Emperor Xuanzong and his Precious Consort Yang Guifei, helping to make her the best-known imperial concubine in Chinese history. People in all walks of life bought his poems in urban markets, and courtesans set his verses to music. He was one of China's first international celebrities. The great Japanese novel from the tenth century, *The Tale of Genji*, quotes dozens of poems by Bo Juyi and his friends.

The Tang court, like all subsequent courts in imperial China, patronized many artists, and Chang'an became a magnet drawing the best painters in the land. Members of the elite continued in the Tang to be buried in tombs with elaborate paintings on the walls, but Tang artists also painted on vertical hanging scrolls or horizontal hand scrolls designed not for tombs but for private ownership by the living. Although few Tang paintings have survived the ravages of war and time, scholars now regard the Tang as the first great period of Chinese landscape painting. In the cosmopolitan atmosphere of Chang'an Chinese artisans quickly learned Persian metalworking techniques for making delicate objects in gold and silver. Merchant caravans from the West were so common that people began placing in tombs cheap painted and glazed porcelain representations of Western merchants and entertainers and their camels. Music from Central Asia also became popular in China and transformed Chinese popular musical tastes and styles. The *pipa*, a four-stringed lute originally from Persia, became a popular instrument in China during the Tang and has remained so ever since.

For several reasons, the Tang period was marked by an openness to foreign influences that has seldom been seen in China before or since. The imperial family of the Tang had long intermingled and intermarried with nomadic peoples of the northwest. Many foreign influences came to China with the unprecedented popularity of Buddhism during the Tang. And by extending Chinese power and influence into Central Asia, the Tang Empire greatly facilitated the flourishing trade of the Silk Roads. As the most powerful, prosperous, and creative civilization in the world in its own time, the Tang dynasty has ever since been a source

This glazed terracotta funerary statue of a Central Asian caravaneer with his loaded camel was found in a Tang tomb. So popular was the Silk Road trade in Tang times that these ceramic camels with their "barbarian" caravaneers were frequently buried in the tombs of officials and royal families, in order to continue the supply of exotic goods from the far west to the ancestral souls of Tang aristocrats in the next world. Bridegman-Giraudon / Art Resource, NY

of great cultural pride for the Chinese people. The meaning of the Cantonese name for Chinatown still today is "the streets of men of Tang." Perhaps the clearest measure of the Tang's success in building an empire is that in stark contrast to the Han, after the Tang collapse in 907, it only took half a century for a new dynasty to reunify the country again into one integrated whole.

CHAPTER 5

Diminished Empire and Nomadic Challengers: Song (960–1279) and Yuan (1279–1368)

The half century between the Tang and Song dynasties is known as the period of the Five Dynasties and Ten Kingdoms, in reference to five short-lived regimes in the north and ten minor kingdoms competing in the south during these years. Chang'an and Luoyang, the two Tang centers of power, were devastated in the civil wars that finished off the Tang, and the city of Kaifeng, at the mouth of the Grand Canal and three hundred miles closer to the grain-producing regions of south China, became the center of competition among the generals of the north. In 960, General Zhao Kuangyin seized control of Kaifeng and proclaimed a new dynasty, the Song (pronounced Soong).

Zhao Kuangyin, known to history by his reign title of Song Taizu, was one of the pivotal emperors in Chinese history because he created a more centralized state than ever before. From 960 to his death in 976, he conquered the south and brought the best troops in the empire under his own direct control to protect the capital. He persuaded his most powerful generals to retire with generous stipends, and he placed their armies in outlying areas under the direct control of his own civil bureaucrats. Many of the powerful aristocratic families of the Tang era were killed or greatly weakened in the civil wars that ended the Tang, and so the Song emperors had far fewer rivals for power than their Tang predecessors. In the Song dynasty, civil bureaucrats were much more likely to become government officials through competing in the civil service examination system rather than through blood ties to other officials.

In the Song period, China came closer than ever before or since to achieving the Confucian ideal of a central bureaucratic state ruled by the emperor with the advice and management of civil bureaucrats who were deeply committed to the Confucian classics. Perhaps in reaction against the perceived excesses of the Tang empress Wu, Song emperors prevented threats to their power from their wives and in-laws. And unlike their Han and Tang predecessors, they suffered no threats to their power from the eunuchs who served the imperial household.

Yet the Song—because Taizu and his brother, who succeeded him, elevated their Confucian scholar-officials over their military commanders—were never as militarily powerful or assertive toward their neighbors as the Han and Tang had been. A powerful nomadic group, the Khitans, occupied the entire northeast, including much of Mongolia and Manchuria, and began to adopt Chinese methods of ruling under a strong leader, Abaoji, who rose to power just as the Tang collapsed. When Abaoji died in 926, his Chinese Confucian advisors suggested that his wife should follow him to the grave. She responded that with only young children in line to succeed him, she would have to remain alive to carry on his work. But to the astonishment of all, she cut off one of her hands to be buried with the deceased emperor, proving her loyalty to him even as she refused to join him in death. She then led the Khitans on a successful campaign to capture sixteen prefectures in the area of today's Beijing, and she proclaimed a new Khitan dynasty, the Liao.

For the first few decades of the Song dynasty, the Khitan Liao administered Chinese communities in Chinese style and Khitan nomadic communities in their traditional tribal ways. They also continuously threatened Chinese settlements in the north and even managed to wound the Song emperor in 979. In 1004, after the Liao had successfully occupied much of the Yellow River valley, the Song and Liao courts signed a treaty meant as an agreement between coequal states. The Liao agreed to withdraw from their recently occupied territory, and the Song state agreed to pay the Liao court 200,000 rolls of silk and 100,000 ounces of silver annually. This was virtual extortion of the weak Song state by the powerful Liao, but the payments were cheaper than war, and a small fraction of the Song military budget (which came to absorb over 80 percent of all state spending).

The Khitan Liao was not the only threat to the Song dynasty. To the northwest the Tanguts, another nomadic group who came from Tibetan stock, ruled over their own state, the Xi Xia. Like the Khitans, the Tanguts ruled with a combination of Chinese and nomadic tribal methods. And like the Khitans, they occupied northern territory once held by the Tang dynasty and were a continual military threat to the new Song dynasty. In 1040 the Song court agreed to pay the Tangut Xi

Xia court substantial annual payments as well, thus buying peace on the northwestern frontier.

The constant border threats required continuous expansion of the Song military, which swelled from 387,000 troops in 975 to 1,259,000 troops in 1045. The cost of training and equipping such a large army, on top of the very large annual "ransom" payments to the Liao and Xi Xia rulers, threatened to bankrupt the state in the eleventh century. In response to this crisis, Song officials in these years carried on the most thorough debate since the Warring States period over the nature of "good government" and the proper relationship between the state and the society it ruled. The result was factional bureaucratic argument and infighting that lasted a generation and has echoed through the halls of Chinese government ever since.

At the heart of the debate was Wang Anshi (1021–1086), an eccentric idealist who argued that the state needed drastic reforms to fulfill its classical Confucian obligations to serve the people. Wang believed that most Confucian officials had lost touch with the true meaning of the classics and had grown too comfortable to perceive the crisis faced by the state. In 1069, Wang Anshi rose to the position of chief councilor (like the prime minister) under the young and ambitious Emperor Shenzong. Wang immediately declared a series of reforms, starting with a government program to make low-interest loans to poor peasants, both to prevent their exploitation by private loan sharks and to use money-lending to raise state revenues. He ordered a land survey to assess new tax rates based on the actual productivity of the land. He declared that taxes would be collected in money, not in labor services, a change aimed particularly at the wealthy. He vowed to reduce the size of the expensive professional army and to train local citizens in self-defense militias. He proposed a nationwide school system to educate those of modest means and called for changing the emphasis of the civil service examinations from poetry and memorization of the classics to current political and economic problems. Wang's government would become more directly involved in the economy, compete with private merchants, set up government pawnshops nationwide, and buy local products to transport and sell elsewhere. This would increase state revenues and undercut excessive profits of the merchant class.

When officials opposed Wang's ideas, he was quick to dismiss them from office. He frightened the wealthy and well established, the very people who dominated the government. He tried to do too much too quickly, and his loan program backfired, for local officials ended up charging interest rates as high as the loan sharks, thereby defeating the purpose of the program. Wang stirred up such powerful opposition that he was forced to resign from office in 1076. After Emperor Shenzong died in 1085, all of Wang's reforms were repealed, and the dynasty continued to limp along financially, not recognizing the disasters that were approaching.

One of the most articulate critics of Wang Anshi's policies was the brilliant scholar-official Su Shi, better known as Su Dongpo (1036–1101). Su had a sharp tongue and suffered through two periods of exile for his opposition to Wang's reforms, but it is indicative of the nature of political battles in the Song that he remained on friendly terms with Wang. They exchanged poems with each other even in old age. In this regard, the Song dynasty represents the high-water mark of civil political debate in imperial China. Before and after the Song, factional political conflicts were more often resolved through force—the arrest, exile, or execution of one's opponents.

Despite his political persecution, Su Dongpo became one of the most admired of all Chinese literati. He was a student of the *Book of Changes* and the *Analects* of Confucius, as well as Daoist alchemy and Chan Buddhist meditation. Known for his compassion, he worked tirelessly to provide flood control measures and famine relief, found orphanages and hospitals, and provide medical care for prisoners. Su's main legacy to Chinese culture was in his poetry, his calligraphy, and his writings about art. He saw poetry as a way of painting, painting as wordless poetry, and both as precious vehicles of self-expression. He left behind 2,400 treasured poems and 300 song lyrics—a new genre of poetry he did much to popularize. One of the few Chinese literati to master every style of poetry as well as painting and calligraphy, he epitomized the ideal that inspired Chinese scholars from Song times into the twentieth century: the brilliant scholar, versatile artist, and conscientious official who would risk his political career to do the right thing and, when driven out of power, would take great solace and pleasure in the beauties of nature and the arts.

In 1101, the year Su Dongpo died, another new emperor, Huizong, took the throne and stated his intention to restore Wang Anshi's reforms. The result was only to intensify rivalries and tensions among Huizong's officials without addressing the fundamental problems of financial and military weakness. Huizong was frankly more interested in art and literature than in the nitty-gritty problems of government. He was a skilled painter and calligrapher and a passionate collector of paintings, ancient bronzes, porcelain ware, and beautiful stones. He particularly excelled at delicate paintings of flowers and birds, and he perfected an exquisite form of calligraphy called "slender gold." He brought many painters to his court, where he supervised and instructed them as if the survival of the empire depended on their artistic abilities. Unfortunately, it did not.

In the early twelfth century another nomadic group, the Jurchen, formed a powerful coalition of tribes to the northeast of the Khitan Liao under a new leader, Aguda. Aguda had his own dynastic ambitions and proclaimed himself emperor of the Jin dynasty. When Aguda's forces attacked the Song's dangerous neighbor, the Khitan Liao, Huizong's court allied with the Jin in hopes of eliminating its strongest nomadic threat. The strategy backfired as the Jin defeated the Liao with Song help and then kept right on marching in 1127 into Kaifeng, the Song capital. Huizong and his son were captured by the Jin and later died in captivity. Many court officials and another of the emperor's sons fled to the south. They established a new capital south of the Yangzi River at Hangzhou, where the many rivers and canals and wet rice fields prevented easy invasion by nomads on horseback. Thus, the Song dynasty is divided into the Northern Song (960–1127) and the Southern Song (1127–1279).

It is easy in retrospect to blame the self-absorbed emperor-artist Huizong for "painting while Kaifeng burned," but there was a self-perpetuating weakness built into the Song state that went far beyond Huizong and his artistic passions. Without control over the northern and northwestern territories that had been held by the Han and Tang, even the Northern Song lacked the capacity to breed the large numbers of horses needed to fend off its powerful nomadic neighbors. In the Southern Song, the main focus of debate among Confucian officials was whether to mount an aggressive counterattack against the Jin occupiers of the north or rest content to maintain a reduced empire in the south.

In 1139 the Southern Song court, under the leadership of chief councilor Qin Gui, signed a peace treaty with the Jin. The fiery Southern Song general Yue Fei attacked the idea of conceding the north to the barbarians as a treasonous betrayal of the nation's best interest. When the Jin broke the treaty and sent troops southward in 1140, Yue Fei led Song forces in repelling them. However, Yue Fei was seen by the court as dangerous, reckless, and sure to invite a deeper invasion by the Jin or else, in his frustration, to threaten the Song ruling family itself. He was ordered to withdraw from the territory he had taken in the north. Recalled to the southern capital of Hangzhou and held under house arrest, Yue Fei was accused of plotting against the emperor and killed in prison in early 1141. Qin Gui concluded a new peace treaty with the Jin on even less favorable terms to the Southern Song. Since Song times,

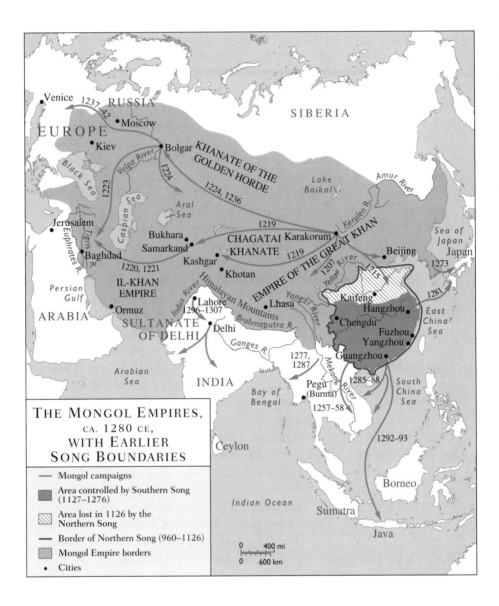

THE MONGOL EMPIRES,
CA. 1280 CE,
WITH EARLIER
SONG BOUNDARIES

— Mongol campaigns

▓ Area controlled by Southern Song (1127–1276)

▨ Area lost in 1126 by the Northern Song

— Border of Northern Song (960–1126)

▓ Mongol Empire borders

• Cities

0   400 mi
0   600 km

the Chinese have regarded Yue Fei as a great heroic patriot and Qin Gui as the ultimate traitor to his nation.

The fate of General Yue Fei reflected the Song dynasty's assertion of civilian control over the military and some shifting cultural assumptions in the Song that helped prevent an aggressive military campaign against the Jin regime in the north. Song Confucian officials were much more self-consciously condescending toward their nomadic neighbors than their Tang predecessors had been. Many of them scorned the martial values they saw in their nomadic neighbors. Whereas horseback riding and archery had been considered perfectly respectable pastimes for the Tang aristocracy, the scholar-official class in Song times became much more concerned with Confucian scholarship, literature, and the arts.

One reason for this cultural shift was the changing nature of Chinese society in the Song period. In the Tang, powerful aristocrats often inherited their official positions, but in the Song, the Chinese elite became much more dependent on the civil service examinations to win positions in government. Consequently, families who wanted to maintain their elite status in society had to provide an extensive classical education for their sons. Examinations were very difficult, requiring years of intense study in preparation, and only a small percentage of candidates could pass them and win official appointments. The invention of printing in the Tang and its spread in the Song made more books available to more families, greatly intensifying the competition for civil service examination degrees and official appointments. Confucian scholar-officials came to see their main task as intellectual and cultural—to master the best of Chinese culture in art, literature, and philosophy.

In self-conscious contrast to the uncivilized "barbarians" of the north, Chinese officials looked to men of genius like Su Dongpo for reassurance that China's was after all a far superior culture. In the strong negative reaction to the reform attempts of Wang Anshi, Song Confucian scholars made a clear choice to reject his aggressive moves to build a strong state. Instead, they opted for a more idealistic form of Confucianism that put less emphasis on governmental institutions and more emphasis on what we might call China's moral and spiritual rearmament.

Convinced by Mencius that moral goodness is ultimately the most powerful force in the world, Neo-Confucian scholars called for individual self-cultivation and rectification of moral faults through study of the Confucian classics and "quiet sitting," a Buddhist-influenced form of meditation and self-reflection. The most important Neo-Confucian scholar was Zhu Xi (1130–1200), who synthesized the work of many Neo-Confucians into one great philosophical system. He wrote commentaries on and edited all the early Confucian classics. His interpretations became the only accepted answers in the civil service examinations from late Song times until the examination system was abolished in 1905.

Another consequence of the growing concern in Song times to differentiate China from its nomadic neighbors was a change in gender relations and gender ideals. As noted, Tang court women were often very active physically and, at times, very assertive politically (e.g. Empress Wu). In the Song period, male Confucian scholars attacked nomadic cultures for their immorality in allowing women so much freedom of movement and in their custom of the levirate, in which a widow was expected to marry her husband's brother. Song male Confucians saw the levirate as a form of incest and outlawed it in Chinese society. In their horror at the levirate, some scholars argued that widows should never remarry at all, and some went so far as to praise widows who committed suicide in order to avoid remarriage. In reaction against their "uncivilized" nomadic neighbors, many Chinese literati began to emphasize more than ever that a woman's proper place was in the home and nowhere else.

Foot-binding, which first became popular in the Song dynasty, probably began with court dancers who bound their feet in the belief that small feet were more attractive on a female dancer. In the Song, mothers and grandmothers began binding their daughters' feet at four to six years of age. They took a long strip of cloth, bent the four smaller toes down under the foot, leaving the big toe in place, and wrapped the foot tightly, pulling the front and back of the foot together. As the growing foot pushed in vain against the binding, the arch bent and broke, and the heel was pulled under the foot to form its own "natural high heel." The tightly wrapped toes withered, and with circulation impaired, there was always a danger of blood poisoning. The pain was excruciating for at least two years; the result was a tiny, cramped foot three to six inches long.

Why did mothers and grandmothers subject their daughters to such pain so needlessly? Scholars still argue over this question, but the main motivation probably was the quest for social status. Song society was more fluid than Chinese society had ever been, and prominent families were very concerned to marry their daughters to other families of equal or greater prominence. Marriages were arranged by parents for the benefit of the family, and a high-status marriage was very desirable for both the daughter and her family. In this kind of competitive atmosphere, anything that made a daughter seem more attractive, more genteel, and more virtuous would improve her marriage prospects. Foot-binding was associated with virtue because it suggested that the girl with bound feet was not one to "run around wildly" and demonstrated that she came from a good family that could afford to have her confined at home like a "good girl."

Ironically, the bound foot also came to have erotic associations. The foot was always covered, and some males found that unwrapping, fondling, even sucking a woman's bound foot was sexually exciting. Finally, women covered their bound feet with beautiful embroidered cloth shoes, adding to their allure. So the female bound foot came to symbolize many things: wealth, leisure, sophistication, artistic skill, beauty, virtue, and sexiness—a powerful combination of positive associations.

In other ways, the Song marriage system improved women's cultural opportunities, as wealthy families began to educate more of their daughters so they would be able to teach their young sons in the basics of literacy, to give them a head start in their long examination preparation. Female literacy thus became one more qualification in the competitive marriage market. This began a trend that was to continue on into the twentieth century.

China's greatest female poet, Li Qingzhao (1084–c. 1151), lived in the Song period. She had a very close relationship with her husband, Zhao Mingcheng, and they shared a passion for poetry and collecting antique seals, paintings, and bronze inscriptions. Together they compiled an extensive catalogue of early bronze inscriptions and stone carvings. She sometimes celebrated their love in her poems. "Should my beloved chance to ask / If my face is fair as a flower's / I'll put one aslant in my hair / Then ask him to look and compare."[1] When the Jin invaders came in 1127, the couple's home was burned, and they lost most of their precious art collection. They fled to the south, and Zhao died two years later, leaving his wife a widow at forty-five. Little is known of her last twenty-two years apart from the fact that she briefly remarried an abusive man and filed for a divorce within three months. Such behavior was scandalous to Chinese scholars in later periods, when chastity was seen as the only proper course of action for a "cultured" woman as a widow.

Given the Song's assertion of civil authority over military leaders, its elevation of civil over martial values, and the growing military power of its nomadic neighbors, it may seem surprising that the dynasty was able to survive as long as it did. The main reason for this was a virtual economic revolution that made Song China the most prosperous and highly developed society on earth. Agricultural productivity increased dramatically in Song times, in part because more land came under cultivation as the population continued to move southward. New strains of early-ripening rice were developed in the south, allowing for two rice crops per year. The government began to print agricultural manuals to spread the newest techniques for increasing crop yields. Farmers began specializing in crops such as mulberry trees for silkworms, tea, sugar cane, bamboo, hemp, and ramie to produce fibers for cloth, and eventually cotton (introduced from India in Tang times), which became a major cash crop by the end of the Song. Interregional and international trade expanded, and along with these came a thriving money economy.

This detail from Qingming Festival Along the River, *an eighteenth-century, thirty-holiday in the Northern Song capital of Kaifeng shortly before it was conquered is filled with shops and stalls selling goods and services, and a plethora of vendors,* Museum, Taipei, Taiwan, Republic of China

In 1120, just before the loss of the north to the Jurchen, the Song government collected eighteen million ounces of silver in taxes.

In the early Song period, advances occurred in iron smelting technology, including the use of explosives to mine iron ore and the use of hydraulic machinery to power bellows that could generate higher temperatures for smelting iron and steel. The Song government sponsored the largest iron-smelting industry in the world, which produced 125,000 tons of iron in 1078 (quantities not reached in Europe for about another eight hundred years). Iron was important for making plows, other farm implements, locks, nails, musical instruments, and

eight-foot-long copy of a twelfth-century handscroll, depicts a Spring Festival
by the Jin invaders in 1127. The famous Rainbow Bridge spanning the Bian River
shoppers, and people transporting goods across the bridge. National Palace

pans for making salt. Chinese peasants probably used as many iron
tools in Song times as in the early twentieth century.

Much of the iron industry produced weapons for defense and coins
for the thriving money economy. Chinese coins were round with a
square hole in the middle, so 1,000 coins could be strung on one string.
In 1041, the Song court ordered one army in Shaanxi Province, facing
the Xi Xia on the northwest frontier, to be supplied with three million strings of cash (requiring 29,000 tons of iron). The government
mint produced eight hundred million coins a year by the year 1000 and
six billion coins a year by 1085. The government also sponsored the

manufacturing of iron weapons in great quantities. In 1084, the court sent to one army on its northwestern frontier 35,000 swords, 8,000 shields, 10,000 spears, and a million arrowheads, all made of iron.

As agriculture became more specialized and interregional trade expanded, the government began in the early Song to allow a few merchants to issue paper certificates for cash deposits in one city that could be redeemed for cash in another city, greatly increasing the convenience of long-distance trade. In the early twelfth century, the government took over the printing and issuing of these certificates, creating the world's first paper money. Song merchants organized guilds, formed partnerships, and raised money by selling stocks in their enterprises. The thriving agricultural and commercial economies of Song times can also be seen in thousands of Song-era contracts that survive, including tomb contracts that were drawn up to apply in both the world of the living and the dead.

The Song capitals of Kaifeng and Hangzhou functioned as commercial centers far more than had the Tang cities of Chang'an or Luoyang. Before it fell to the Jin invaders in 1127, Kaifeng was the largest city in the world, with perhaps one million inhabitants. After the fall of Kaifeng, the Southern Song capital of Hangzhou became an equally thriving center of trade and entertainment. A guide to Hangzhou written in 1235 describes its markets for every kind of commodity, artisans' workshops, teahouses, inns, wineshops, restaurants, professional banquet caterers, every kind of entertainment, including trained bears and insects, as well as public and private gardens, and many volunteer organizations of people with hobbies such as music, physical fitness, exotic foods, and antique collecting—and the list went on and on.

Song prosperity also stimulated international trade, particularly along the southeast coast, where Arab Muslim merchants operated huge Chinese-made ships with watertight compartments and used the Chinese invention of the compass to facilitate a thriving long-distance trade between China, Southeast Asia, and the Indian Ocean. By the early twelfth century, Quanzhou, a coastal city in southern Fujian, had half a million residents. The general prosperity of Song times can also be seen in population growth. Scholars now estimate that China's population grew from perhaps 70 million in 750 to about 100 million in 1100 and perhaps 110 million (including the Southern Song and the Jin state in the north) by 1200, a rate of population growth the world had never seen before.

Reflecting the prosperity of these years, Chinese silks, lacquerware, and porcelains reached their highest level of technical refinement in the Song. By the late Tang, Chinese craftsmen had perfected the production of true porcelain, using purified clays, firing at temperatures of 1300 degrees centigrade, and producing the fusion of glaze and body to produce a glossy translucent surface. Song porcelains are particularly treasured by collectors around the world for their beautiful monochrome glazes and simple, elegant shapes. While the Song court sponsored the manufacture of large quantities of the finest porcelain, for the first time in the Song period, highly skilled artisans began to produce such things as porcelain and lacquerware on a large scale for the marketplace. During the Song, porcelain surpassed silk as the premier Chinese export, reaching markets as far west as the Persian Gulf and the west coast of Africa.

Perhaps no cultural symbol is more closely associated with the Song dynasty than landscape painting. Song painters emphasized the beauty, harmony, and magnificence of the natural world, particularly forested mountains amid streams and valleys. In many paintings, human beings are absent or barely visible, blending into the larger harmonies of nature. If a hut or house appears, it blends in with the natural landscape and never dominates or detracts. The busy urban official treasured the rare times when he could get away to the tranquility of deserted mountains and streams and took great pleasure and solace in the landscapes hung on his wall, or rolled in his drawer, to be brought out and shared with friends over wine and the chanting of poetry. Poetry and painting were identified in another way, as painters and calligraphers regularly wrote poems on landscape paintings. The beautiful language and calligraphy of the inscription came to be seen as necessary complements to the painting itself.

Despite the economic prosperity, intellectual brilliance, and artistic greatness of the Song dynasty, it was continuously under military pressure from its nomadic neighbors to the north and west and in the thirteenth century succumbed to a newly arrived nomadic force, the Mongols of Central Asia.

Before defeating the Southern Song, the Mongols created the most effective fighting force and the largest land empire the world had ever seen. The process began with the rise in 1203 of Temuchin, a skilled fighter, who was able to unify a whole federation of Mongol and other nomadic tribes into one large fighting force. In 1206 Temuchin took the title Genghis Khan, or "Ruler of the Oceans" (that is, the world). Skilled and ferocious fighters, the Mongols under Genghis Khan, and later his son, Ögödei, established their capital at the oasis town of Kara-korum in today's Mongolia. Mongol troops were organized in groups of 100, 1,000 and 10,000, and there were 129 thousand-soldier units when Genghis died in 1227. Troops traveled with three to five horses per soldier so they could carry supplies and weapons, change mounts

The tenth-century Buddhist painter Juran used a graceful impressionistic style to portray the idyllic and ever-changing scenery of hills, fields, trees. and clouds along the Yangzi River. In this Song age of urbanization, Chinese scholar officials found solace from the pressures of official life by painting, viewing, and contemplating landscape paintings that made use of empty spaces among towering mountains, trees, stones, and water to depict the beauty, grandeur, and peaceful harmony of nature. Freer Gallery of Art, Smithsonian Institution, Washington, D.C.: Gift of Charles Lang Freer, F1911.168

regularly, and keep moving rapidly for days on end. Military commanders used flags, torches, and message carriers to maintain effective communications between units. Soldiers wore light armor made of leather with metal scales and helmets of leather or iron and carried leather-covered wicker shields. Each soldier carried two powerful compound bows and a large quiver of at least sixty iron-tipped arrows. With the use of iron stirrups, soldiers could shoot arrows accurately from a standing position while riding on horseback at full gallop. Light cavalrymen carried a short sword and two or three light spears; heavy cavalrymen carried a mace or spiked club, a curved long sword, and a twelve-foot wooden spear with a metal blade. With the prospect of rich rewards in war booty for loyal service or death for insubordination, Mongol troops were fearless and disciplined in battle.

With a ferocity and military effectiveness seldom seen in world history, they proceeded over the next fifty years to conquer not only the northern rivals of the Song dynasty—the Jin and the Xi Xia—but also Korea, all of Central Asia, the Russian cities of Moscow and Kiev in the northwest, Hungary and Poland in the far west, and the Persian cities of Baghdad, Aleppo, Damascus, and Ormuz in the southwest.

To succeed in creating the world's largest land empire, the Mongols, with only 150,000 troops, were quick to incorporate other groups into their armies and governmental structures. Given the enormous distances involved and the natural tensions that arose among the descendants of Genghis Khan, it is not surprising that the four large khanates soon broke apart and were never centrally controlled. More surprising than this failure was the success of one of Genghis's grandsons, Khubilai Khan, in conquering and ruling China in the Chinese style.

In 1264, Khubilai moved his capital from Mongolia to Dadu (today's Beijing), and in 1271 he declared himself emperor of the Yuan dynasty and the rightful inheritor of the Mandate of Heaven. As Yuan Emperor Shizu, Khubilai hired many Chinese advisors and officials and quickly set them to the task of conquering south China by hiring Chinese engineers adept at the use of catapults and explosives and commandeering Chinese ships and seamen to defeat the navies of the Southern Song. By the effective use of Chinese, Khitan, Jurchen, Korean, Uighur, and Persian troops, the Mongols were able to take most of south China by 1276, and in 1279 the last Song emperor was killed in a naval battle in the far south.

One of the reasons for the Mongols' military success was their effective use of terror as a weapon. If a city resisted or refused to surrender, the Mongols would burn, loot, kill, and rape indiscriminately and enslave the survivors. If a city surrendered, the inhabitants might survive unharmed and be allowed to continue their lives in a normal fashion. Governing a society as complex as China's was more difficult than conquering it. At most, the Mongol population totaled perhaps two million, ruling over a Chinese population of perhaps sixty to eighty million, much reduced by the wars of conquest from a peak in the Song of 115 million.

Khubilai established a government modeled after the Chinese dynastic institutions, with Mongols and their Central Asian allies in the most important positions but Chinese filling most middle and lower positions. Chinese were forbidden to bear arms, and to punish the Chinese literati for having resisted the Mongol conquest, there were no civil service examinations for Chinese until 1315. Because the south had put up a much greater struggle against the Mongols, strict examination quotas prevented southerners from passing in large numbers. While Mongols were generally tolerant of all religions, Khubilai Khan began to patronize and support Tibetan Lama Buddhism in particular, a form of Buddhism that includes many rituals and the belief that each priest is a lama, or reincarnation of the Buddha. Khubilai and his successors gave Tibetan lamas special privileges and allowed them to convert some Song imperial palaces into Buddhist temples and even to loot the tombs of the Song emperors to sell their treasures for money to build more temples.

The Mongol conquest of China took a terrible economic toll. The Song iron industry was devastated and never fully regained Song levels of productivity. Intense warfare greatly reduced the population, and the spread of infectious diseases, such as bubonic plague, from Central Asia to China produced several terrible epidemics that killed millions in the mid-fourteenth century (and eliminated one-fourth of Europe's population soon thereafter). The wars destroyed farmland and irrigation works, and in places Mongol princes and generals turned rice-producing land into parks and pastures. The combined effects of war and disease greatly reduced the tax base. The Yuan government responded by printing more money, which only fueled inflation and further undermined the economic health of the dynasty.

Following their conquest of southern China, the Mongols ambitiously undertook naval expeditions of conquest against Japan in 1274 and 1281 and against the kingdom of Java in the southern Pacific in 1292–1293. They also launched attacks on Vietnam and Burma, failing in both cases but winning the symbolic "submission" of those countries to the "Son of Heaven," Khubilai Khan. These wars were a serious drain on the state's resources and only served to delay the economic recovery of the Yuan from the dislocations of their early years.

Despite the hardships imposed on the Chinese population during the Yuan dynasty, Chinese life was not greatly changed. The Mongols did not interfere with Chinese customs or religious practices. The Venetian merchant Marco Polo claimed to have spent twenty years (1275–1295) in China during Mongol rule and wrote a bestselling account of his travels. Although some have cast doubt on the truthfulness of his story, many of his observations have been confirmed by other sources. He accurately reported, for example, that relations between Han Chinese and their Mongol rulers were very strained but also that south China was far more economically advanced than any country in Europe at the same time.

Because of the Yuan imperial government's discrimination against the southern Chinese literati, many southerners had to find ways to make a living outside of government service. Some went into medical practice, with benefits to the long-term development of Chinese medicine. Others became lowly clerks with poor pay and no chance for advancement. Others maintained the lifestyle and traditions of the Song literati and worked as scholars, painters, and poets.

Some Chinese literati refused to work in the service of the Mongol conquerors. One famous scholar-general, Wen Tianxiang, won the admiration of many subsequent generations by his refusal to surrender to the Mongol armies long after any chance of success had disappeared. He was captured in 1275 but escaped and continued to lead troops, only to be defeated again and to witness the capture of many members of his own family. Still refusing surrender, he fled to the southernmost province of Guangdong, where an epidemic claimed the lives of many of his troops as well as his mother and one of his sons. When finally captured and taken in chains to Khubilai Khan he refused to accept him as his sovereign and asked only to be executed, a wish granted in 1283.

Other Chinese literati resumed their normal lives but stayed away from the political realm. When the civil service examinations were resumed in 1315, they were based on Zhu Xi's interpretations of the Confucian classics. Cultural trends in painting, ceramics, even philosophy and poetry continued on from the Song with little change or deviation. One painter, Gong Kai, expressed his opposition to Yuan rule in a subtle way that was to provide a model for later dissenters from imperial orthodoxy. Gong Kai had served as a minor official under the Song; he refused to serve the Yuan, lived in extreme poverty, and supported his family by selling his paintings and calligraphy or exchanging them for food. Only two of his paintings have survived; one is a shocking painting of a starving horse, symbolizing China's fate under Mongol rule.

Another lasting contribution of the Yuan period to Chinese culture came in a form of four- or five-act dramatic operas called *zaju*, a term often translated as "Yuan drama." Drawing on popular songs and Central Asian art forms, with stylized costumes and elaborate facial makeup, Yuan drama combines mime, singing, dancing, and carefully choreographed acrobatics to present melodramatic stories of crime, love, war, and politics that have been immensely popular with Chinese audiences of all social classes ever since Yuan times.

Despite the continuities of Chinese cultural trends under Mongol rule, the Chinese people never fully accepted their position as subjects of non-Chinese emperors. They felt oppressed by inflation, by high taxes, and by the quota system that denied most Chinese any high position in government. While epidemic diseases swept through China in the mid-fourteenth century, massive flooding began along the Yellow River in 1344 and lasted for several years. The government forced 150,000 Chinese commoners into labor brigades to repair the Yellow River dikes and then paid the men with worthless paper money. By 1351, antigovernment uprisings began under the banner of a popular Buddhist sect, the White Lotus Society. This sect declared that the end of history was near when the Buddha of the Future, Maitreya, would appear to punish the wicked (Yuan rulers) and reward the good (Chinese people). In 1368, one rebel band grew sufficiently powerful to invade Beijing and declare a new dynasty, the Ming. The last Mongol emperor and his entourage fled beyond the Great Wall to their original homelands of Mongolia.

Ironically, during this period of "foreign rule," the Mongol court came to sponsor the very ideas of the Song Neo-Confucian scholars who had failed to protect the Southern Song from collapse and conquest. Perhaps even more important for the future of China, the Mongols managed to create a much larger land empire than even the Han and Tang and a very much larger empire than the northern Song. By making strategic alliances with the Khitans, Tanguts, Uighurs, and Tibetans and integrating officials from each of these groups into their government, the Mongols incorporated these peoples into one large empire in ways the Chinese had never previously managed. Consequently, when the Yuan dynasty collapsed in the fourteenth century, it was replaced by a Chinese dynasty of much greater extent than anything dreamed of by the Song emperors.

CHAPTER 6

Early Modern China: Ming (1368–1644) and Early Qing (1644–1800)

Zhu Yuanzhang, the Ming dynasty founder, was born into a desperately poor peasant family. He was such a sickly baby that his parents once offered him to the Buddha if his life could be spared. When he was sixteen, during the floods of 1344, his parents and two brothers died during an epidemic, leaving him and one brother alone with no means of support. Finding refuge at a Buddhist temple, he joined in begging on the streets for food and learned basic literacy from some of the monks. In 1352, the Buddhist temple was attacked and burned by the Yuan military because it was seen as part of the Red Turban movement—troops of the White Lotus Society, which had just risen in rebellion against the Yuan government.

With his temple burned to the ground, Zhu Yuanzhang, at age twenty-four, joined a Red Turban army. Physically imposing, very intelligent, and fearless in battle, Zhu quickly impressed his commander, who made him a top assistant and then gave him command of his own troops. Zhu soon married the commander's adopted daughter, and when his commander was killed in battle in 1355, Zhu took his place. In 1356, his troops occupied the important regional city of Nanjing, which had been the seat of several southern kingdoms. He had gained the allegiance of a number of capable men of some learning and experience, and rather than simply loot and plunder, he and his forces began to administer the territory surrounding Nanjing and to impose peace and order in areas that had been in chaos for over a decade.

As Zhu Yuanzhang's ambitions grew with his success, he came to see the limitations of the Red Turbans, whose forces were splintered and poorly disciplined. He formally broke with the Red Turbans in 1366, and within two years he had eliminated his rivals among the

Red Turban commanders. He then declared the founding of a new dynasty, the Ming (meaning "bright" or "light") and sent his largest army in 1368 to invade and take over the former Yuan capital, which he renamed Beiping, "The North Pacified." Zhu Yuanzhang's rise from destitute orphan-beggar-monk at age sixteen to Son of Heaven and Emperor of China at forty is probably the most dramatic success story in Chinese history. Yet his rise to power was only the beginning, because Zhu had an additional thirty years to impose his iron will on the country and its government. If Shakespeare had been Chinese, his greatest tragedy would have been the life of Zhu Yuanzhang.

In 1368, no one could have foreseen the troubles that lay ahead. To have expelled the Mongols and reunify a strong empire under Chinese control for the first time in 250 years gave Zhu and his commanders and officials great pride and cause for optimism. The new emperor took the reign title Hongwu (Abundantly Martial), and he is also known in history as Ming Taizu (the Grand Progenitor of the Ming). He was energetic, smart, dedicated, and determined to ensure that the people of China would never have to suffer as his family had suffered. No emperor of China was ever more sympathetic to the plight of the poor. He ordered an empire-wide land and population survey, kept central government expenses low, and placed the dynasty on a firm financial footing. He built an imposing capital at Nanjing, surrounded by a twenty-four-mile wall, forty feet high and twenty-five feet wide at the top, with thirteen magnificent gates. He refused to employ large numbers of eunuchs and vowed to limit the number of concubines in his palaces. (He succeeded on the eunuch front but still ended up with forty concubines.) And he ordered villages to be self-regulating in units of 110 households, with the village leaders responsible for tax collection and recordkeeping. He also ordered that his Confucian admonitions and teachings be read aloud monthly at every village in the empire, so that the entire population could be taught the virtues of Confucian filial piety and loyalty to the emperor.

Despite all this, he became—whether from deep character flaws, the terrible insecurities of his youth, or the corruptions of power itself—a paranoid emperor who ultimately tried to control his officials through the blunt use of force and terror. He put out many pleas in 1368 and later for men of talent and dedication to come forward and aid in the great enterprise of government. Yet with the empire fully in his hands, he found it increasingly difficult to trust his subordinates. In 1376, he suddenly ordered the execution of up to a thousand officials for committing the crime of having some government tax documents "prestamped" before being filled out. What might have been a simple move toward efficiency the Hongwu emperor interpreted as proof of corruption.

In 1380, he discovered that his chief councilor and head of the Confucian bureaucracy, Hu Weiyong, was plotting against him, so he had the councilor killed, along with perhaps 15,000 other officials, including anyone with any ties to the traitor. He abolished the position of chief councilor and determined to manage the Confucian bureaucracy himself.

The only person the Hongwu emperor trusted was his wife, Empress Ma, and after she died in 1382, he became even more paranoid. "In the morning I punish a few," he wrote in exasperation, "by evening others commit the same crime. I punish these in the evening and by the next morning again there are violations. Although the corpses of the first have not been removed, already others follow in their path. The harsher the punishment, the more violations."[1] Unfortunately, he did not have the presence of mind to see the self-defeating destructiveness of his own lethal policies. The "Abundantly Martial" emperor probably executed 100,000 officials during his thirty years in power.

When the Ming founder died in 1398, there was no doubt a gigantic sigh of relief felt throughout officialdom, but more blood was soon to be spilled. Emperor Hongwu had placed on the throne his twenty-one-year-old grandson, the son of his eldest son, who had died earlier. But Hongwu's fourth son, the Prince of Yan, commanded a sizable army around the former Mongol capital, now Beiping, defending the all-important northern borders of the empire. As the oldest surviving son of the founding emperor, he felt he deserved the dragon throne. In August 1399, he announced his intentions to "save" his nephew from corrupt advisors and commanded his troops to move on Nanjing.

The young emperor was mismatched with his battle-toughened uncle, and the troops of the Prince of Yan took Nanjing by force in 1402, burning the imperial palace with the young emperor and his mother in it. The prince declared himself the Yongle Emperor (Emperor of Perpetual Happiness), presided over the burial of his nephew, and erased his name from the official records of the dynasty. He was desperate to get the endorsement of one or more high officials from his nephew's court, but they steadfastly refused, choosing death (and posthumous fame) instead.

Fears about his own legitimacy were to haunt the Yongle Emperor for the rest of his life, but despite the violent beginning of his reign, after his nephew's loyalist officials were eliminated, he did not repeat the terrible and destructive purges of his father. He was a vigorous and forceful emperor who consolidated the power of the Ming dynasty during his reign of twenty-two years and tried very self-consciously to fulfill the Confucian model of a great emperor. He had scholars prepare the definitive edition of *The Four Books* (*Analects, Mencius, Doctrine of the Mean,* and *The Great Learning*), as interpreted by Zhu Xi, for use in the civil service examinations. He also commissioned the compilation of all known works in Chinese into the massive *Yongle Encyclopedia,* which had 22,000 chapters and fifty million words—the largest work of its kind in the fifteenth century.

The Yongle Emperor led five military campaigns into Mongolia to prevent any powerful federation of Mongols from threatening China. He rebuilt the Grand Canal, and late in his reign he built a magnificent new capital (with three massive concentric walls) in Beiping, now renamed Beijing, "Northern Capital." He designed the awesome Imperial Palace in the heart of Beijing. Its large courtyards between massive ceremonial halls on raised marble platforms comprised the Outer Court, where the emperor met with his officials and attended to his public duties. To the north of these were smaller buildings and courtyards, the Inner Court, where the emperor lived with his many servants and consorts. With some 9,000 rooms, the entire complex extended for 961 meters from north to south and 753 meters from east to west. The Ming and Qing emperors lived in this large complex, known as the Forbidden City, from 1421 to 1911.

The most unusual undertaking of Emperor Yongle was to commission Zheng He, a Muslim eunuch admiral, to assemble the largest naval fleet the world had ever seen, or would see for the next five hundred years. In 1405, Zheng He led a fleet of 62 large "treasure ships" and 225 smaller ships carrying 28,000 men southward around Vietnam through the Indonesian archipelago and into the Indian Ocean as far as Ceylon (today's Sri Lanka) and the southern coast of India. Some of these treasure ships were 400 feet long and 160 feet wide, about ten times the size of the ships Columbus used to sail to the New World almost a century later. From 1405 to 1433, Admiral Zheng led seven such expeditions, all of a similar size, and some as far as the Arabian Peninsula and the east coast of Africa. The Yongle Emperor claimed that the missions were to find the young emperor he had deposed, as there had long been rumors that he had escaped when his palace was burned in 1402. But the main reason was to display the power of this new Ming dynasty and to solicit more tributary states to recognize and send tribute to the Ming court.

Admiral Zheng He presented foreign rulers with Chinese luxury goods like silks and porcelains as well as everyday goods such as clothes, calendars, books, and Chinese money. The foreign rulers presented Zheng He in return with luxury goods from their own country, and in the case of Africa, with such rare animals as giraffes, zebras, lions, tigers,

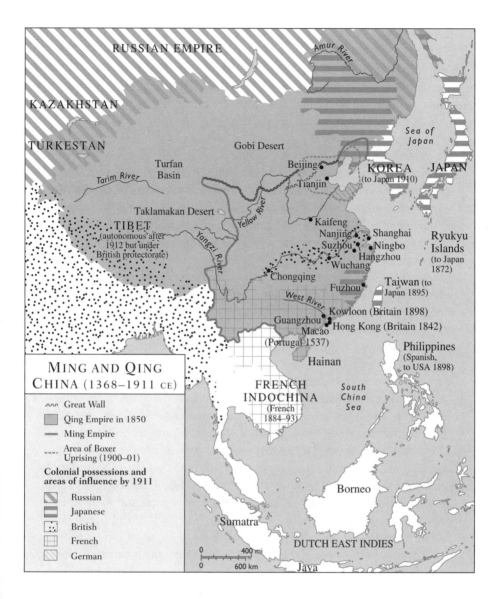

MING AND QING
CHINA (1368–1911 CE)

~~~ Great Wall

▨ Qing Empire in 1850

— Ming Empire

---- Area of Boxer
Uprising (1900–01)

**Colonial possessions and
areas of influence by 1911**

▨ Russian

☰ Japanese

⠿ British

▦ French

▨ German

RUSSIAN EMPIRE

KAZAKHSTAN

TURKESTAN

Gobi Desert

Amur River

Sea of Japan

Turfan
Basin

Tarim River

Beijing

Tianjin

KOREA
(to Japan 1910)

JAPAN

Taklamakan Desert

TIBET
(autonomous after
1912 but under
British protectorate)

Yellow River

Yangzi River

Kaifeng

Nanjing

Shanghai

Suzhou   Ningbo

Wuchang   Hangzhou

Chongqing

Fuzhou

Taiwan (to
Japan 1895)

Ryukyu
Islands
(to Japan
1872)

West River

Guangzhou

Macao
(Portugal 1537)

Kowloon (Britain 1898)

Hong Kong (Britain 1842)

Hainan

FRENCH
INDOCHINA
(French
1884–93)

*South
China
Sea*

Philippines
(Spanish,
to USA 1898)

Borneo

Sumatra

DUTCH EAST INDIES

0   400 mi
0   600 km

Java

rhinoceroses, and ostriches. The Chinese took the giraffe to be the fabled
unicorn of Chinese folklore that appeared only rarely in history to signal
the appearance of a sage emperor. Since the main purpose of these trips
was to demonstrate the power and majesty of the Ming court, they were
not financially profitable, and once Zheng He died, they were discontinued. We can only speculate how different the modern world would

have been if the Chinese had used their naval superiority in the fifteenth century as the Europeans did two and three centuries later—to conquer people and territory and seize control of international trade.

Unfortunately, none of the succeeding Ming emperors were very effective political or military leaders. In one famous case, the Wanli Emperor spent much of his nearly fifty-year reign, from 1572 to 1620, in a mental and political tug-of-war with his Confucian officials. After his officials would not allow him to elevate the consort he loved most to the position of empress because he already had an empress, he refused for two decades to hold court, read official documents, or make decisions about government policy. His officials and eunuchs were forced to carry on a charade of normality while the emperor devoted himself to the pleasures of private life in the palace. Meanwhile, increasing factionalism in the bureaucracy was accompanied by sometimes lethal power struggles between Confucian bureaucrats and palace eunuchs, who grew in numbers and influence in the middle and late Ming. By the end of the dynasty, the government supported perhaps 100,000 eunuchs and another 100,000 members of the extended imperial family.

In a pattern not unlike the Song period, the political problems of the Ming did not prevent a second commercial revolution from transforming Chinese society. During the Ming period, more land came under cultivation in southwest China, and by the late sixteenth century, new crops from the Americas—tobacco, corn, peanuts, tomatoes, sweet red peppers, potatoes, and sweet potatoes—were all introduced into China. These crops could often be grown on hilly or sandy soil not previously farmed. They helped produce another dramatic burst of population growth in the late Ming and entire Qing period. Interregional trade grew steadily, and as merchants accumulated significant wealth, they began to challenge, in practice if not yet in theory, the traditional Confucian prejudice against merchants.

The southern lower Yangzi valley region around Nanjing, Suzhou, and Hangzhou became by far the most prosperous area in China. Cotton production grew dramatically during the Ming. Farmers increasingly specialized in cash crops such as fruits, vegetables, rice, wheat, sugar, cotton, tea, and tobacco, and silver became the main medium of exchange in the economy. Vast quantities of silver flowed into China from Japan and, from 1570 onward, from the Spanish production of silver in Peru and Mexico. The Spanish took silver to Manila, where they bought Chinese products, especially silk and porcelain. The export trade grew rapidly as the world began to discover the attractions of Chinese silks, tea, and porcelain. The imperial kilns at the southern town of Jingdezhen came in the Ming to employ more than 10,000 workers. Using a special clay from that area and firing pieces at temperatures exceeding 1,300 degrees Centigrade, they produced elegant blue and white porcelain wares that have been world famous ever since.

By the late Ming, China was widely seen as the most prosperous country on earth. Some economic historians have estimated that three-fourths of all the silver produced in the New World from 1500 to 1800 found its way to China, because the Chinese economy was the most highly developed in the world and its products were better and cheaper than those of any other country.[2] In addition, Portuguese traders had already become involved in the China trade in the 1540s, when they occupied the small peninsula of Macao on China's southeast coast, and in 1619 they established a fort and trading post on the southern coast of Taiwan. From the sixteenth century onward, Chinese merchants began to migrate throughout Southeast Asia, where by the late nineteenth century they formed a substantial prosperous minority in almost every country. As prosperity grew, China's population more than doubled during the Ming period.[3]

Along with unparalleled prosperity in China in the sixteenth century came many other social and cultural changes. Growing contradictions in the life of the Chinese literati helped stimulate more creative philosophical analysis in the sixteenth and seventeenth centuries than at any time since the Neo-Confucian revival of the Song. Every scholar admired the Confucian ideal of public service, but the only route to officialdom was examination success, which required rote memorization and the mastery of a deadly dull prose genre called the eight-legged essay. The good Confucian official was duty bound to criticize the emperor if he erred, and in Ming times he often did, even though any Ming official who spoke up was likely to be publicly beaten within an inch of his life, exiled, or even executed. One response was to avoid public service; another was to try to rethink the whole Confucian tradition.

The only later Confucian thinker ever to rival the great Zhu Xi was the Ming scholar-official and visionary Wang Yangming. Even as a youngster, Wang had the ambition to become a Confucian sage. He passed the exams and served with distinction in officialdom, but that wasn't enough for him. In 1506, when he was thirty-four, he wrote a memorial criticizing the emperor for protecting a corrupt eunuch. The emperor had Wang beaten with forty strokes of a bamboo rod and exiled to a remote region of southern China. While in exile, Wang had a breakthrough experience much like what the Buddhists called enlightenment.

Wang drew on the idealism of Mencius, who had proclaimed the goodness of every person, and on the Chan Buddhist teaching that all people carry the Buddha-nature within themselves. Wang declared that to find moral truth one needed above all to look deeply into one's own heart. The followers of Zhu Xi, in Wang's view, made Confucianism an abstract philosophy dependent on detailed study of ancient texts. He argued that knowing and doing are one and the same thing: "I have said that knowing is the intent of acting and that acting is the work of knowing and that knowing is the beginning of acting and acting is the completion of knowing."[4]

The implications of Wang's new views were profound. If all people have the seeds of goodness within themselves, they can cultivate goodness, even greatness, without necessarily being brilliant scholars. Some of Wang's followers emphasized that this principle applied to women as well as men, challenging the traditional Confucian assumption of male superiority. Some of his followers preached his vision to commoners and refused to dress in the silk robes and caps of scholar-officials. Wang Yangming's philosophy seemed made for the times; more and more people were becoming literate, and the wealth and prosperity of society provided new outlets for creativity besides examination success and government service.

The publishing industry flourished in the Ming as never before, producing guidebooks to cities, examination preparation books, morality books for men and women, almanacs, popular stories in vernacular Chinese (rather than the more difficult classical language), popular songs, poetry, and dramas for reading as well as performing. Four great novels, or long pieces of narrative fiction, were published in the sixteenth century, including *The Romance of the Three Kingdoms*; *Water Margin*, a Robin Hood–like story about a band of righteous outlaws from Song times; *Journey to the West*; and *Plum in the Golden Vase* (*Jin Ping Mei*), a social satire and highly erotic tale of a rich, hedonistic urban merchant and his wife and five concubines.

Status competition in the late Ming embraced various forms of connoisseurship, including collections of art, calligraphy, ancient bronzes, odd-shaped stones, old books, and expensive new editions. Urban merchants and scholar-officials hired landscape artists and architects to build elegant gardens with ponds, rocks, trees, bamboo groves, pavilions, bridges, and meandering pathways to simulate in a small space the beauty and grandeur of mountains and natural forests. These gardens were scenes of endless poetry readings, calligraphy parties, dramatic productions, and philosophical discussions. Connoisseurs even competed to see who could assemble the most highly cultured circle of friends.

Some of the most creative landscape painters in Chinese history worked during the Ming period. As in earlier dynasties, the court employed many painters to make imperial portraits, supply murals for palaces and temples, and commemorate official occasions of all types. The most famous Ming painters were poet-painters from the central China region of the southern lower Yangzi valley, particularly the beautiful canal-laced city of Suzhou, where many literati built their private estates and gardens. The peace and prosperity of Ming times allowed these amateur artists to travel widely, and to see the paintings of earlier masters, which were now being assembled in private rather than official collections. Ming landscape painters were deeply aware of the Song and Yuan traditions and often made direct references in their work to the earlier masters. At the same time, some Ming artists self-consciously manipulated the earlier traditions in order to use painting as a vehicle for their own artistic creativity.

Women in Ming times reveal an interesting paradox. On the one hand, the Hongwu Emperor tried to promote a very orthodox brand of Confucianism that emphasized a woman's "Three Bonds": her subordination to her father, her husband, and her adult sons. The Ming government began to provide a cash reward for families whose widows committed suicide or lived out their widowhood in celibacy. Scholars compiled biographies of virtuous widows and began to emphasize sexual purity and chastity as the greatest of all female virtues. Some encouraged and celebrated lifelong chastity or suicide even among young betrothed "widows" who had not yet married when their fiancés died.

On the other hand, with the publishing boom in Ming times, more women than ever before became literate, and those in the scholar, landlord, and merchant classes began to develop the same passions as the male literati for art and literature. In late Ming poetry, fiction, and drama, romantic love was a very popular theme. Some of the most prominent literati in the country had open, much-celebrated affairs with courtesans—high-class prostitutes who worked in semibondage yet gained fame themselves as great poets, painters, calligraphers, and musicians.

One of the most famous of these was the courtesan Liu Shi, who was sold to a courtesan establishment (the less polite term is brothel) when still a child. This often happened to young women from poor families. They worked first as maids in the brothel and once they were old enough were taught to "serve" the brothel's male customers. At fourteen, Liu Shi was sold to a government minister to become his concubine. She quickly became his favorite in the household, and he spent many hours teaching her the arts of poetry, painting, and calligraphy. This made her the least popular person in the household, and the minister soon sold her back to the same establishment.

As the former concubine of a famous government minister, she became one of the most expensive courtesans in the Songjiang area (a city south of the Yangzi where many government officials lived). In subsequent years, Liu Shi had love affairs with several other very prominent men, including Chen Zilong and Qian Qianyi, two of the most prominent poet-scholar-officials of the Ming period. During a pleasure boat trip that lasted several months, Qian married Liu in a formal wedding ceremony even though he already had a proper wife. This caused a great scandal, but Qian was prominent enough that the episode did little to hurt his career.

When the Ming dynasty collapsed in 1644, Liu Shi urged Qian to commit suicide as loyal officials were expected to do in such circumstances. Incapable of following her advice, he defected to the Manchus and held an official position for a couple of years before resigning his post. For such irresolution, he was widely criticized. He and Liu Shi turned increasingly to Buddhism in their later years, seeking detachment from passion as consolation for their lost dynasty. In 1663, two years after her daughter was married, Liu Shi shaved her head in the style of a Buddhist nun. Qian died the next year. When relatives descended on his estate to try to claim his property for themselves, Liu Shi took her own life by hanging herself. Qian's son had her buried with Qian as his second wife.

Despite the low status of courtesans and concubines in Chinese culture, Liu Shi has been widely admired ever since for her abundant talents in poetry and painting, and even more for her courage and strength of character, as seen in her steadfast loyalty to the Ming dynasty and her final act of suicide to protest the greed, arrogance, and malice of her husband's relatives. She showed to one and all that a mere courtesan could match the artistic sophistication of the greatest of Chinese male literati and the highest ideals of Chinese civilization.

Themes of romantic love in literature initially grew out of the flourishing Ming courtesan culture, but the proper wives of scholar-officials also enjoyed romantic literature along with their husbands, and some developed companionate marriages in which husband and wife enjoyed the same intellectual and cultural interests and developed deep emotional ties as both lovers and friends.

A time of great cultural ferment, the late Ming also witnessed growing political and economic problems. The sixteenth-century surge of prosperity was concentrated in the southern lower Yangzi valley and did not extend far toward north or southwest China. The wealthy found ways to avoid taxes and shift more of the tax burden onto the poor. Increasing impoverishment forced many peasants to become tenants paying high rents to wealthy landlords. A major tax reform in the sixteenth century, the "Single Whip Tax Reform," combining land and labor taxes into one annual payment in silver, increased efficiency but did little to ease the growing tax burden on the poor.

To make matters worse, the Ming government in the early seventeenth century became increasingly paralyzed by deadly factional struggles between powerful eunuchs and crusading scholar-officials. Wei Zhongxian, the most notorious eunuch of the late Ming, gained control of the court in 1625. He lashed out against the Donglin Movement (named after the Donglin Academy where moralistic, reform-minded scholars studied) and had thousands of scholar-officials jailed, tortured, and killed. When a new sixteen-year-old emperor came to the throne in 1627, he soon arrested Wei, who then hanged himself in prison. This gave officials some hope that the dynasty might be saved, but the Ming decline had progressed too far to be reversed. The state was nearly bankrupted already in the 1590s by providing aid to Korea to help it resist attacks from Japan, and by the 1620s, the Ming government had lost the capacity to keep peace within its own borders.

Famines in northwest China provoked peasant uprisings beginning in 1628, and by 1634 large areas were under the control of rebel bands of peasant soldiers, led by two different bandit leaders, Li Zicheng and Zhang Xianzhong. In 1639, Japanese and Spanish merchants both stopped shipping silver to China, which quickly drove up the price of silver and led to many riots by peasants against high rents and high taxes. In 1642, anti-Ming rebels destroyed the dikes of the Yellow River, leading to extensive floods, famine, and a smallpox epidemic.

All the unrest came to a head in 1644, when Li Zicheng's forces captured Beijing and the last Ming emperor hung himself on a hill overlooking the Forbidden City. Li's forces were badly disciplined and proceeded to terrify the population of Beijing and surrounding areas. The strongest military commander under the Ming, Wu Sangui, guarded the Great Wall north of Beijing. Although the details remain murky, Wu invited a powerful army of Manchu troops to join him in taking Beijing back from the rebel forces. The Manchus were descended from the Jurchen Jin dynasty rulers who had taken north China during Song times. They had already declared a Chinese-style Jin dynasty in 1616, and in 1636 they changed the name of their dynasty to the Qing, meaning pure.[5]

Wu Sangui surely knew of the power and ambition of the Manchus, though his initial invitation to them to breach the Great Wall was stated in terms promising only wealth in exchange for helping defend the Ming state. In any case, it quickly became apparent that the Manchu forces were the most capable and well-disciplined in the empire.

The Manchus' professional military forces were organized under eight different colored flags or banners (four solid colors and four with borders). There were eight Manchu banner divisions, eight Chinese banners, and eight Mongol banners, all expert riders and archers and all under Manchu leadership. They quickly took Beijing, restored order, and proclaimed that the Mandate of Heaven had passed to the Qing dynasty.

Where the Chinese people surrendered, they were assured that Chinese life and culture would continue on in peace and prosperity. If they resisted they would be killed, as was demonstrated vividly when the southern city of Yangzhou refused to surrender. Manchu forces took

This Manchu bannerman, part of the Imperial Bodyguard, tests his bow from a crouching position. Manchu troops were all skilled archers who carried a powerful bow and a quiver full of arrows and were able to shoot accurately while riding a horse at full speed. Only the best and most reliable soldiers were made part of the elite Imperial Bodyguard. Courtesy of Sotheby's, New York

the city and for ten days were given free rein to rape, loot, and kill the entire population at random. Some Chinese officials chose to resist to the death and to kill their families to prevent their violation by the invading forces. But many other Chinese, including Wu Sangui, opted to cooperate closely and fully with the Manchu invaders. They saw that the Ming cause was hopeless and that the disciplined rule of the Manchus offered their best chance for a peaceful future. The peasant rebellions and rent riots of the late Ming proved in the end much more terrifying to the Chinese landlord-scholar elite than the prospect of being ruled by the Manchus.

The one serious Manchu intervention in Chinese life was that all Chinese males had to adopt the Manchu hairstyle: to shave the front half of the head and grow the remaining hair into one long braid at the back, the queue. Hairstyle can be a powerful symbol, and Chinese men had always been proud of their long hair tied in a topknot (something like Japanese sumo wrestlers today). Forcing the queue on Chinese males probably increased the resistance rate among the Chinese, but it also worked as a visible and omnipresent symbol of Chinese submission to Manchu power.

Despite the effectiveness of the Manchu forces and their Chinese collaborators, it took a full generation to put the dynasty on a firm footing. At age fifteen, the Kangxi Emperor took control of the government in 1669 by arresting his regent, the powerful Prince Oboi, believing that he was plotting against him. Just four years later, as the emperor turned nineteen, three former Ming generals, including Wu Sangui who had been awarded large independent fiefdoms in south China, had risen in revolt against the dynasty. The Kangxi Emperor led the successful suppression of these forces by 1681, and two years later Qing forces took the island of Taiwan, wiping away the last remnants of Ming loyalist resistance to Manchu rule.

Often compared with his contemporary Peter the Great of Russia, the Kangxi Emperor was one of the most effective rulers China ever had. He was to hold the throne for sixty years until his death in 1722, the longest reign in Chinese history to that point. In 1712, he froze the tax assessment (based on the number of able-bodied males in each area) so that taxes would not increase in the future even as the population increased. He extended the empire northward and established the borders with Korea and Russia that remain in place (with some disputed areas) today. He also led successful campaigns against the Mongols in Central Asia, and his troops occupied Tibet, extending the dynasty's borders westward far beyond anything imagined by the Han or Tang.

An itinerant barber in Beijing, photographed in 1865, tends a customer with the Manchu hairstyle (head shaved in front and the queue, a long single braid, in back) that was forced on all Chinese males in 1644 as a universal symbol of Chinese submission to Manchu rule. Itinerant barbers carried all their equipment on a shoulder pole; on one side were a bowl, razors, and brushes in a chest that doubled as a seat for the customer, and on the other side were a water container, bowl, and charcoal burner. Adoc-photos / Art Resource, NY

What made Kangxi a great emperor were not just his military conquests but his ability to recruit able and dedicated Chinese officials to the service of his dynasty. He was a diligent, hardworking emperor and a good judge of character who valued and rewarded honest answers from his officials. This in turn inspired their loyalty and devotion to him. Kangxi honored Ming loyalists who refused to serve the Qing as long as they did not engage in forceful resistance. He held special examinations to recruit eminent Chinese scholars to work on the official history of the Ming dynasty, an effective way to enlist proud Chinese in the service of Manchu rule. He opened the examination system to Chinese from the south, where resistance to Manchu rule had been widespread. He also patronized Chinese art, philosophy, and poetry by recruiting scholars and officials to compile a massive encyclopedia, several kinds of Chinese dictionaries, authoritative editions of important works in philosophy, and the complete poems of the Tang dynasty.

The Kangxi Emperor was interested in Western learning, which Jesuit missionaries brought to China starting in the sixteenth century. Several Jesuits working in the late Ming court explained Western theories of astronomy, calendar calculations, mathematics, geography, and military technology. The Jesuits saw Chinese ancestor worship as mere civil ceremonies of respect, not idolatrous pagan rites. Thus, they allowed their Chinese converts to maintain their social obligations under Chinese beliefs and customs. In the early eighteenth century, a papal envoy to the Qing court declared that ancestral worship could not be performed by Chinese Christians. This intolerance, plus the national jealousies and competition among Western Christian missionaries, led Kangxi to place more restrictions on missionary activities, thus ending the Jesuit dream of converting a Chinese emperor.

In 1722, the Kangxi Emperor died and was succeeded by another powerful and competent ruler, the Yongzheng Emperor. Some people accused the Yongzheng Emperor of poisoning his father and seizing power. Whether true or not, he was a much more guarded and suspicious man than his father. He took several steps to reduce the power of Chinese officials and to make the government more responsive to the emperor's will. He expanded a secret memorial system (begun by his father) whereby high officials could send him confidential messages quickly by an empire-wide, pony express–type system. He also instituted a thorough tax reform to try to eliminate tax evasion among the wealthy and privileged classes.

The Yongzheng Emperor died in 1736 and was succeeded by the Qianlong Emperor, who, like his grandfather, Kangxi, also reigned for sixty years. He tried in many other ways to emulate his grandfather. He made a number of southern tours of the empire as the Kangxi Emperor had done. He intensified Qing involvement in Tibet and sent more troops there in the late eighteenth century to help defend the Tibetans against attacks from the Gurkhas of Nepal. He also extended Qing control further west into the Mongol regions of Chinese Turkestan (today's Xinjiang Autonomous Region). The boundaries of China today are based largely on the Qing borders as established in the Qianlong reign.

The Qianlong Emperor also imitated his grandfather as a patron of Chinese culture, including the arts, philosophy, and poetry. He became the most avid art collector and sponsored the greatest library building effort in the entire history of China.[6] *The Complete Works of the*

Four Treasuries was to include a copy of every significant work ever published in Chinese. Part of the emperor's concern was to collect all known works in order to suppress anything that was judged harmful to the dynasty or to public morals. Therefore, some military works, all works with anti-Manchu content, and works judged to be heretical as pornographic or as anti-Confucian were to be burned. Anyone who harbored subversive writings faced the death penalty, but if they turned in such works they were not punished.

The three great emperors of the Qing—Kangxi, Yongzheng, and Qianlong—saw themselves as sage-kings in ways that extended the Chinese model of emperorship beyond the Chinese-speaking world. They presided over a multiethnic empire, uniting the Manchus with the Chinese, the Mongols, the Uighurs, the Tibetans, and many minority tribes in south and southwest China. They were very conscientious, deeply versed in the traditions of Confucianism and Buddhism themselves, and not about to tolerate criticisms of their rule.

The Manchu emperors and their Chinese officials saw the eighteenth century as one of China's greatest eras of peace and prosperity. Culturally and politically it was a conservative time, partly enforced by strong-willed emperors and partly embraced by Chinese scholar-officials who came to reject the late-Ming trends of individualism and creativity in philosophy and art as somehow responsible for the Ming collapse and the Manchu conquest. The school of Wang Yangming fell into general disfavor in the early Qing, but there were also creative developments in art and philosophy, even if they were not as exuberant as in the late Ming. Some painters and writers found subtle ways to express their unhappiness with Manchu rule or with Chinese society.

Two of China's greatest novels were written in the middle of the eighteenth century. Wu Jingzi, a failed examination candidate, wrote a brilliant satirical novel, *Unofficial History of the Scholars*, poking fun at ignorant and arrogant scholars who cared only about examination success, wealth, and status. Cao Xueqin, whose Chinese grandfather had been a close personal bondservant of the Kangxi Emperor, wrote *The Dream of the Red Chamber* (also known as *The Story of the Stone*), which is universally acknowledged as China's greatest novel. Set in a framework of Buddhist reincarnation and proclaiming the illusory nature of material life, *The Dream of the Red Chamber* is a compelling psychological portrait of a very large and powerful family gradually falling into poverty and disgrace.

These two novels seem prophetic, in that the Qianlong reign was glorious on the surface but showed by its end the unmistakable signs of dynastic decline. Government institutions and revenues did not keep pace with the rapid population growth of the eighteenth century. In his last twenty years, the Qianlong Emperor became overly fond of one of his imperial Manchu bodyguards, Heshen, who used his privileged position to embezzle millions of ounces of silver for his own private fortune. This coupled with the continuous military campaigns of Qianlong's later years left the state near bankruptcy by the end of his reign.

When Qianlong died in 1799, officials were finally free to speak out against Heshen. Qianlong's son, the Jiaqing Emperor, had Heshen imprisoned, charged with corruption, and forced to hang himself. When his fortune was assessed, it equaled in value about half of all the state revenues for the past twenty years. Heshen was one symptom of dynastic decline in the Qianlong Emperor's later years. An even more ominous symptom was a serious peasant rebellion, lasting a decade and ranging over five provinces, under the same White Lotus banner that had sealed the fate of the Ming dynasty. The rebellion was suppressed by 1804, but the difficulty Qing forces faced in putting it down showed how much the Manchu banner garrisons scattered around the empire had declined in fighting effectiveness during the century of relative peace.

CHAPTER 7

Decline, Fall, and Aftermath of the Qing Empire (1800–1920)

I t was a cruel coincidence of history that Qing dynastic decline coincided precisely with the early Industrial Revolution and the rise of aggressive western European powers competing for world domination through two major enterprises: trade and warfare. Spain and Portugal had first dominated the Asia trade in the fifteenth and sixteenth centuries, the Dutch dominated the trade in the seventeenth century, and Britain emerged as by far the dominant European power in the eighteenth century. As western European countries competed during these years in trade and warfare, they began to enslave millions of Africans and to conquer and colonize much of the New World, Africa, and India. The Qing court remained largely ignorant of these processes.

In the late eighteenth century, British traders came to feel increasingly frustrated with problems in the China trade. The British had grown very fond of Chinese silks, porcelains, and tea and were losing millions of ounces of silver annually to the China trade. Merchants ranked very low in the Confucian value system, and the Qing government saw international trade not as a way to generate new wealth but as a privilege granted to less-developed "barbarians" in exchange for their paying respects to the Son of Heaven and his court. British merchants were allowed to trade only at the southeastern seaport of Guangzhou (known in the West as Canton), where they were confined to a few warehouses and allowed to reside only temporarily to load and unload their ships.

In frustration, the British government sent two official missions to the Qing court in Beijing, in 1793 and 1816, to seek the opening of new trading ports to British merchants and to request that an official envoy from the British government be allowed to reside in Beijing. Both of these missions ended in complete frustration. In 1793, the Qianlong Emperor dismissed every British request as ridiculous, warning that British merchants would be expelled if they tried to come ashore anywhere other than Guangzhou and concluding with a standard emperor's command to his lowly subjects: "Tremblingly obey and show no negligence!"[1]

The emperor's condescending attitude reflected how little he understood the power realities of the world at the end of the eighteenth century. Lord Macartney, the British envoy to Qianlong's court in 1793, was struck by the inefficiency and fragility of the Chinese government, as he perceptively observed that China's ship of state had fallen into serious disrepair. "She may, perhaps, not sink outright; she may drift some time as a wreck, and will then be dashed to pieces on the shores; but she can never be rebuilt on the bottom."[2]

The problems of the China trade might have remained a minor irritant to the expanding British Empire in the early nineteenth century, but frustrations increased dramatically on both sides in the next few decades because of one additional factor: opium. From 1800 to 1810 China accumulated about twenty-six million ounces of silver through its trade with western (mostly British) merchants, because the British public became a nation of tea drinkers, while the Chinese remained largely indifferent to British products. British merchants found the answer to this economic problem in the growth and sale of the addictive drug opium. They began to grow opium on British-controlled plantations in India and to ship the drug to China in order to pay for the ever-increasing British imports of tea, silk, and porcelain.

Opium, produced from the poppy plant, had long been known in China as a pain reliever and treatment for diarrhea, but opium addiction had not been a serious social problem. In the eighteenth century, it was discovered that by vaporizing the sap from the opium poppy and inhaling the vapors through a long-stemmed pipe, the drug could be efficiently introduced into the blood stream, producing a strong sense of euphoria. This kind of opium smoking relieved boredom along with physical and mental pain. It was also highly addictive, and withdrawal produced chills, trembling, severe cramps, and nausea. As British traders discovered this magical solution to their balance-of-payments problem with China, opium addiction spread rapidly through a Chinese population that had little understanding of the poisonous dangers of the drug.[3]

The economic effects of the growing drug trade were just as bad as the social effects. By the mid-1820s, China's trade surplus with the West had disappeared. Between 1831 and 1833, ten million ounces of silver flowed out of China, as Britain paid for its tea, silk, and porcelain imports with opium profits. By 1836, British merchants sold about $18 million worth of opium in China and bought $17 million worth of tea. The Qing court became aware of the opium problem as early as

Opium smoking induced feelings of elation and also lethargy, as these men show by indulging in their habit in prone positions on their portable mat in a garden. After British traders began selling opium in Guangzhou in the eighteenth century, opium addiction spread rapidly among all social classes, producing serious social and economic problems as addiction led to crime and broken families, while Britain financed its entire consumption of tea, silk, and porcelain with the profits from opium and still came away with a growing trade surplus. Adoc-photos, Coll. Gérard Lévy, Paris, France / Art Resource, NY

1807, when a government official complained that China's laws against opium smoking were too lax. Occasionally foreign opium dealers were arrested in Guangzhou, but because Qing government salaries were low, foreigners were generally able to bribe local Chinese officials to look the other way. In the mid-1830s, some Chinese officials argued for the legalization of the opium trade so that the Qing government might at least tax the trade. Other officials raised strenuous moral objections to the legalization of such a harmful drug, and they prevailed.

In early 1839, an upright official, Lin Zexu, became the commissioner of trade in Guangzhou, where he was determined to suppress the opium trade. When he announced a ban on opium, the Western merchants handed over 1,000 chests of the drug, a small fraction of the total supply in the waters around Guangzhou. Lin responded by arresting 350 Westerners and confining them without their servants in their "factories" (warehouses). They would be released, he declared, only when they handed over all the opium in their control. Within two months, Commissioner Lin collected more than 21,000 chests of opium (each weighing about five hundred pounds), which was about half the annual total trade. Much to the shock of the Western merchants in Guangzhou, and to the British government in London, Lin proceeded to publicly destroy this entire supply of opium, which could have sold for somewhere between $10 and $20 million.[4]

What Commissioner Lin and the Qing government saw as a wholly justified law enforcement operation the British government saw as an act of piracy against free trade, a severe violation of the rights of British subjects, and an insult to the British Crown. Great Britain sent an expeditionary force of sixteen warships, four armed steamers, twenty-seven transport ships, and one troop ship to China in 1840, with a total of 4,000 British troops. The Chinese had no naval forces capable of defeating such a force and little comprehension of how deadly serious the British government was in its determination to force the opium trade to continue and to grow.

After two years of failed negotiations alternating with fighting, the British forces (increased to 10,000 troops) eventually blockaded China's major eastern seaport cities and sailed up the Yangzi River to Nanjing, threatening to cut the Qing Empire in half. The court at this point had little choice but to surrender and to accept every humiliating condition the British demanded. The result was the Treaty of Nanjing in 1842, which stipulated that China would pay for all the British expenses in the Opium War ($12 million), the market cost of the opium destroyed (conservatively set at $6 million), and the accumulated debts of Chinese merchant houses owed to British merchants ($3 million). In addition, Great Britain took control of Hong Kong, an island of fishing villages off the south China coast, which had what turned out to be one of the best deepwater harbors in the world. Four new coastal cities were opened to trade with the British, and China promised to deal with Western governments as equals in the future.

In a supplementary treaty following the Opium War, China agreed to set a fixed tariff rate on its trade with the Western countries, to extend its agreements with Britain to every other Western country, and to allow Westerners in China to be subject not to Chinese law but to Western laws, under what was called extraterritoriality. The Qing court agreed to these stipulations without realizing that they were in effect giving up control of their own policies in trade and foreign relations. Opium was politely not mentioned in any of these agreements, but it was understood on both sides that the opium trade would continue without being regulated or taxed. By 1880, China imported about 80,000 chests of opium per year, twice the amount imported in the late 1830s.

As painful as it was, the Opium War was only the beginning of the Qing court's troubles in the nineteenth century. The serious economic and social dislocations caused by the war and by the opium trade itself produced conditions ripe for rebellion. In 1850, a religious and military uprising threatened the immediate survival of the dynasty: the Taiping Rebellion, named for a peasant movement called Taiping Tianguo (Heavenly Kingdom of Great Peace), which was inspired by Hong Xiuquan, a failed examination candidate from south China. Hong was from the Hakka people, a small minority group in south China whose women did not bind their feet. He had a nervous breakdown and suffered hallucinations after failing the civil service examinations several times. When he recovered, he recalled having read a Christian missionary pamphlet that he now felt explained the visions he had experienced. He came to believe he was the second son of the Westerners' Christian God and the younger brother of Jesus Christ.

Hong inspired his followers to pool their wealth, to worship this new Western god, Jehovah, and to destroy Confucian and ancestral temples as heathen idols. When local government officials tried to suppress this movement in 1850, Hong and his followers rose in open revolt against the Qing dynasty. They quickly recruited desperate peasants and unemployed workers to their cause, trained them to fight fiercely, and by 1854 had occupied the major city of Nanjing on the Yangzi, where they established the capital of their self-proclaimed Heavenly Kingdom. They asserted control of the prosperous Yangzi valley, and their armies came within twenty miles of Beijing in 1855, but poor planning for the northern winter and the dispersal of their forces in too many directions at once doomed that effort to failure.

The Taiping movement was a curious combination of Western Christianity with many traditional Chinese elements. Hong Xiuquan lived as a Chinese-style emperor in Nanjing, in palatial splendor with many concubines, while his movement outlawed opium use, declared equality of land ownership and taxation, and abolished the painful custom of foot-binding for women. Western missionaries were at first amazed and delighted at the thought of a Chinese Christian uprising that might overthrow the Qing dynasty. But when they learned of Hong's claim to be the younger brother of Jesus Christ and his direct visions from God, they quickly lost their enthusiasm. Western traders successfully pressured their governments to support the Qing forces battling the rebels, as they feared above all the Taiping threat to the opium trade.

Hong Xiuquan's power was based heavily on his direct access to divine revelation through his visions, and soon another Taiping leader, Yang Xiuqing, began to have his own visions, which posed a threat to Hong. This led to a bloody power struggle in Nanjing that decimated the Taiping leadership in 1856. Despite this setback, Nanjing was not recaptured by the government until 1864. By the mid-nineteenth century, the Manchu banner forces were so weak and ill-trained that the Qing court was forced to give several Chinese officials more military power and authority than ever before under Qing rule. The man most responsible for the eventual Qing victory over the Taiping forces was Zeng Guofan, a conservative Confucian who saw the Taipings as a much greater threat to the Chinese way of life than the Manchu rulers. Zeng and several other Chinese officials recruited and trained their own armies from their own home districts. These Chinese armies could have posed a grave danger to the Qing court, but in the heat of the Taiping Rebellion, the court had no choice but to give more power and autonomy to its top Chinese officials.

An estimated twenty million people were killed in the Taiping Rebellion, and there were several other rebellions that occurred during and after the Taiping. In the middle of these rebellions, in 1858–1860, what could be called a second opium war broke out when a joint Anglo-French force invaded Beijing, burned the emperor's Summer Palace, and forced more unequal treaties on the Qing. This marked something of a turning point in relations with the West, as Western governments now got almost everything they wanted from the Qing court, including the right to have diplomats reside permanently in the capital. Fourteen treaty ports were now opened to Western trade, with whole sections of treaty ports completely under Western control. After 1860, Westerners also took over the entire administration of China's taxes on trade and commerce. The once-great Qing Empire had become a semicolony of the West.

Western "coolie" (after the Chinese word, *kuli*, "bitter laborers") traders recruited poor illiterate Chinese men with false promises, or simply kidnapped them, put them on virtual slave ships, and sent them to work in gold mines, to build railroads in the western United States, or to work on sugar and other plantations in Western colonies in Southeast Asia, the Caribbean, and South America. Treated as indentured servants, these workers were charged for their meals and transport and forced to work for years to pay off their "debts" to their overseers. The Qing government was powerless to protect its own citizens from this kind of exploitation.

The internal rebellions and the external wars of the nineteenth century served to keep the court engaged in a daily struggle for survival, leaving no one with time or energy to assess the dynasty's need for long-term political and economic reforms. There were Confucian officials in the late nineteenth century who called for "self-strengthening," learning from the West, and who began to build modern weapons, steamships, railroads and telegraph lines. But the Qing Empire was a vast, poor, mostly agricultural and overpopulated territory with a small, weak government, and the modernization efforts were confined to tiny coastal areas that had little impact inland.

No Qing emperor in the nineteenth century was very capable, and in any case the problems facing the dynasty were so great and complex that even a capable and engaged emperor would have had great difficulty in meeting the twin challenges of internal rebellion and external aggression. In 1860, the Tongzhi Emperor took the throne as a young man while real power was shared between his uncle, Prince Gong, and his mother, the Empress Dowager Cixi. Having entered the palace as a low-ranking concubine, Cixi became, through her combination of beauty, ambition, and shrewdness in cultivating allies among officials, the most powerful single individual in the Qing court, from her initial rise as empress dowager in 1860 to her death in 1908. No woman since the Tang Empress Wu had ever held as much power and influence in Chinese politics as the Empress Dowager Cixi.

The Empress Dowager has often been blamed by modern Chinese nationalists for selling out the interests of the Chinese people and living in splendid luxury in the palace while foreigners continued to increase their power and influence over China. She rebuilt the Summer Palace, which Western troops had burned down in 1860, and among other excesses she used funds originally intended for naval expansion to have a pleasure boat carved in marble beside the lake there. Today, tour groups from all over are shown this boat as a symbol of Cixi's selfish indulgences and the corruption of the late Qing court. In retrospect, she was more a symptom than a cause of Qing weakness. The court was torn between conservative and reformist officials, and she maintained her power by alternating appeals to each group, allowing neither to dominate for long.

In 1894–1895, fighting over influence in Korea, Japanese troops quickly and soundly defeated Qing forces. This was a great shock to China and to the whole world, as the small island nation of Japan was roughly the size of one Chinese province and had long been regarded as a weak peripheral state. The Qing court agreed to pay Japan two hundred million ounces of silver and to cede to Japan the island of Taiwan, and the Pescadores chain of islands. Suddenly, all Western nations feared the coming collapse of the Qing dynasty, and each nation pressured the court

Empress Dowager Cixi rose to power in 1860 when her young son was enthroned as the Tongzhi Emperor. Because of the importance of filial piety, even adult emperors often felt obliged to obey their mothers. By manipulating the imperial succession when the Tongzhi Emperor died in 1874, Cixi was able to become one of the most powerful women in all of Chinese history, second only to Tang Empress Wu. Library of Congress, LC-USZ62–56127

to grant it special trading and taxation privileges in its own "sphere of influence," in what became known as the "scramble for concessions."

Preoccupied with the anti-Spanish rebellion in Cuba and the Spanish-American War, the United States did not get deeply involved in the scramble for concessions, but after defeating Spain and taking over the Philippines in 1899, the U.S. government became worried that the European powers and Japan might start fighting colonial wars with each other in China. In September 1899, John Hay, America's secretary of state, issued a series of "Open Door Notes" to Britain, France, Germany, Russia, Italy, and Japan, calling on all foreign powers in China to allow free trade in all spheres of influence. The scramble for concessions soon subsided, not because of Hay's Open Door Notes but because the foreign powers decided to ease pressures on the Qing court since they, too, feared the breakup of China.

The humiliating defeat of Qing forces at the hands of Japan pushed some Chinese to begin to call for the overthrow of the Qing dynasty, while others called for radical reforms within the dynastic system. In the summer of 1898, Kang Youwei, a brilliant Confucian scholar who admired Japan for its rapid adoption of Western institutions and industrialization, gained an audience with the young Guangxu Emperor, who was growing impatient with his subordination to the Empress Dowager Cixi. The emperor was so taken with Kang that within the short space of one hundred days, he issued edict after edict announcing sweeping reforms, including the introduction of Western subjects in Chinese education, the abolition of thousands of sinecure positions, a crackdown on government corruption, and a crash program of industrialization and Westernization.

Conservative officials quickly grew alarmed at the direction of these pronouncements and approached the empress dowager to intervene. When disciples of Kang Youwei countered by asking Yuan Shikai, the leading military official in the empire, to back the reformers in any conflict with conservatives at court, General Yuan reported this move to the empress dowager, who immediately ordered the reform movement crushed. The Guangxu Emperor was in effect imprisoned on the small island in the lake of the Summer Palace, and Kang Youwei and his closest disciple, Liang Qichao, fled to Japan to escape arrest and execution. Six of Kang's closest followers, including his younger brother, were arrested and executed. One of them, Tan Sitong, refused to flee when offered the chance, saying that effective change in China would require the blood of martyrs.

With the reformers crushed after only one hundred days, conservatives now seized control of the court, a dangerous turn of events that happened to coincide with the boiling over of a sense of rage and frustration in the north China countryside. During the severe drought of the summer of 1899, secret society groups of peasants and illiterate day laborers called the Boxers went on a rampage, capturing and killing any foreigners they could find. Most of this anger was directed at Western

Christian missionaries who moved into many parts of the Chinese countryside in the late nineteenth century. Western missionaries were courageous people, and some of them did amazing medical and social work in China. The first women's movement against foot-binding was inspired by Western missionary women. But many Chinese could not forgive the fact that Western Christianity and opium came to China at the same time and in the same way, backed by Western guns pointed at Chinese heads. Much wealthier than most Chinese peasants, Western missionaries lived in their own walled compounds apart from the Chinese, under the protection of extraterritoriality. Some poor Chinese "converted" to Christianity for economic reasons, gaining the label "rice Christians," and authorities suspected Chinese criminal elements of becoming nominally Christian only to use extraterritoriality to avoid Chinese prosecution. All of these practices angered poor Chinese peasants, as did all the foreign wars and unequal treaties of the past half century.

After initially trying to suppress the Boxers' attacks on foreigners, the Qing court in the summer of 1900 decided to support the Boxers and to try to use them to drive the foreigners out of China once and for all. One factor in the empress dowager's decision to back the Boxers was that foreign governments had strenuously objected to her plans to depose the Guangxu Emperor in 1898, an act she saw as an intolerable level of foreign interference in Chinese affairs. Some court officials also told her that the Boxers' religious rituals made them immune to Western firearms, and this appeared to be true when she was given a demonstration (with the shooters using blanks).

All that saved the dynasty from collapse at this point was the fact that southern Chinese officials ignored the court's orders to declare full-scale war on all foreigners. An eight-nation invasion force (the Western powers plus Japan) quickly took Beijing in 1901, and the empress dowager fled the capital disguised as a Buddhist nun. On her trip through the desolate countryside, she was confronted for the first time with the realities of China's poverty and weakness. Once a new truce was negotiated, with China agreeing to pay four hundred million ounces of silver in damages, the empress dowager returned to Beijing, invited the wives of Western diplomats to her court for tea, and vigorously promoted the same kinds of modernizing reform she had violently suppressed just three years earlier.

The Boxer Rebellion brought the Qing dynasty's reputation to an all-time low throughout the world. China was now seen as a backward, dangerous, and barbaric place. One Westerner who perceived the larger significance of the event was Robert Hart, an Irishman who oversaw the China Maritime Customs Office from 1865 to 1908. In the aftermath of the Boxer uprising, Hart predicted with uncanny accuracy that in fifty years' time, twenty million or more Boxers "will make residence in China impossible for foreigners, will take back from foreigners everything foreigners have taken from China, will pay off old grudges with interest, and will carry the Chinese flag and Chinese arms into many a place that even fancy will not suggest today..."[5]

In the first decade of the twentieth century, the Qing government tried finally to promote the reforms that might yet save the dynasty. However, it was too little, too late, as more and more Chinese concluded

A stereographic photograph labeled "Some of China's trouble-makers" shows Boxer prisoners captured by the 6th U.S. Cavalry in Tianjin. The United States joined the European powers and Japan in sending troops to free the foreign legations in Beijing and quell the Boxer uprising in 1901. Library of Congress, LC-USZ62–68811

that the Manchus had in effect betrayed China by giving in to Western demands in order to preserve their own power. Many young Chinese began to study in Japan, Western Europe, and the United States, while Sun Yat-sen and others agitated for the overthrow of Qing rule. The court promised the adoption of a constitutional monarchy (basically what Kang Youwei had proposed in 1898), but as provincial assemblies were set up after 1908, they became centers of opposition to, rather than support for, the Qing imperial system.

Sun Yat-sen was a charismatic visionary from Guangzhou who went to Hawaii at age thirteen to live with his brother. He became a Christian, attended a British medical school in Hong Kong, and practiced medicine briefly in Macao. But his true calling was politics, and his great desire was to save his country. After the Sino-Japanese War, he decided the only hope for China was to overthrow the Qing dynasty and replace it with a democratic republic. In 1895, Sun and several friends were discovered plotting an armed uprising in Guangzhou, and he escaped to Japan. He cut off his queue, grew a mustache (then the popular style in Japan), adopted a Japanese name, Nakayama (Zhongshan, or "Central Mountain," in Chinese), and started wearing Western clothes. He attracted a following among Chinese students in Japan and inspired audiences with his vision of a modern democratic China. He called for three principles of the people: racialism, meaning China for the Chinese and not the Manchus or foreigners; democracy, or people's rights; and socialism, or people's livelihood. To answer the argument that China was not ready for democracy, Sun suggested a transition period of "tutelage" during which military rulers would gradually turn over power to an elected civilian government.

Sun's career was almost ended in 1896 when he was seized and held in the Qing embassy in London when officials there recognized him as a revolutionary. Fortunately for Sun, his British friends successfully lobbied the British government to pressure the embassy to release him. Thereafter, Sun stayed safely out of China and raised money for his revolutionary cause among overseas Chinese communities around the world. He plotted many uprisings against the Qing government in the first decade of the twentieth century, and some of his co-conspirators were caught and executed.

One of the most impressive of the anti-Manchu revolutionaries was a woman, Qiu Jin. When her merchant husband wanted to take a concubine in 1904, she left him in disgust, sent their two children to her parents, and sold the jewelry in her dowry to finance a trip to Japan to study. She dressed like a man, carried a sword, and wrote fiery calls for revolution against both the Manchus and the traditional Chinese family system. She returned to China in 1906 to work for the end of Qing rule. In the second week of July 1907, she heard that her cousin had been arrested for plotting to assassinate a Manchu provincial governor and knew they would soon be coming for her. She refused to flee and instead wrote these lines to a friend: "The sun is setting with no road ahead / In vain I weep for loss of country. Although I die, yet I still live / Through sacrifice I have fulfilled my duty."[6] Qiu Jin was soon arrested and beheaded for treason. Her death made her a national celebrity and only intensified the populace's growing anger at their Manchu rulers.

When the Qing dynasty finally fell, after a century of decline, rebellion, and humiliation, it seemed almost accidental. The examination system was abolished in 1905, leaving many upper-class Chinese uncertain how they could relate to the Qing government, which had promised a constitutional monarchy but seemed to be dragging its feet. The empress dowager died in 1908, one day after the Guangxu Emperor (whom she was rumored to have poisoned so that he would not be able to assume power himself). The throne was passed to the three-year-old imperial prince, Puyi, who became the Xuantong Emperor. The court was now at its weakest point in two and a half centuries.

On October 9, 1911, in the central Chinese city of Wuchang on the Yangzi River, a group of revolutionaries loosely affiliated with Sun Yat-sen were preparing to rise in revolt when one of them carelessly set off an explosion as a live ash from his cigarette fell into the gunpowder he was putting into rifle shells. The explosion brought the authorities to investigate, and they found revolutionary tracts and plans for a rebellion. Facing immediate arrest and execution, the revolutionaries in the Wuchang vicinity decided to declare themselves at war with the Qing state on October 10. The local governor-general had recently sent his best troops west to Hunan to suppress riots over disputed railroad rights in the area. Rather than calmly commanding the suppression of this ramshackle uprising, he fled Wuchang, and the rebels found themselves in control of a major city.

Word of this local revolt spread quickly, and some provincial assemblies began to declare their independence from Qing rule, while some troops, newly trained in the Western style, refused to support the Qing and instead began fighting for the rebels. Sun Yat-sen read about the Wuchang uprising on a train outside Denver, Colorado, where he had been raising money among overseas Chinese in America. Knowing the battle for China was just beginning, he headed east to London, where he hoped to raise more money for his cause. At this point, the Manchu court looked to the top Chinese military official in the empire, Yuan

Shikai, who had earlier sided with the empress dowager against the reformers of 1898. But the revolutionaries also appealed to Yuan to support a new republic of China, free of Manchu imperial rule. Yuan in effect negotiated the end of the Qing dynasty.

The Qing court agreed to the six-year-old Xuantong Emperor abdicating the dragon throne in exchange for the promise that he and his family would continue to live in the imperial palace with a generous annual stipend while maintaining possession of the immense imperial palace collection of art treasures. Much to the relief of the revolutionaries, the Qing dynasty had been overthrown without China's descending into chaos and without the Western powers and Japan carving up the country like a melon. Because Yuan Shikai controlled the military forces of the fledgling state, he rather than Sun Yat-sen assumed the presidency of this new republic on February 12, 1912.

While the anti-Qing revolutionaries were united in their desire to overthrow the dynasty, they were divided on most other issues. Sun Yat-sen and his followers now organized a new political party, the Guomindang (Nationalist Party), which they saw as a "loyal opposition" party that would compete in electoral politics with the followers of Yuan Shikai. A number of other parties were formed as well, and National Assembly elections were held in December 1912. Only men who owned property, paid taxes, and had an elementary school education could vote. Some forty million men were qualified to vote, about 10 percent of the population. Given China's lack of experience with electoral politics over the previous 2,000 years, this was an impressive start, and the elections of 1912 went remarkably smoothly. The manager of the Nationalist Party campaign effort was Song Jiaoren, an articulate advocate of democracy from Hunan who hoped to become prime minister in President Yuan's cabinet. The Nationalists won 43 percent of the vote, far more than any other single party, and Sun Yat-sen, who had agreed to become the director of railroad development, was very pleased.

To Yuan Shikai, the idea of a "loyal opposition" was a contradiction in terms; he saw the Nationalist Party's criticisms of his policies and their electoral success as a threat to his attempts to create a strong central government. Song Jiaoren had been outspoken in criticizing President Yuan's cabinet choices and his policies. As Song was waiting in Shanghai to board the train for Beijing on March 20, 1913, a stranger walked up to him and shot him twice at close range. He died in a Shanghai hospital two days later, two weeks short of his thirty-first birthday. The gunman was never caught, but most assumed, with good reason, that Yuan Shikai had ordered the assassination.

President Yuan was a heavy-set, jovial man who charmed his dinner guests with his witty comments, but he was very traditional in his outlook (having for himself a dozen concubines) and quite ruthless toward his political opponents. The Nationalist Party responded to the assassination of Song Jiaoren with calls for Yuan's resignation and soon rose in open revolt. As the man who had overseen the military modernization program at the end of the Qing dynasty, Yuan enjoyed the loyalty of most military commanders in the nation. In 1913, he made short work of the Nationalist Party uprising, crushing their armed forces very quickly and sending Sun Yat-sen fleeing once again into exile in Japan.

Yuan took all the power he could for himself and borrowed huge quantities of money from foreign banks and governments to buy weapons for his armies. He wanted a strong, modern industrialized state, but he could not quite imagine any effective political system other than the monarchy he had known as a Qing official. In 1915, he plotted with his advisors to restore the monarchy with himself as emperor. But too much had changed since 1911, and almost no one outside Yuan's personal circle supported such a move. Yuan died of kidney failure in 1916, leaving a power vacuum at the center, with no national consensus about how political power should be created and exercised.

The period from Yuan Shikai's death in 1916 until 1927 was one of the darkest and most violent in China's long history. Yuan's former generals could not unite in support of one leader but began to compete with each other and use their troops as personal armies loyal only to themselves. The period is thus known as China's Warlord Era, when the country was splintered into dozens of small warlord kingdoms. Whoever controlled Beijing was recognized as the "president of the republic," but the republic was really a fiction as warlords large and small competed by raiding, looting, or taxing to death the areas under their control. The number of armed soldiers in China grew from 500,000 in 1913 to 2.2 million in 1928. Much of the wealth created during that time was absorbed in the training and equipping of these forces.

Some warlords were little more than bandits, while others actually tried to build a viable government in the area under their control. One of the "best" was Feng Yuxiang, who rose from a humble peasant background to become one of the most powerful military commanders in the country. Widely known as the Christian General, he indoctrinated his troops in Christian teachings as well as good military discipline, built orphanages and schools, and occasionally held mass baptisms for his troops, using a fire hose for sprinkling water on the converts. Zhang Zuolin was a former bandit from Manchuria, which he ruled with an iron hand; Yan Xishan controlled the northwest province of Shanxi, where he promoted public morality and industrialization.

With nearly complete fragmentation of power, the central government had little control of the areas outside the capital, Beijing, and no way to collect taxes from the nation as a whole. During World War I, Chinese businessmen were able to begin some successful modern industries because Westerners were so preoccupied with the war in Europe. Japan took advantage of World War I by issuing to Yuan Shikai's government a list of "21 Demands" in 1915, demands that would have given Japan de facto control of the Chinese government. When public protests broke out against Japan, the Japanese dropped their most outrageous demands and settled for increased economic rights and privileges.

After the United States, Britain, and France defeated Germany, ending World War I, the victors at the Versailles peace negotiations decided that the former German-held concessions in north China would be turned over directly to Japan. News of this decision hit Chinese students, professors, and businessmen like a bolt of lightning. The Chinese had allied with the United States, Britain, and France in World War I and had sent 100,000 workers to Europe to support the allied powers. Woodrow Wilson had taken the United States into World War I declaring his idealistic desire to make the world safe for democracy and to promote self-determination for all countries of the world. For the Western democracies to reward Japan with formerly German property in China struck all informed Chinese as the height of hypocrisy, reminiscent of the Opium War being justified as a defense of "free trade."

Word of this decision reached Beijing on the evening of May 3, 1919, and the next day, 3,000 Chinese students marched to the Gate of Heavenly Peace in front of the Forbidden City to protest the Versailles peace treaty. They marched to the home of a pro-Japanese government official and looted and burned it to the ground. Two dozen protesters were arrested, and in the following months students, professors, businessmen, and workers all organized protests and anti-Japanese strikes and boycotts. The May Fourth Movement came to be the name for these protests as well as a whole movement promoting cultural change that had begun already several years before.

Four years earlier, in 1915, two Beijing University professors, Chen Duxiu and Hu Shi, had begun a new journal called *New Youth*. In the first issue, Chen wrote an essay calling on Chinese young people to reject Chinese traditions, suggesting that they follow six principles: (1) be independent, not servile; (2) be progressive, not conservative; (3) be aggressive, not retiring; (4) be cosmopolitan, not isolationist;

Student demonstrators surround the Gate of Heavenly Peace in Beijing on May 4, 1919. Their protest against the Versailles Peace Treaty quickly grew into a popular urban movement against both foreign imperialism and traditional Chinese culture. Kautz Family YMCA Archives, University of Minnesota Libraries, Minneapolis, MN

(5) be utilitarian, not formalistic; and (6) be scientific, not imaginative. China was backward, Chen argued, because it was too conservative and gave too much respect to tradition and to the elderly. Young people should rebel against the authority of their elders, reject the "wisdom of the past," and embrace independence, individualism, and freedom.

The events of 1919 suddenly brought many young people into the camp of the critics of Chinese tradition. In analyzing the foreign and domestic crises of the Warlord Era, students, teachers, writers, and journalists published periodicals, short stories, poems, and propaganda posters all blaming China's weakness on two things: foreign imperialism and the conservative Confucian culture of Chinese tradition. The pace of change began now to accelerate.

CHAPTER 8

Civil Wars, Invasion, and the Rise of Communism (1920–1949)

The betrayal of China in 1919 by the Western democracies marked a major turning point in Sun Yat-sen's political career and in the history of modern China. Before this time, Sun had looked primarily to the West for support of a progressive and democratic China. Now, the Western democracies seemed more concerned with foreign rights and privileges in China, and with the warlords of Beijing, than with Sun Yat-sen and his cause. Moreover, the Bolshevik Revolution in 1917 in Russia suggested to many that a Marxist movement could seize power in a poor backward country and jump-start the process of rapid modernization, building a wealthy, powerful, and independent nation.

The German thinker and revolutionary Karl Marx had argued that capitalism was a major historical advance over feudalism, releasing new powers of productive capacity that promised to liberate human beings from the precarious struggle for survival. But capitalism, in Marx's view, required such severe exploitation of workers by their capitalist overlords that it would inspire a lethal class struggle and eventually collapse under the weight of its own contradictions. The industrial workers leading this struggle would establish an egalitarian socialism in which all workers would enjoy the full fruits of their labors. Co-owning the factories where they worked, they would develop their full potential as well-rounded and cultured human beings.

Marx thought socialist revolutions could only occur in the most advanced capitalist countries with a large industrial proletariat. In Russia, the Bolshevik leader Vladimir Lenin argued that a highly disciplined socialist party with its own army could seize power in a poor, backward country like Russia and move directly from precapitalist feudalism to a workers' socialism, tolerating enough capitalism on the way to bring prosperity and equality to the country simultaneously. In a very influential pamphlet, *Imperialism as the Last Stage of Capitalism*, Lenin argued that Western imperialism was not just an accident of history but the logical result of the ever-expanding demands of industrial capitalism for raw materials, exploitable workers, and new markets. To educated Chinese readers, Lenin helped explain the Western exploitation of China for the past hundred years with compelling force.

Sun Yat-sen did not fully embrace Marxism-Leninism, but he was impressed by the effectiveness of the Russian Bolsheviks in seizing power and even more by their immediate renunciation of the unequal treaties Czarist Russia had forced on the Qing court in the nineteenth century. In 1920, Sun began meeting with agents of the Soviet-sponsored Communist International, or Comintern, an organization dedicated to spreading workers' revolutions throughout the world. They offered Sun military assistance and political advice if his Nationalist Party would join in a formal alliance with the tiny recently founded Chinese Communist Party. The two parties would remain separate but would work together to promote workers' organizations, to develop a joint army, and to try to seize power from the warlords who were bleeding the country.

In 1923 Sun and his supporters formally reorganized their Nationalist Party along Leninist lines, meaning that members would have to observe party discipline and implement whatever policies the leadership adopted. Communist Party and Nationalist Party members would cooperate wherever possible, and together they formed a military officers' training school, the Whampoa Military Academy, on an island in the Pearl River ten miles downstream from Guangzhou. The first leader of this academy was Chiang Kai-shek, an ambitious young soldier who had undergone military training in China and Japan before 1911 and who went to Russia for a few months in 1923 to study Soviet governmental and party organizational methods.

There were always tensions in this alliance between the more radical Communist Party organizers and more conservative Nationalist Party members. The former wanted to promote workers' and peasants' rights and overturn the traditional Chinese social hierarchies. The latter were more concerned about seizing power from the warlords and unifying China into a strong industrialized state. Sun Yat-sen had enough prestige with both groups to hold the alliance together, but suspicions were growing on both sides in early 1925, when Sun went to Beijing to negotiate a possible truce with the Manchurian warlord Zhang Zuolin, who was then in control of Beijing. Sun fell seriously ill in Beijing, was diagnosed with liver cancer, and died on March 12. On May 30, Japanese troops fired on Chinese workers demonstrating in Shanghai, and suddenly many Chinese cities erupted with strikes, demonstrations, and boycotts. The May Thirtieth Movement, as it came to be known, swelled the membership of the Chinese Communist Party from 1,000 to 10,000 between May and November 1925 and to 30,000 by July 1926.

Having supervised the first three classes of military officers to graduate from the Whampoa Military Academy, Chiang Kai-shek was appointed commander in chief of the new National Revolutionary Army in June 1926. He enjoyed a strong personal loyalty from the vast majority of 6,000 newly trained officers who commanded an army of 85,000 soldiers recruited from peasant and worker families in south China. One of Chiang's main rivals to become leader of the National-ist Party after Sun's death was Liao Zhongkai, who had been a close associate of Sun Yat-sen and who, like Sun, maintained cordial relations with the more radical Communists. In August 1925, Liao Zhongkai was assassinated, eliminating one of the obstacles to Chiang Kai-shek's rise to power.

In July 1926, Chiang Kai-shek and the National Revolutionary Army launched the Northern Expedition, a two-pronged campaign along the east coast and through the center of south China to oust the regional warlords and unify south and central China under Nation-alist Party rule. The Communist Party labor and peasant organizers infiltrated areas in advance of the troops and helped undermine local warlord forces through strikes and nationalistic propaganda calling on people to resist foreign imperialism and support the Nationalists against the warlords. Within one month, the National Revolutionary Army was in control of the southwestern city of Changsha. In September and October, Nationalist forces took Nanchang and the major Yangzi River port city of Wuhan. By December, they had taken the coastal city of Fuzhou. In March 1927, they took the city of Nanjing (the early Ming capital), and by April, the great seaport and commercial capital Shang-hai was in Nationalist hands.

Chiang Kai-shek had never trusted his Communist collaborators. Since the May Thirtieth Movement of 1925 had radicalized many work-ers and pushed them toward the Communist camp, he feared his move-ment and his army might be taken over by its most radical elements. In his early days, he had briefly been a stockbroker in Shanghai, where he developed close ties with the banking community and with the Green Gang, a mafia-style organization that ran the prostitution, gambling, and opium dens of Shanghai. With support of the Green Gang and its henchmen, Chiang's forces struck against their Communist "allies" without warning on April 12, 1927, and murdered any and all known or suspected Communists in all the cities under their control. Thousands were killed without trials or hearings.

The Russian advisors to the Nationalist Party fled as quickly as they could, but Joseph Stalin, with little understanding of the real situation in China, urged the Chinese Communist Party to cooperate with "progressive" elements in the Nationalist Party and to resist Chiang Kai-shek with armed opposition. This was disastrous advice, as Chiang had most military commanders under his control. The end result was the death of perhaps 20,000 of the most loyal and committed Communists and non-Communist labor organizers in the spring of 1927.

The northern warlords Yan Xishan and Feng Yuxiang now threw their support to the anti-Communist Chiang Kai-shek. In June, the Manchurian warlord Zhang Zuolin was killed when his railroad car was blown up by Japanese troops. Zhang's son, Zhang Xueliang, inherited his father's troops and immediately declared his allegiance to a new government headed by the Nationalist Party. Thus, after thirteen years of warlord domination of China, civil war, and near anarchy, the country was at least nominally unified under its new president, Chiang Kai-shek. Chiang established his capital at Nanjing, since his real power base was in the Yangzi valley of central China, renaming Beijing (Northern Capital) Beiping (Northern Peace).

The northern warlords now donned Nationalist uniforms and declared themselves loyal to the Republic of China under Chiang Kai-shek. For the next decade, known in history books as "the Nanjing decade," Chiang attempted to promote rapid industrialization and the development of a modern government and a strong nation that would participate in the international community as an equal rather than as a semicolony of foreign powers. Chiang was a very strict disciplinarian and demanded (and usually received) the utmost loyalty from his troops. He was attracted to the doctrines of fascism, which were developing in Europe in the 1930s, and he came to rely heavily on German advisors in training his army and organizing his government in Nanjing. Although never able to suppress his political rivals completely, he was a master manipulator of factions within the Nationalist Party and an effective speaker, despite a high, squeaky voice and heavy Zhejiang accent, in rallying his followers against the "evils" of communism.

An additional factor in Chiang's rise to power was his much-publicized marriage in December 1927 to Soong Meiling, the daughter of one of China's wealthiest families and the sister of Sun Yat-sen's widow, Soong Qingling. Soong Meiling had been educated in the United States and would become an extremely effective ambassador for her husband and his government to the United States and the entire international community. The Soong family was Christian, and Chiang (who already had one wife) had to promise to consider becoming a Christian as a condition of the family's consent to the marriage. He was baptized as a Christian in October 1930.

Chiang's connections with the Soong family had a profound effect on his government. His wife's brother, T. V. Soong, became prime minister, and her brother-in-law, H. H. Kung, minister of finance. These men managed to create a modern centralized banking system that brought some much-needed economic stability to the cities. A beginning was made to establish a functioning tax system, though many provincial revenues never made it to the central government. Economic growth occurred mainly in the cities where foreign capitalists still tended to dominate the urban economy, but Chinese merchants and entrepreneurs began to grow in both numbers and prosperity.

To provide a counterweight to the anti-imperialist, anti-capitalist, and anti-Confucian ideology of his left-wing opponents, Chiang promoted the "New Life Movement" in the 1930s, which called for a revival of traditional Confucian values, including reverence for elders, for the nation, and for its political leaders. In the wake of the May Fourth Movement, which had discredited much of Chinese tradition in the eyes of young people in particular, Chiang Kai-shek's attempts to revive traditional values was often viewed with cynicism by urban Chinese youth and by journalists, writers, and university professors.

One of the most vibrant developments in the 1910s and 1920s was a women's movement to abolish foot-binding, end concubinage, eradicate widow suicide, and promote education for women and the freedom of young people to choose their own marriage partners. Many older women had suffered a great deal to achieve bound feet that had long been regarded as beautiful, so it was confusing and distressing to be told now that they were backward and ignorant victims of an oppressive custom. It also caused almost as much pain to unbind one's feet as to bind them in the first place. Despite the persistence of some women's pride in their bound feet, Chinese society as a whole quickly abandoned a custom that had become the norm over a period of eight centuries.

In the same years, the leaders of the May Fourth Movement called for the promotion of vernacular written Chinese and the abandonment of the cumbersome classical language, which required years of study just to acquire basic literacy. Within a few years classical Chinese became a dead language, except that a few continued to write poetry in classical forms. Vernacular Chinese became the universal means of written communication in newspapers, books, and periodicals.

In 1931, the best-selling novel in China was *Family*, by Ba Jin, a writer drawn to the political philosophy of anarchism. Based on his own upper-class family's life in the western province of Sichuan, Ba Jin's novel dramatized the oppressive nature of the old family system by showing three brothers in varying degrees of rebellion against the Confucian-style family. The youngest brother in the novel rebels against his family almost completely, while his eldest brother sees its injustices but cannot bring himself to challenge his elders directly. Ba Jin had no concrete proposals for organizing a new social and political system, but he very effectively condemned the old order and helped to infuse a whole generation with the May Fourth spirit.

In China's major cities, Western styles of dress became the norm, and girls began going to school with boys for the first time. Conservatives in the Nationalist Party resisted many of these changes. Nationalist Party zealots formed the Blue Shirts, an organization patterned in part after the Brown Shirts of Nazi Germany. These "morality police" sometimes went so far as to imprison young women for wearing their short bobbed hair with Western-style permanent waves. They also intimidated and even assassinated intellectuals who spoke out publicly against Chiang Kai-shek's policies. Chiang and his closest followers began to promote fascism as the answer to China's problems. All Chinese, in their analysis, should cultivate a greater sense of self-sacrifice to the needs and goals of the nation and an ever greater sense of loyalty to the one leader of the country, Chiang Kai-shek.

One of the major accomplishments of Chiang's government was to regain some aspects of Chinese sovereignty that had been lost in all the humiliating unequal treaties forced on China in the nineteenth and early twentieth centuries. From 1928 to 1933, China regained control of its own trade tariffs, something lost after the Opium War, and Chiang's government took complete control of the China Maritime Customs Service and reduced the number of foreign concessions in China from thirty-three to nineteen. Later, during World War II, China's Western allies ended extraterritoriality, that century-long symbol of Chinese subordination, and Chiang met personally with Roosevelt and Churchill as a full partner in the Allies' coalition against the Axis powers.

Despite these advances and some growth of a modern industrial economy in the major cities, the vast majority of Chinese peasants continued under Nationalist rule to live in dire poverty. Without the benefits of modern medicine, peasants suffered especially from parasitic worms and snails that multiplied in the night soil that peasants had used as fertilizer for millennia. If the night soil was not properly heated to

From the fifteenth century on, Beijing (renamed Beiping, or Northern Peace, in 1927) was known for its magnificent walls and gates, including Qianmen, the 138-feet-high "Front Gate" of the inner city, photographed here with a mixture of rickshaw pullers, cars, trucks, and electric trams in 1931. Modernization sometimes caused serious social tensions, as when 25,000 rickshaw pullers (who traditionally hired themselves out to move people about the sprawling city) rioted in October 1929, attacking the newly installed electric trams and their passengers. Library of Congress, LC-USZ62–137015

kill them, tapeworms and other parasitic organisms survived and easily bore into the skin and infected peasants who waded with bare feet and legs through muddy rice paddies. Millions of Chinese peasants died every year from such parasitic diseases.

The traditional sources of peasant misery—floods, droughts, and famines—continued to inflict great damage in the Chinese countryside in the 1920s and 1930s. A major problem in the countryside was a very high rate of tenancy, with many farmers owning no land and paying up to 50 or even 70 percent of their crops in rent. Landlords and loan sharks charged high interest rates, often 30–40 percent annually, so that peasants who fell into debt were unlikely ever to be free of debt payments. The great British economist R. H. Tawney spent a year in China in the early 1930s studying China's rural economy. After describing the desperate position of Chinese peasants in his classic book *Land and Labor in China*, he made a chilling historical prophecy with typical British understatement. "The revolution of 1911 was a bourgeois affair. The revolution of the peasants is yet to come. If their overlords continue to exploit them as hitherto, it will not be pleasant. It will not, perhaps, be undeserved."[1]

At the very moment Tawney was writing, Mao Zedong a young, ambitious Communist, and his comrades in a poor rural area were beginning to organize Chinese peasants to turn the traditional rural power structure upside down. A tall, thin young man with sad eyes, Mao was born into a wealthy peasant family in rural Hunan Province, near the provincial capital of Changsha. Rebellious from his youth, Mao often came into conflict with his father. After his high school education, Mao went to Beijing for six months, where he was deeply influenced by Li Dazhao, the Beijing University librarian, one of the founders of the Chinese Communist Party. In sharp contrast to Marxist orthodoxy and the views of Stalin, Li Dazhao argued that Chinese peasants should be the heart and soul of the Chinese revolution.

What gave Mao a chance to rise in the Chinese Communist Party hierarchy was Chiang Kai-shek's successful suppression of Communist organizational activities in the cities of south and central China in the spring of 1927. While Moscow continued to emphasize the urban labor movement, even after Chiang Kai-shek's violent purge of Communist and labor organizers, Mao and two military leaders, Zhu De and Peng Dehuai, went in a different direction. In the early 1930s, they began to organize their own soviet—a Communist-controlled network of villages and market towns—in Jinggang Mountain, a poor, remote mountainous district in the border area between the provinces of Hunan and Jiangxi.

In these isolated mountain villages, Mao worked on political questions of party organization and land reform, while Zhu De and Peng Dehuai organized peasant sons into a disciplined Red Army. The army could protect and secure rural villages, where land seizures and landlord executions could be implemented without fear of reprisals from the provincial or national government. Mao and his comrades adopted the Leninist model of the party controlling the army, but they also went far beyond Lenin in their organizational approach and philosophy. Mao had studied the ancient Chinese military classic *The Art of War*, by Sunzi, and he loved the stories of military battles and inventive strategies in the sixteenth-century novels *Water Margin* and *Romance of the Three Kingdoms*. From these varied sources, Mao developed a unique philosophy of guerrilla warfare that was made to order for the weaker side in any battle.

The basic principles of guerrilla warfare are captured in slogans the Red Army soldiers learned at Jinggang Mountain: "The enemy advances, we retreat; the enemy camps, we harass; the enemy tires, we attack; the enemy retreats, we pursue."[2] The guerrilla army evades its more powerful foe and, through superior intelligence, fights only the battles it can win. This army depended on strong political indoctrination. Knowing who they fought and why, the Red Army troops were well disciplined and taught not to raid, rape, loot, or destroy the property of the people. By winning the support of peasants in the remote countryside, the Red Army also gained superior intelligence that yielded precise information about the movements, strength, and plans of the enemy.

These principles were first developed in local skirmishes around Jinggang Mountain, and it did not take long for Mao's organizing efforts to attract the attention of Chiang Kai-shek. From 1931 to 1934, Chiang sent his Nationalist troops on five separate "extermination campaigns" against the Communist forces on the Hunan-Jiangxi border. Each of Chiang's first four campaigns ended in defeat as his armies were outmaneuvered by the smaller Communist forces, divided into subunits, and lured into ambushes. By the fifth such campaign in 1934, Chiang Kai-shek adopted a more deliberate approach: he encircled the Communist forces with his overwhelming superiority in numbers and weaponry and slowly tightened the noose, trapping the Red Army for a final showdown. When these tactics began to succeed, Mao argued for a radical response: to break out of the blockade and flee, with the entire Red Army, to northwest China. This was a move both desperate and brilliant: desperate in that it risked annihilation for an uncertain outcome and brilliant in that it would demonstrate to the world that the Red Army was disciplined and, as Japanese aggression mounted, dedicated to defending China's peasants against Japan, whose role in China's internal politics would soon prove crucial.

From October 1934 to October 1935, Mao, Zhu De, and Peng Dehuai led the Red Army—about 86,000 troops (including thirty-five women)—on what has become known as the Long March, one of the most impressive feats of endurance in the history of warfare. Losing 80–90 percent of their troops along the way—to injury, frostbite, desertion, death, disease, or capture—the Long Marchers traversed, mostly on foot, over 6,000 miles in 368 days, enduring frequent harassment or attack. They crossed twenty-four rivers, moved through twelve provinces, and crossed over eighteen mountain ranges. Though pursued by an army that was much better equipped, the Red Army survived through ingeniously daring tactics and sheer force of will. In the middle of the Long March, Mao was recognized for his strategic brilliance and made head of the Chinese Communist Party.

Zigzagging their way through southwestern and western provinces, the Communists arrived in October 1935 in northwest China, one of the poorest regions of the country, where they made their headquarters in peasant-built caves in Yan'an in Shaanxi Province. This area was chosen in part because it was far removed from Chiang Kai-shek's base in south central China and in part because it was much closer than Jinggang Mountain to Chinese areas now occupied by Japan. Japanese aggression in China accelerated in the early 1930s, in part because Japan feared a truly unified Republic of China. The Japanese had seized control of Manchuria, the original homeland of the Manchus, in 1931–32. This large area north and east of Beiping was rich in forests and coal and oil deposits and, unlike most of China, it was not heavily populated.

Preoccupied with the growing worldwide economic depression, the United States and European countries paid little attention to Japan's takeover of Manchuria. The League of Nations sent an investigating team that pronounced Japan the aggressor, but beyond verbally condemning Japan, the League did nothing to contest Japan's fait accompli, and Japan protested the League's censure by withdrawing from the League.

Throughout the early 1930s, Chiang Kai-shek repeatedly complied with Japanese demands and shied away from any military confrontation. Japan set up a puppet state, Manchukuo, in Manchuria, under the nominal leadership of the last Manchu emperor, Henry Puyi. Japan also seized territory in Inner Mongolia and made ever more demands on the Nationalist government for rights and privileges. Comparing Japanese aggression to a disease of the skin and Chinese communism to a disease of the heart, Chiang argued that he must first wipe out the Communists before he could confront Japan. This policy made Chiang begin to look to his own people like an appeaser, ready to sell out part of his country to maintain his own power.

Chiang's policy almost cost him his life in December 1936 when he flew into the northwest provincial capital of Xi'an to meet with the young Marshall Zhang Xueliang, son of Zhang Zuolin, the Manchurian warlord whom the Japanese had murdered in 1928. Zhang's troops had fled their homeland when Japan took over Manchuria in 1931, and now Chiang Kai-shek was urging them to attack the Communist camps around Yan'an. Increasingly resistant to fighting fellow Chinese while Japan colonized their homeland, Zhang Xueliang and his troops rebelled against Chiang's authority and literally kidnapped him at gunpoint. They invited Mao's confidant Zhou Enlai to sit down with Chiang and negotiate an anti-Japanese truce between the Communists and Nationalists. Chiang reluctantly agreed and flew back to Nanjing, after a two-week captivity, to announce an end to the Chinese civil war.[3]

Japan was quick to see the significance of the growing anti-Japanese hostility in China, and in July 1937, Japanese troops south of Beiping opened fire at Marco Polo Bridge in what was to become the opening round of World War II. As Japan had modernized and Westernized in the late nineteenth century, it had quickly adopted the Western version of imperialism, which viewed the world as locked in a struggle for survival between the weak and the strong, the backward and the progressive. As the most advanced eastern nation, Japan saw itself as the most logical power to colonize and modernize China. In Japan's view, it was only following the example of Britain in India, Holland in the East Indies, the United States in the Philippines, France in Indochina, and the French, British, and Belgians in Africa.

Assuming that Chiang Kai-shek would soon seek a truce, leaving Japan in a strong position in north and northeast China, Japan expected the fighting in China to be brief and decisive. But instead of seeking a peaceful compromise, Chiang and his entire Nationalist government evacuated the eastern half of China and set up a wartime capital in the far western provincial city of Chongqing on the Yangzi River. To slow the Japanese advance westward, Chiang's air force bombed the dikes of the Yellow River in June 1938, thereby flooding millions of acres of farmland, drowning perhaps 300,000 people, and leaving two million people homeless.

The Japanese forces often operated with considerable autonomy from Tokyo, and they reacted with fury when Chinese refused to surrender quickly. When local forces resisted the Japanese occupation of Shanghai and its advance on Nanjing in late 1937, the Japanese military adopted a deliberate policy of raping, looting, and murdering the

Ill equipped and no match for Japan's powerful modern army, Chiang Kai-shek's Nationalist forces enter the Shandong city of Tai'an in 1937 as they retreat from the invading Japanese. Too weak to offer much resistance, Chiang's forces beat a hasty retreat westward, and his fledgling air force bombed the dikes of the Yellow River in June 1938 to slow the Japanese advance. Library of Congress, LC-USZ62–137679

civilian population with impunity. In six weeks' time, they raped at least 20,000 Chinese women and killed 100,000 to 300,000 Chinese civilians (historians still debate the numbers) in what has become known to the world as the Rape of Nanjing, one of the more infamous atrocities of the twentieth century.

The Western world, preoccupied with the Nazi movement and its growing threat in Europe, looked on this Japanese butchery in China with some indifference. A stalemate was reached in China by 1939, when Japan controlled the eastern third of the country, the Chinese Communists controlled its small base area in the northwest, and the Nationalists controlled the southwest. Chinese Communists and Nationalists cooperated only nominally, and Chiang Kai-shek often positioned his best troops not so as to engage the Japanese but so as to contain his Communist "allies" in the northwest.

When Japan moved into French Indochina and occupied a naval base there in the summer of 1941, the United States declared an embargo on further trade with Japan. Since the United States had been its main supplier of oil and scrap metal up to this point, Japan saw the trade embargo as a virtual declaration of war. Japan offered to pull out of French Indochina in exchange for the lifting of the embargo. The United States refused, and Japan attacked the U.S. naval base at Pearl Harbor without warning on December 7, 1941. Chiang Kai-shek and Mao Zedong both rejoiced to have the United States, finally, as a full partner in the war with Japan.

China's war against the invading Japanese was made to order for the Maoist style of guerrilla warfare. Japanese troops were easily identifiable anywhere in China, and Chinese Communist forces now subordinated their class warfare to the task of uniting all Chinese in the struggle against Japan. In August 1940, Communist forces launched a major offensive against the Japanese in north China, cutting railway lines and roads, blowing up bridges, and sabotaging strategic assets like coal mines. Japanese commanders responded with a scorched-earth policy of "kill all, burn all, loot all," designed to terrorize the Chinese population into submission. What it did instead was to send ever-increasing numbers of Chinese into the Communist Party. Throughout the war, the Communists modified their land policies—they reduced rents while guaranteeing their payment, thus winning the support of all classes. Peasants were so grateful to the Chinese Communist Party for organizing resistance to Japan that they happily sent their sons to join the Red Army. In 1935, the Communists commanded some 30,000 troops and controlled perhaps two million people. By the end of World War II, the Communist Party had a well-trained, highly motivated army of nearly one million troops and controlled a total population of about one hundred million people.

During World War II, the Chinese Communist Party developed many of the techniques it would later use to rule all of China. In the heat of a war that everyone saw as a struggle for survival, the Party developed an iron-clad discipline and a strong spirit of self-sacrifice for the sake of the Party and the nation. Mao delivered a stirring eulogy of Norman Bethune, an idealistic Canadian surgeon who went to Yan'an to help the Chinese Communists resist Japan, worked tirelessly to teach Chinese doctors and nurses the techniques of battlefield surgical operations, blood transfusions, and so on, and died of blood poisoning after failing to treat a cut he had suffered during surgery: "Comrade Bethune's spirit, his utter devotion to others without any thought of self, was shown in his boundless sense of responsibility in his work and his boundless warm-heartedness towards all comrades and the people. Every Communist must learn from him.... We must all learn the spirit of absolute selflessness from him."[4]

Mao seemed such a brilliant military and political strategist that he gained ever-increasing authority. Once he and his small group of Party leaders (including Zhou Enlai, Zhu De, and Peng Dehuai) determined and announced the military strategies and political policies for the day, every Party member was obligated to implement these strategies and policies with enthusiasm. Every Party member was obliged to read and study the speeches and essays of Party Chairman Mao.

When many writers and intellectuals fled to the wartime base of Yan'an, they were quickly indoctrinated against writing the kinds of critical essays or short stories that showed the seamy side of society. Instead, they were told to write clear propaganda in support of the Chinese people and their war effort. In 1942 Mao delivered a series of lectures on literature and art in which he declared that writers and intellectuals must identify themselves with the peasant class and write for the sake of the nation (and the Communist Party). What the country needed from its writers, he concluded, was not "more flowers on the brocade" but "fuel in snowy weather."[5]

China's greatest woman writer in Yan'an, Ding Ling, fled to Yan'an after having been imprisoned by the Nationalists. She was disappointed to discover the low status of women in the Communist Party and wrote a story showing the contrast between Party rhetoric about women's equality with men and the realities of life under Party control. In keeping with Mao's policies on art and literature, she was harshly criticized for her efforts, forced to confess her "bourgeois outlook," and pressured to write only propaganda favorable to Mao and the Party.

As for Mao's "fuel in snowy weather," the Party organized mass associations to communicate Party policies to every person in Party-controlled areas. Propaganda teams went into villages to perform plays, puppet theater, songs, and folk dances, all carrying the message that the Chinese Communist Party would lead China to victory against the Japanese aggressors. Peasant associations worked to reduce rents and interest rates while being careful not to attack landlords, who were also enlisted in the anti-Japanese war. Women's associations mobilized women to work collectively in support of the war effort, confronted men who beat their wives, and worked to promote women's freedom of marriage and divorce. Youth associations rallied young people in the war effort as well, stirred their idealistic impulses, and recruited thousands to become members of the Communist Party.

Chiang Kai-shek's forces, by contrast, grew in numbers but not in strength. He appointed commanders on the basis of their personal loyalty to him rather than their competence or honesty. Commanders often inflated their troop rolls, sold off their allotted rations on the black market, and left their troops starving and weaponless in the field. Nationalist forces died more often from disease and starvation than enemy bullets. American diplomats in China often contrasted the high morale and discipline of the Communist forces with the corruption and incompetence of the Nationalist forces. The crusty American general George Stilwell, known as "Vinegar Joe" for his sharp tongue, felt nothing but contempt for Chiang Kai-shek, who seemed to care far more about his own power and Communist rivals than defeating Japan. Eventually the United States recalled Stilwell from China in order to try to improve America's relationship with Chiang Kai-shek.

When World War II ended, the United States was anxious to avoid a renewed civil war in China between the Communists and the Nationalists. General George Marshall, one of America's most respected generals, went to China to try to negotiate a peaceful compromise between the two sides, but his efforts were doomed by the deep suspicions on both sides based on their long history of lethal conflict and feigned "cooperation." Having suffered through an eight-year war that left twenty million Chinese dead and millions more wounded, sick or starving, the Chinese people desperately wanted peace. But Chiang Kai-shek was not about to tolerate an independent Communist army in China, and Mao would never again agree to lay down arms and trust the goodwill of Chiang.

On paper, the Nationalists had about a four-to-one advantage in numbers of armed troops (four million to one million); overwhelming technical superiority in terms of tanks, aircraft, and weapons; and the clear and strong support of the United States, which provided Chiang's forces with about $2 billion in military aid from 1946 to 1949. But Chiang was overconfident in thinking the United States could not and would not let him lose a shooting war with his Communist rivals. Against American advice, Chiang used U.S. air transport to fly his best forces into northeast China and Manchuria in 1946–1947 in order to try to prevent the Communists from taking the Japanese surrender and establishing Communist power in those areas. When full-scale civil war broke out in early 1947, the Communists abandoned their wartime capital of Yan'an, scattered into the countryside in classic guerrilla fashion, and renamed their forces the People's Liberation Army.

Chinese Communist forces had moved into Manchuria with some tactical help from the Soviet Union (which had also sent troops into

China on the request of the United States when the overwhelming concern was to force Japan's quick surrender). In mid-1947, the Communists seized the initiative in Manchuria, surrounded the Nationalist forces in the cities, and cut railway and communication lines. Chiang refused to recognize the looming defeat of his troops there and sent in reinforcements. In late 1948, the Communist general Lin Biao led a final massive assault in Manchuria, capturing in two months' time 230,000 rifles and 400,000 of Chiang's best soldiers.

Even then, the Nationalists still enjoyed numerical superiority in men and a virtual monopoly on tanks and planes. That changed in the central Yangzi valley battle of Hwaihai (Xuzhou) from November 1948 through January 1949. When the Nationalist general at Hwaihai found himself encircled and cut off by Communist forces, he heard that Chiang Kai-shek was preparing to bomb his troops to keep them and their equipment from falling to the Communists. He quickly surrendered his force of 460,000 troops to the People's Liberation Army. The Nationalist effort was further undermined by rampant inflation that swept through Nationalist-controlled territory with the force of a hurricane. From January 1946 to August 1948, prices multiplied sixty-seven times. In late 1948, all confidence in the Nationalist government collapsed. Prices multiplied 85,000 times in six months, and the Nationalist currency became as meaningless as a Qing dynasty copper coin. Chiang Kai-shek fled first to Sichuan Province in the far west and then to Taiwan, along with nearly two million Nationalist troops and officials and their families. (Taiwan, a Japanese colony from 1895 to 1945, had been returned to the Republic of China upon the surrender of Japan in August 1945.) On October 1, 1949, Mao Zedong stood atop the Gate of Heavenly Peace in the center of Beijing and proclaimed the founding of the People's Republic of China.

The People's Republic of China (1949 to the Present)

T he Chinese people have stood up…. Ours will no longer be a nation subject to insult and humiliation,"[1] Chairman Mao Zedong proclaimed upon his arrival in Beijing in the autumn of 1949. The Chinese Communist Party had risen to power on three converging currents of public opinion: (1) Chinese nationalism that had been building since the Opium Wars; (2) class resentment, mainly of peasants against landlords; and (3) growing frustration shared by all classes over the corruption, incompetence, and financial collapse of the Nationalist government. As the civil war had begun in earnest in 1947, the Communist Party had changed its tactics in vast stretches of countryside under its control. No longer feeling any need for a united front of all social classes against the Japanese enemy, the Party launched a violent rural revolution.

In the wake of the rapid victories of the People's Liberation Army, Communist Party work teams now spread over the entire nation, extending to the remotest villages, to organize peasants, recruit leaders, and categorize everyone as poor, middle-class, or rich peasants or as landlords. In public "struggle sessions," peasants denounced landlords and pressured them to confess their past crimes and give up their land and property. These struggle sessions served to humiliate all the members of the rural upper classes and to destroy the prestige they had enjoyed in the past. Gradually, from 1949 to 1957, all the land in China was "collectivized," or put under the supervision of cooperatives called "production teams." Individual families were allowed to keep small plots of land for their own use, though the sum of these "private plots" could not exceed 10 percent of the total land held by the production team, which usually consisted of all the members of one village. The land was worked collectively, and the state took 5 to 10 percent of the grain production as a tax. Each family received a portion of the agricultural produce based on a work-point system administered by the village head, who was now a representative of the Communist Party. The state bought the rest of the produce at whatever price it set.

One of the first acts of the new government in 1950 was to issue its New Marriage Law, which forbade arranged marriages and awarded women the rights to divorce and to inherit property. Equally momentous was the move of the Chinese Communist Party to promote the legitimacy of women working outside the home and to facilitate that work by providing child care. Even in the early twentieth century, to be employed outside the home was seen by many as shameful for a woman. With their own incomes, women gained more influence over family decisions and more independence than ever before.

In the early 1950s, the Communist Party also took control of the urban economy, with less violence than in the countryside but with equal thoroughness. Former capitalists who cooperated with the Party were allowed to remain as state-employed managers of the enterprises they once owned. Many capitalists and Nationalist Party members fled to Taiwan or the British colony of Hong Kong, escaping persecution and leaving their factories and properties behind. Private commerce and private enterprise were effectively outlawed.

Party chairman Mao and state premier Zhou Enlai traveled to Moscow in early 1950 to negotiate a treaty of friendship and to secure Soviet aid in China's modernization. As a result, 20,000 Chinese young people went to the Soviet Union for training, and the Soviets sent 10,000 scientists and engineers to China to give technical aid and advice in the building of new roads, dams, bridges, and factories.

The United States realized the Communist revolution in China represented a stunning defeat for American foreign policy, but the Truman administration concluded by the late 1940s that Chiang Kai-shek had completely lost the support of the Chinese people and no longer deserved American aid. In 1950, as Communist military forces were preparing to invade Taiwan and finish the civil war once and for all, the U.S. government was reconciled to watching the last chapter of the Chinese civil war from the sidelines. The Korean War abruptly changed all that.

After Japan's surrender in 1945, Korea, which had been a Japanese colony since 1910, had been divided and occupied by Soviet forces north and American forces south of the 38th parallel. Near the end of World War II, the United States had agreed to this in order to enlist Soviet help to hasten the defeat of Japan. Kim Il-sung, the Communist leader of North Korea, was determined not to tolerate a permanently

Against a background of modern industrial plants with smokestacks, Mao Zedong holds blueprints for the future in this 1953 poster, which reads, "Chairman Mao leads us to build a great country." These popular posters, painted in the style of *"revolutionary romanticism,"* communicated state goals and policies to the general populace, always portraying the Communist Party and Chairman Mao in the most positive light possible. Hoover Political Poster Collection, CC 202

divided Korea. On June 25, 1950, with Soviet equipment and probably with the permission of Stalin, Kim launched an invasion across the 38th parallel in an attempt to unify the Korean peninsula under Communist control. The United States quickly sent American troops to Korea under the banner of the United Nations and the leadership of General Douglas MacArthur.

When MacArthur's forces pushed the North Korean troops back behind the 38th parallel and then proceeded toward the Yalu River (marking the Korea-China border), hundreds of thousands of Chinese troops surged into North Korea and entered the war. The United States and China were now in direct military conflict, with each side prepared to believe the worst of the other's motives. The United States assumed China was behind the Korean War in the first place, proving that Communism was a dangerous uncontainable virus. The Chinese Communist leaders believed the United States wanted to use Korea as a launching pad from which to invade China, reverse the Communist revolution, and restore Chiang Kai-shek to power. At the outbreak of war, President Truman ordered the U.S. Navy's Seventh Fleet to the Taiwan Strait, reversing the United States' earlier policy of nonintervention in the Chinese civil war.

Against the overwhelming technological superiority of the U.S. forces, the Chinese compensated by sending wave after wave of foot soldiers into battle against American tanks and artillery units. Despite incredibly high casualties—one million Chinese combat deaths—the People's Liberation Army fought the American and United Nations forces to a stalemate near the 38th parallel. A truce was finally signed in 1953. The Korea War had dire consequences for U.S.-Chinese relations. For two decades, the United States refused to recognize the People's Republic of China and forbade American citizens to travel to or trade with China. During those years, Chiang Kai-shek's government sat as China's permanent representative on the United Nations Security Council, as if the People's Republic did not exist. Chinese Communist leaders, despite their alliance with America during World War II, now assumed America was their premier enemy in the world.

Chairman Mao had come to power as a great military leader and strategist, and he continued to look at the challenge of governing the country as though politics was simply warfare by other means. If external enemies did not actually invade China, Mao was quick to find internal enemies to be rooted out, exposed, and destroyed. The Communist Party controlled all aspects of the government and military and all communications media. Mao's preferred style of governance was through a succession of massive campaigns, mobilizing the entire population to carry out Party policies. Early campaigns included attacks on prostitution, venereal disease, drug addiction, illiteracy, and bribery and corruption. These were largely successful in educating people in the ideals and national goals of the Party. There were also strong pressures in some more destructive campaigns to find, expose, and attack "enemies" of the Party and the Chinese people within their own midst.

Everyone in the nation now belonged to a "work unit" (*danwei*). Factories, schools, trading companies, villages, and farms were all organized into work units, and every work unit was under Communist Party supervision. The work unit controlled every aspect of a person's life: salary, housing, medical care, and so on. No one could move, change jobs, or travel any distance without permission of the work unit. Thus, the Chinese Communist Party exercised a degree of control over people's lives that was never imaginable under the strongest emperors of the past.

In 1956, Mao was startled by the uprising of the Hungarian people against the Soviet Communists and their Hungarian collaborators. Mao argued that the Chinese Communist Party needed to remain close to the masses of the people in order to prevent such a rebellion against its rule in China. Under the slogan "Let a hundred flowers bloom," Mao and the Party leadership invited all people to write their criticisms of the Party and the government, so that its leaders might "learn from the masses" and get in closer touch with the people. At first, people were reluctant to speak up in the Hundred Flowers Campaign, but after a few received public praise for their criticisms, many began to express their unhappiness with heavy-handed Party control over all aspects of intellectual work, including art, literature, and historical scholarship. In June 1957, Mao changed course dramatically and called for harsh criticism and suppression of all these "class enemies" who had attacked the policies of the Chinese Communist Party.

In the blink of an eye, the Hundred Flowers Campaign turned into an antirightist campaign that sent 400,000 to 700,000 intellectuals to labor camps, ending their careers and robbing the country of many of its best educated minds. At the same time that he was lashing out at intellectuals, Mao was growing impatient with shortcomings in the economy. In 1958, he called for a massive new economic campaign.

Presiding over a mostly agricultural economy, the government had to finance its industrialization by extracting every possible surplus from agricultural production. Some surpluses were achieved in the early 1950s by the restoration of peace, collectivization, and reclaiming new land. But the economy was not growing fast enough to satisfy Mao, and he was disturbed by what he saw as a growing gap between the urban industrial economy and the rural agricultural one. He was frustrated that China's private plots (only 10 percent of the land) were producing much more than 10 percent of its agricultural product, suggesting that people had not really learned the beauty and utility of collectivization. Mao was also growing increasingly impatient with China's Soviet partner, particularly after the Soviet leader Nikita Khrushchev denounced Stalin (who died in 1953) at a Soviet Congress in 1956. This was easily interpreted in Beijing as an attack on Mao.

Thus, in 1958 Mao announced a new campaign, the Great Leap Forward, which he promised would launch China into the leading ranks of the industrialized world within a few years. The Chinese Communist Party moved to collectivize agriculture completely, abolishing all private plots, and called for the self-industrialization of the countryside by the peasants themselves. Rural cadres mobilized peasants in the winter months to build dams, roads, irrigation canals, and terraced fields. They directed peasants to make their own machinery, to smelt steel in their own backyard furnaces—to industrialize the nation from the bottom up all at once.

To further increase economic efficiency, all women were freed from the cooking of meals by having everyone eat in mass cafeterias. Child care likewise was completely collectivized, freeing more mothers for productive labor. Peasants had to hand over all their own draft animals to the collective. Soviet leaders were so horrified by the madness of the Great Leap Forward and its implicit criticism of the Soviet model that they withdrew all Soviet aid from China, and the 10,000 Russian engineers and scientists returned to the Soviet Union, taking their plans, blueprints, and technical expertise with them. Mao soon denounced the Soviet Union as bitterly as he denounced the United States.

The Great Leap Forward is a textbook example of how badly a dictatorship can go wrong when it believes its own propaganda and all criticism is forbidden. The Party organization was so strong and so all-pervasive in society that no one could safely call attention to the unrealistic goals and promises of the Great Leap Forward. Everyone was pressured to work longer hours and to increase production. Since no one could admit that this was madness, every local leader did his duty and reported increases in annual production in 1958. Since the state based its own allotment of the crop on reported yields, it took more and more of the harvest for urban areas, leaving rural villages with little to eat.

In fact, grain production was rapidly plummeting. Peasants resented the loss of their private plots and in some cases butchered their draft animals rather than hand them over to the collective. The mass cafeterias produced poor-quality food that everyone resented and that caused massive waste. The backyard steel furnaces produced nothing but useless brittle pig iron, and the massive labor mobilizations took peasants away from the fields at crucial times in the planting and harvesting cycle. All these mistakes cumulatively produced the largest man-made famine in world history. In the "three hard years," 1959–61, an estimated thirty million Chinese starved to death or died from disease and other complications of malnutrition.

The Great Leap Forward was the first catastrophic failure of Mao Zedong's leadership. At a high Party meeting in the summer of 1959, defense minister Peng Dehuai wrote Mao a private letter expressing his concern about the disastrous mistakes of the misguided campaign. Mao reacted with bitterness, circulated the letter to other leaders, threatened to go "back to the mountains" and organize another Red Army to seize power anew, and demanded Peng Dehuai's resignation for his "betrayal" of the revolution. No one else was willing to resist Mao or speak up for Peng, who was dismissed from his posts. Mao did step down from his position as president of the People's Republic, and he turned over the daily administration of the government to the new president, Liu Shaoqi, and his deputy, Deng Xiaoping. They relaxed the Great Leap policies, disbanded the cafeterias, and restored private plots. The economy made a slow recovery as Mao backed away from his utopian policies, at least for the time being.

In the 1960s, China became increasingly isolated diplomatically both from the West and from the Soviet Union. In 1959, Tibetan Buddhists rose in open revolt against Beijing, and the People's Liberation Army sent troops into Tibet. The Dalai Lama, the spiritual and political leader of Tibet, fled to India. China had tolerated most practices of Tibetan Buddhism in the 1950s but now began to close monasteries and temples and to forbid the open practice of Buddhism. China bitterly criticized the Soviet Union in 1960 for its policy of peaceful coexistence with the United States. In 1962, China soundly defeated India in a border dispute in the Himalayan Mountains. These actions all served to alarm the Western world about China's power and its expansive intentions. To further feed such fears, China detonated its first atomic bomb in 1964, thanks to the work of Western-trained Chinese physicists who had returned to China in 1949.

From 1962 to 1966, Liu Shaoqi and Deng Xiaoping tried to restore a sense of order and predictability to Chinese life. During these few years, some intellectuals in Beijing felt secure enough to write critical and satirical essays about the excesses of Mao. The very appearance of such writings suggested that Mao had lost much of his former power, but Mao was not about to recede quietly into the background. He countered these trends by building up his image in the armed forces. Lin Biao, a career military man, had replaced Peng Dehuai as minister of defense, and in 1964, Lin created an edition of some of Mao's writings, the *Quotations of Chairman Mao*. Known as the "Little Red Book," it became required reading for all members of the People's Liberation Army.

In 1966, Mao made a dramatic move to restore his power within the Chinese Communist Party. Adopting his guerrilla warfare model to political competition within the Party, with Lin Biao's help, Mao began to spread the cult of Mao from the army to all of society. Mao needed other allies, particularly in the mass media, and for this he turned, with the help of his wife, to Shanghai. Mao had divorced his third wife in about 1939 to marry a Shanghai actress, Jiang Qing.[2] Jiang Qing had great ambitions but had been frustrated for years because the Party leadership had insisted that she not be deeply involved in political affairs.

Now Jiang Qing's ambitions and Mao's desire to regain power were linked as Jiang made an alliance with several radical intellectuals in Shanghai, where they published a virulent attack on criticisms of Chairman Mao as "counterrevolutionary" (a very strong term implying a capital crime). When a student at Beijing University posted a big-character poster criticizing professors as unprogressive for putting too much emphasis on technical knowledge and not enough on Communist ideology, Mao responded with his own big-character poster giving students the exhilarating message that "to rebel is justified."[3] Mao called on all young people to organize themselves into Red Guard units to find and expose all examples of "capitalist-roader" sympathies or Soviet-style "revisionism" in the universities and in society at large.[4] Mao further declared that revisionists and capitalist-roaders existed at the very highest levels of the Communist Party, an accusation people quickly understood as directed at none other than Liu Shaoqi and Deng Xiaoping.

Mao and his radical Shanghai comrades dubbed this nationwide movement the Great Proletarian Cultural Revolution. All schools were closed in 1966, and young people were given free rein to "smash the four olds"—old ideas, habits, customs, and cultures. In a poisonous atmosphere in which anyone could be accused of counterrevolutionary thoughts or deeds at any time, youthful bands of Red Guards raided people's homes to find evidence of revisionism, foreign influence, or secret anti-Maoist sentiment. Red Guard factions quickly became polarized as each one tried to prove it was more revolutionary than its rivals. In 1968, Liu Shaoqi was removed from office, expelled from the Party, beaten, and denied medical treatment. He died of pneumonia in prison in 1969. Deng Xiaoping was sent into exile in south China to "reform himself through labor" by working in a tractor plant.

For a time Mao tolerated the chaos of the Red Guards, but by the summer of 1968, when anarchy and civil war seemed close, he retreated and called in the People's Liberation Army to restore order. He proclaimed that the Cultural Revolution was a great success but said the Red Guards had gone too far. As if simply concluding one phase of the revolution and moving on to the next "higher stage," Mao now urged that all former Red Guards be sent to the countryside themselves, to live

This 1967 poster glorifies young Red Guards carrying the banner of Chairman Mao and attacking the "four olds" ("old ideas, old culture, old customs, old habits of the exploiting classes"), trampling traditional Confucian virtues, Buddhism religion, and foreign influences alike. In the heady atmosphere of unprecedented freedom from adult supervision and the intense propaganda about class struggle and the evils of revisionism, young people often beat and tortured their teachers and anyone else they could identify as revisionists or secret enemies of Chairman Mao. Library of Congress, LC-USZC4–3346

with the peasants and to be reformed through hard labor, just as they had sent their victims to a similar fate. For thousands of young people who had been members of the Red Guards, this was a sudden awakening from the dream of the glorious Cultural Revolution.

In poor rural villages, these "sent-down" youth discovered how poor China really was, and they were often resented by the peasants who saw them with their soft hands and city ways as burdensome intruders. More shocks followed in quick succession. Actual shooting between Russian and Chinese troops occurred at two points on the long Soviet-Chinese border in 1969, and there were rumors that the Soviet military might actually strike China's nuclear facilities. In part to counteract the Soviet threat, Mao and Zhou Enlai now decided to resume official contacts with the United States. In early 1972, in perhaps the most dramatic diplomatic reversal in the twentieth century, the avid cold warrior President Richard Nixon and his national security advisor, Henry Kissinger, visited Beijing for extensive talks with Premier Zhou Enlai and an ailing Mao Zedong. Nixon had his own reasons for seeking improved relations with China, both to help the United States find a graceful way out of its war in Vietnam and to play off China against the Soviet Union.

It was difficult for Maoists to explain to the Chinese people how the United States could go in one day from being China's greatest enemy to being a potential friend, and another development at almost the same time was even more difficult to explain. In 1972 it was officially announced that defense minister Lin Biao, the hero of the Cultural Revolution and Chairman Mao's "closest comrade-in-arms," was a traitor. He had plotted to kill Mao, and when his plot was discovered, he died in a plane crash on September 13, 1971, along with his wife and son, as they were trying to escape to the Soviet Union. No one knew if this report was true, but everyone had to ask how such "traitors" as Liu Shaoqi and Lin Biao could ever have risen to such heights of power if Mao was as wise as always claimed.

From 1949 onward, Mao dominated the People's Republic of China as no one else, so when his health steadily worsened in the early 1970s (from amyotrophic lateral sclerosis), anxieties mounted over who could possibly replace him. Zhou Enlai had survived the Cultural Revolution only by backing Mao and sacrificing some of his own closest associates. Surprisingly, when Zhou fell ill in 1974, Mao brought Deng Xiaoping back from political exile to assume the reins of government. Zhou died in early 1976, and in April there were riots in Tiananmen Square when police removed memorial wreaths dedicated to Zhou. Mao's wife, Jiang

Qing, and the other leaders of the Cultural Revolution blamed this open defiance of the Communist Party on Deng Xiaoping, and Mao agreed once again to Deng's dismissal. Then in July, one of the most severe earthquakes on record devastated the coal-mining town of Tangshan, near Tianjin, killing as many as 600,000 people. Many Chinese could not help seeing such a natural disaster as foretelling a change of the Mandate of Heaven.

As if to confirm such an interpretation, Mao Zedong died on September 9, 1976, a momentous event that left everyone feeling anxious and uncertain about the future. Before his death, with high party leaders increasingly polarized into moderate and radical camps, Mao had appointed a little-known provincial official, Hua Guofeng, as his successor. Within one month after Mao died, Hua arrested Jiang Qing and her three Shanghai associates. They were now labeled the Gang of Four—Mao had once cautioned his wife not to form a "gang of four" with these three. In November 1980, they were put on trial and convicted

Curious crowds absorb the fall of the "Gang of Four," caricatured in Shanghai wall posters in mid-October, 1976. The closest associates of Chairman Mao, his wife and three of her Shanghai colleagues, were arrested in early October, about one month after Mao's death, and their fall from power was first announced, beginning October 15, in a flurry of wall posters covering the streets of Shanghai, the city they had controlled for the past decade. Photo by Paul Ropp

for wrongfully persecuting millions during the Cultural Revolution.[5] Hua Guofeng had few strong supporters in the Party, and Deng Xiaoping soon returned from political exile to replace him as Party leader. After all the purges, policy reversals, and persecutions of the Maoist era, Deng moved quickly to try to restore some level of popular faith in the Chinese Communist Party.

Nearly all the victims of the Cultural Revolution, including some who had been killed or committed suicide, were now pronounced innocent and restored as Communist Party members in good standing. Deng ended the Maoist-style political campaigns, opened China to foreign investment, and allowed people for the first time in more than a decade to enjoy their private lives without being swept up into political campaigns. He never explicitly repudiated Maoism, but in effect he reversed almost every Maoist policy. He quickly reprivatized agriculture through a "responsibility system" by which peasants were given lifetime tilling rights to land that they could pass on to their descendants. Peasants were responsible for their own production, and after meeting a minimal state quota, a tax in effect, they could sell any surplus in private markets based on supply and demand.

Deng Xiaoping called his reforms the Four Modernizations (in agriculture, industry, science and technology, and the military) and argued that the main goal of the Communist Party was to make China prosperous. The government implemented business and contract laws to attract foreign investors and assure them that their investments would be safe. Deng created special economic zones with low tax rates along the coast to attract foreign investment and speed economic development. For the first time since 1949, individual Chinese were again free to invest in business enterprises. Foreign investment poured into China in the 1980s, and the country began a remarkable thirty-year economic boom of unprecedented proportions. Chinese universities quickly expanded to resume training the best students in China, now recruited by entrance examinations on academic subjects rather by class background or political ideology. Tens of thousands of Chinese students began studying abroad in the United States and Europe.

In some ways, Deng Xiaoping brought more radical changes to Chinese society than Mao had. For example, one aspect of Maoist rule in China had been to promote a very puritanical (one might almost say Confucian) attitude toward sexuality and sexual freedom. From 1949 until after the death of Mao, women wore long, baggy pants and baggy shirts, as all China adopted a kind of peasant unisex look. Makeup and jewelry were condemned as wasteful bourgeois products, and advertising for anything but revolutionary politics was forbidden. Romantic love was regarded as a bourgeois sickness, and adultery was treated much as under the Confucian family system.[6]

After Mao died, Deng Xiaoping promoted drastic changes in allowing capitalist style advertising and in allowing men and women to dress as they pleased. Western-style dress became the accepted mode of attire in China's cities. Fiction writers in the 1980s began to write candidly about romantic love, and some even wrote erotic or pornographic stories, evading censors by publishing in underground publications sold on street corners by highly mobile hawkers. Advertisers once again used beautiful scantily clad women to sell products. Art schools allowed drawing from human nudes; the cosmetics industry took off; fashion shows became commonplace in large cities; and some urban women began to have their eyelids cut to make them look more "Western."

Despite the promises of the Marriage Law of 1950, the Communist Party had aggressively discouraged divorces in the Maoist era and had set up mediation committees to mobilize troubled couples' families and friends to pressure them not to divorce. In the post-Mao era, these regulations were greatly relaxed, and divorce rates quickly rose in China's cities in the 1980s and 1990s. In the countryside changes were less drastic, as old attitudes continued to hold sway.

Upon his return to power in 1978, Deng Xiaoping encouraged people to write honestly and truthfully about their mistreatment in the Cultural Revolution. He himself had suffered at Mao's hands, and he thought the cathartic sharing of such feelings would unite people behind his leadership. However, when people went beyond condemnation of the Gang of Four to question the entire system, Deng turned against them. One of the most outspoken critics to emerge in 1978–79 was Wei Jingsheng, a young electrical engineer. At an intersection in Beijing that became known as Democracy Wall, where people could post their criticisms, Wei was shockingly direct in mocking Deng Xiaoping's "four modernizations": "Democracy, freedom and happiness are the only goals of modernization. Without this fifth modernization, the four others are nothing more than a new-fangled lie."[7]

Wei Jingsheng was arrested in March 1979 and sentenced to fifteen years in prison. Democracy Wall was abruptly closed down, and the Party announced Deng Xiaoping's doctrine of the Four Principles (to counterbalance the Four Modernizations): it would tolerate no opposition to socialism, to the proletarian dictatorship, to Communist Party leadership, or to Marxism–Leninism–Mao Zedong Thought. Deng, like Mao before him, tended to alternate between competing factions in the

Party. On the one hand, he hoped to free people from the deadly political campaigns of the Maoist era and to liberate China's economy from the waste and inefficiency of state socialism. On the other hand, he was determined to maintain the Party's monopoly on political power, and he resisted some of his younger associates when they began to argue for gradual moves toward a multiparty state with open political competition.

In a brief period of relaxation in the mid-1980s, students demonstrated in Beijing and elsewhere for more personal freedom and against rampant corruption within the Communist Party. Fang Lizhi, a famous astrophysicist and president of a major university, openly spoke to students as no one had dared since 1949: "I am here to tell you that the socialist movement, from Marx and Lenin to Stalin and Mao Zedong, has been a failure. I think that complete Westernization is the only way to modernize."[8] Deng Xiaoping responded to these demonstrations with another round of crackdowns and arrests and the dismissal of one of his top associates, Hu Yaobang, who had pushed for more intellectual freedom and was thus blamed for the demonstrations. Fang Lizhi and several other dissident intellectuals were expelled from the Party.

In the spring of 1989, there was increasing unrest in China's cities as prices on more and more commodities were deregulated and wages fell behind inflation.[9] As managers could now fire workers to cut costs, unemployment rose, producing new inequalities. Students were becoming frustrated by corruption within the Communist Party and by their own lack of freedom to choose where to work after they graduated from college. This combustible mix was ignited by the sudden death of Hu Yaobang of a heart attack on April 15. Immediately students at Beijing University and other campuses began holding rallies to commemorate Hu Yaobang, to criticize the Communist Party for having dismissed him from office, and to call for immediate reforms. They urged the government to open up China's political system, to rehabilitate critics like Wei Jingsheng who were in prison, to publicize the salaries of top Party leaders, and to crack down on nepotism and corruption.

The designated heir to Deng Xiaoping, Zhao Ziyang, saw in these demonstrations an opportunity to edge his more conservative opponents out of power. But his opponents saw the demonstrations as proof that Deng's reforms had gone too far and should be rolled back. When a *People's Daily* editorial used the word "turmoil" to describe the demonstrations, the students were outraged, for they saw themselves as true patriots calling for much-needed improvements in Chinese life. The international news media came to Beijing in mid-May to cover the much-anticipated visit of Soviet leader and reformer Mikhail Gorbachev to China. Both Deng and Gorbachev were anxious to repair relations between their two countries, but for the reporters from around the world, massive student demonstrations in Tiananmen Square easily overshadowed Gorbachev's visit.

Zhao Ziyang argued for a more conciliatory approach to the students, but when students learned of Zhao's sympathies, they optimistically intensified their protests, confirming to the hard-liners that Zhao's approach would backfire. Some students began a hunger strike to demonstrate their determination to die for their cause if necessary. Even worse, from the Party's perspective, hundreds of thousands of ordinary citizens took to the streets in Beijing and other major cities to express their support for the students. For weeks the Communist Party leadership seemed paralyzed and unable to respond effectively to this growing crisis. Deng Xiaoping, who had seen Gorbachev's visit to Beijing as the crowning event of his reforms, felt humiliated by this open show of disrespect for his leadership.

As soon as Gorbachev departed on May 18, Deng sided with the hard-line faction in the leadership and agreed to end the demonstrations by force. Zhao Ziyang refused to declare martial law and was expelled from the Party a few days later. Premier Li Peng went on national television to declare martial law on May 20. Even at this point, many remained hopeful, as citizens filled the streets and turned back the first attempts of the People's Liberation Army troops to enter Beijing. On May 30, students assembled a plaster model they called the Goddess of Democracy in the middle of Tiananmen Square, directly facing the portrait of Chairman Mao, a final symbolic defiance of the Chinese government.

Many student leaders argued in late May for the evacuation of Tiananmen Square and a return to their campuses. They could declare victory in having peacefully demonstrated for six exhilarating weeks and vow to continue their crusade more quietly. But in the heat of the moment, the most radical students had come to believe that bloodshed was needed to move China forward by discrediting the Chinese Communist government once and for all. Not very familiar with the democratic principle of majority rule, the students refused to leave the square as long as some students insisted on staying.

In the early dawn of June 4, after six weeks of hope and uncertainty, army troops entered Beijing by force, shooting live bullets at unarmed crowds. It was a night of horror, bloodshed, and anger, as many in the crowds fought back with rocks and homemade Molotov cocktails.

Everyone publicly associated with the demonstrations was ordered arrested. Although the government cut off the satellite feed to kill live broadcasting from China, television reporters smuggled videotapes out of China showing the world horrific scenes of carnage. Some rioting occurred in other Chinese cities as well, but China's newscasters, who had been free to cover the demonstrations during much of the spring, now praised the brave soldiers for putting down an uprising of "bad elements." Near dawn, the remaining students evacuated Tiananmen Square just before the tanks and troops rolled in, so no one was killed in the square itself, as the government was quick to point out. Yet in the bloody streets of Beijing somewhere between four hundred and eight hundred civilians had been killed and perhaps 10,000 wounded.

The government urged people to turn in friends and neighbors who might have participated in the demonstrations, but in contrast with the Cultural Revolution era, most people refused to cooperate with the witch hunt. Thousands of ordinary people helped to hide students and other demonstration leaders from the authorities and to smuggle them safely out of the country.

Some hard liners in the Communist Party hoped that the 1989 demonstrations would enable them to reverse the entire direction of Deng Xiaoping's reforms, but Deng stuck to his economic policies. For about a year, foreign businesses cut their investments in China because they feared for its stability. Once it became clear that the regime was not going to collapse in chaos, foreign investment again came pouring into China, sending the economy into another rapid burst of growth.

The fall of communism in Eastern Europe and the breakup of the Soviet Union convinced Deng and his successors that they made the right decision in 1989. Deng died in 1997, the same year that Hong Kong was returned from British to Chinese control. Because Britain had colonized Hong Kong as part of the Opium War, this was a highly symbolic transfer of power that all Chinese, including many Hong Kong residents, took pride in. Deng Xiaoping's successor, Jiang Zemin, who had supported Deng in 1989, maintained Deng's dual emphasis on strict political control and greater economic openness. In 2002, Jiang Zemin retired and was replaced by Hu Jintao in the first relatively smooth generational transfer of power in the People's Republic. Hu has continued to push economic growth and repress political dissent.

China today is the world's sixth largest economy and its third most active trading nation after the United States and Germany. Between 1978 and 2004, China's GDP grew by a factor of four. With China's enormous domestic market, deep talent pool, and vast supply of disciplined and skilled workers, the country's economic takeoff may have been the most important single world event in the last half of the twentieth century. In 2004, China produced 325,000 engineers, five times the number produced in the United States.

In its capitalist form, albeit with a one-party political system, China has much more impact on American life than Mao Zedong ever did. By mobilizing its vast workforce to become the manufacturing capital of the world, China is now creating tremendous new demand and thus driving up prices for the world's natural resources, including oil, rubber, timber, cotton, and all types of precious metals. While Chinese workers replace American workers in manufacturing jobs, Chinese productivity has had a profound impact in lowering prices on a vast array of consumer goods.[10] China's rise also has profound implications for the global environment, as China is competing with the United States to lead the world in emission of carbon dioxide gases.

There are many uncertainties in China's future. Its population continues to grow, despite a one-child policy since 1979. With at least

Nanjing Road in Shanghai is the busiest shopping street in China, with an estimated 1.7 million visitors on a single weekend day. Whether or not that figure is accurate, the density of Chinese shoppers on Nanjing Road reminds us that China in the first decade of the twenty-first century has by far the world's largest middle class. Photo by Brad Stern

1.3 billion people today, China will probably have 1.5 billion by 2015, in part because the one-child policy is difficult to enforce in rural areas and is now being relaxed to address the problem of an increasingly aging population. There are serious resentments of Chinese control of traditionally non-Chinese regions, particularly in Muslim Xinjiang and in Buddhist areas of Tibet and Inner Mongolia. Buddhist and Islamic practices are tolerated in China today (in contrast to the Cultural Revolution era), but any sign of challenge to the Chinese government is met with quick and severe repression. When 10,000 practitioners of Falun Gong, a form of meditation and spiritual and physical exercise, demonstrated outside the living quarters of top government leaders in 1994, the Communist Party immediately cracked down on the movement, even though it had encouraged it in the 1980s as a traditional, cost-effective way to promote health and well-being.

Deng Xiaoping and his successors have made a gamble that the Chinese people will be willing to tolerate a one-party political system as long as they have relative economic and cultural freedom, and freedom from the forced political participation of the Maoist era. Chinese fiction, art, music, film, and fashion are thriving today as never before under Communist rule. There is once again room for subtlety and irony in Chinese art, as long as artists make no frontal attacks on the Chinese Communist Party.

In some ways, the status of women, ironically, has declined in China since the Maoist era. Prostitution has returned, and in very poor regions, women are sometimes kidnapped and forced to marry into families that could not persuade any women to join them willingly. Social inequalities usually impact women especially, and when some people are desperately poor in a society where some are rich, those at the bottom easily find themselves in degrading circumstances, such as prostitution, for the sake of their own survival. Nonetheless, despite this seamy side of the post-Mao reforms, few women (or men) today would advocate returning to the Maoist era.

The Chinese government has promoted rapid economic development in such "minority regions" as Tibet, Xinjiang, and Inner Mongolia and has also sponsored massive Chinese migration there, making the minority cultures more difficult to maintain. The most immediate threat to China's economic stability is the more than one hundred million rural migrants who have flocked in recent years to the cities, where they often live in poverty and look for jobs. The industrial economy needs to create so many new jobs every year to employ this floating population that anything below 8 percent annual economic growth could present serious problems. Should an economic crisis lead to rapid inflation or rising unemployment, the resulting labor unrest could make the student demonstrations of 1989 look mild by contrast. In response to the U.S. and global financial crisis, the Chinese government in late 2008 announced a two-year, $586 billion (7 percent of China's GDP each year for two years) economic stimulus program of infrastructure building to help maintain rapid economic growth.

The environment also presents a steep challenge to the People's Republic. In its rush to industrialize, China tries to use every energy source it can, including its abundant reserves of low-grade soft coal, which—along with its rapidly growing automobile industry—has made China's major cities today among the most polluted in the world. At the same time, the government is investing heavily in wind and solar power and in building environmentally efficient buildings, putting China on par with Western Europe and considerably ahead of the United States in green technology.

In the last twenty years, Taiwan has become a functioning democracy. From 2000 to 2008, the Nationalist Party in Taiwan lost power to the Democratic Progressive Party, which at times called for an independent Taiwan, despite threats from Beijing that China would invade Taiwan if it ever declared formal independence. Taiwanese businesses have invested billions of dollars in factories in China, and both sides have become highly dependent on their economic ties. The twenty-five million people of Taiwan now enjoy a fully modern industrial economy with one of the highest standards of living in Asia, making the ambivalent status quo with China quite attractive. Appealing to the need for stability and improved relations with the People's Republic, the Nationalist Party's Ma Ying-jeou won the presidency in Taiwan in 2008.

In the summer of 2008, Beijing hosted the Summer Olympics, with 10,500 athletes participating from 204 countries. Spending an estimated $42 billion on new infrastructure, including the architectural marvels of the Beijing National Stadium (the "Bird's Nest") and the National Aquatics Center (the "Water Cube"), the Chinese government was determined to demonstrate to the world the wealth and cutting-edge modernity of today's China. While hosting the Olympics did not visibly change the Chinese Communist Party's tight control of information and intolerance of political dissent, it was clearly a source of pride to the Chinese people to host such a successful Summer Olympics and to see Chinese athletes win more gold medals (fifty-one) than any other nation.

The United States and China have developed a relatively cooperative relationship over the past twenty years, despite lingering suspicions on both sides. The United States often criticizes China's human rights record, but since the 1990s, economics has trumped human rights in U.S.-China relations. China and America have become, surprisingly, deeply interdependent. As the largest holder of U.S. debt in the world, China props up the U.S. dollar, thereby enabling Americans to keep interest rates low, despite a ballooning national debt, and to purchase Chinese products with money borrowed from China.[11] The American banking crisis of 2008–09 is likely to speed China's relative rise, because China is unburdened by debt and can readily encourage more domestic consumption to keep its economy growing despite the worldwide recession.

Today it is much more than cheap labor that draws investors to China from all corners of the world. With a relatively new industrial plant, China now has the world's most modern productive processes with cutting-edge efficiency, and any entrepreneurs who want to enjoy the benefits of this technology are in China or feel they need to be there.

After the terrorist attacks on the World Trade Center in New York City on September 11, 2001, Jiang Zemin and Hu Jintao proclaimed China Washington's ally in the "war on terror" that was proclaimed by U.S. president George W. Bush (as they see separatist movements in Tibet and Xinjiang as terrorist). Since then, America's preoccupation with the Middle East, coupled with China's economic boom and the American financial crisis, has led many Asian countries, for the first time since World War II, to see China as politically and economically more important than the United States.

No history is predetermined. The past 3,000 years of Chinese history have been shaped by millions of choices by the Chinese people. For about two hundred years, starting in the late eighteenth century, China was seen by the world as weak, poor, and backward. Now China has reemerged as one of the world's most powerful countries, as it was through much of its 3,000-year history. China has many problems and many shortcomings, as well as an immensely talented and energetic population. Whether it can continue its rapid economic growth without changing its political system or suffering serious instability is a major question. Whether, in the process, it can avoid an environmental catastrophe, is another.

One of the key principles of the ancient Chinese classic the *Book of Changes* is sure to apply still today: change is an unavoidable constant in human history. The past is never a straitjacket, and the Chinese people will continue to make choices in the future as they have in the past. The pace of change in China has been accelerating for the past century, and

Chinese society today is more open to outside influences than at any time since the Tang dynasty. The Chinese people may continue to seek out and embrace new values and new roles, yet the Chinese cultural identity has proven remarkably strong and enduring. The history of China and its interactions with the world, with its deep patterns four millennia in the making, will surely continue to shape Chinese life.

China has the world's largest population, 1.3 billion, approximately four times the size of the United States and one-fifth of the entire world population of 6.6 billion. It is the largest authoritarian state in the world, and for the past thirty years it has had by far the most rapidly growing economy in the world. More Chinese are traveling, studying, and working abroad than at any previous time in China's long history. In this light, it seems clear that China in the future will have a more profound impact on the rest of the world than ever before.

Chronology

10,000–8,000 BCE
Beginnings of settled agriculture in the north China plain

5000–1500 BCE
Neolithic settlements grow in sophistication of agriculture, of pottery, and of jade tools

ca. 1500–1045 BCE
Shang kings dominate north China plain, develop stratified feudal-type society with writing and sophisticated bronze culture

1045 BCE
Zhou people conquer Shang settlements, develop idea of Mandate of Heaven

1045–771 BCE
Western Zhou dynasty continues Shang bronze and artistic culture, king rules through feudal-type division of outlying territories

770–256 BCE
Spring and Autumn period (after the *Spring and Autumn Annals*); gradual decline of Zhou court as vassals in outlying territories become increasingly independent

481–221 BCE
Warring States period (after *Intrigues of the Warring States*); independent kingdoms compete in attempt to conquer and absorb competing states

221–206 BCE
Qin dynasty; Qin Empire, under Qin Shi Huangdi, defeats and unifies all the Warring States into a central bureaucratic empire

206 BCE–220 CE
Han dynasty; Han Empire maintains Qin imperial institutions while moderating harsh Qin laws and promoting Confucianism as a state ideology

220–589
North-South Division; nomadic peoples (with Chinese collaborators) dominate north China; series of weak Chinese regimes in south China; Buddhism grows dramatically in both south and north

581–618
Sui dynasty; Sui Empire unifies north and south militarily and politically in 589 and builds Grand Canal from central to north China

618–907
Tang dynasty; great age of Buddhism and of poetry; Tang Empire maintains strong central state and becomes cosmopolitan center of world trade

755–763
An Lushan Rebellion weakens Tang politically and militarily

907–960
Five Dynasties period of division and civil war

960–1279
Song dynasty; growing prosperity and trade; revival of Confucian thought (Neo-Confucianism); increasingly threatened by neighboring nomadic peoples

960–1127
Northern Song dynasty; capital at Kaifeng falls to Jurchen invaders in 1127

1127–1279
Southern Song dynasty; capital moved to Hangzhou

1279–1368
Yuan dynasty; Mongols conquer all of China in 1279 and rule the south harshly

1368–1644
Ming ynasty; Zhu Yuanzhang defeats Mongols and establishes more authoritarian monarchical rule; growing prosperity in sixteenth century; China again becomes center of world trade (tea, silk, porcelain for New World silver)

1644–1911
Qing ynasty; Manchus from northeast of Beijing conquer all of China with collaboration of many elite Chinese

ca. 1700–1799
Height of Qing influence over Tibet, Central Asia, and Inner Mongolia

1839–1842
Opium War demonstrates weakness of Qing dynasty in face of industrializing western European states

1840s–1911
Qing weakness invites Western and Japanese encroachment on Chinese sovereignty

1912–1949
Republic of China; Yuan Shikai, first president, asserts dictatorship but dies in 1916

1916–1927
Warlord period; no strong central government; warlords compete for power mainly through training and equipping of armed troops

1925–1927
Nationalist Party and Communist Party cooperate to seize military control of southeast and central coastal areas by 1927

1927–1937
Nanjing Decade; Chiang Kai-shek purges Communist Party allies in 1927 and wins allegiance of northern warlords to "unify" north and south under Nationalist Party control

1931
Japan seizes control of Manchuria

1937–1945
Sino-Japanese War; Japan occupies eastern third of China; Chinese Communist Party occupies northwest, and Nationalist Party occupies southwest

1945–1949
Communist-Nationalist Party negotiations break down; civil war begins in 1947; Communist forces quickly defeat Nationalists, who flee to Taiwan

1949–present
People's Republic of China on mainland; Republic of China on Taiwan

1957
Hundred Flowers campaign leads to persecution of intellectuals

1958–1961
Great Leap Forward leads to massive famine and thirty million deaths

1959
Suppression of revolt in Tibet

1966–1969
Great Proletarian Cultural Revolution produces chaos and isolates China diplomatically

1971–1972
China readmitted to the United Nations; U.S. president Richard Nixon visits China

1976
Zhou Enlai dies in January; Mao Zedong dies in August; Hua Guofeng succeeds Mao and arrests his closest associates, the "Gang of Four"

1978
Deng Xiaoping returns to power, promotes "the four modernizations," and ends the decades of Maoist-style class struggle

1979
Special Economic Zones created to stimulate foreign trade and investment

1987
In Taiwan, President Chiang Ching-kuo (Chiang Kai-shek's son) lifts martial law and permits opposition political parties

1989
Prodemocracy demonstrations suppressed in early June after six weeks of occupying the streets of Beijing and other cities

1992
Deng Xiaoping on "southern tour" to Shenzhen reaffirms commitment to economic reform and rapid development (with Communist Party monopoly on political power)

1994
Jiang Zemin succeeds Deng Xiaoping and continues his policies

1997
Hong Kong reverts to Chinese control

1998
Pragmatist Zhu Rongji succeeds conservative Li Peng as premier

2000
Chen Shui-bian of the Democratic Progressive Party wins Taiwan presidency, putting the Nationalist Party out of power on Taiwan for the first time

2001
China becomes a member of the World Trade Organization

2003
Hu Jintao succeeds Jiang Zemin as president and general secretary of the Chinese Communist Party; continues policies of Deng Xiaoping and Jiang Zemin

2008
Ma Ying-jeou regains Taiwan presidency for Nationalist Party, calling for improved relations and negotiations with the People's Republic of China; China hosts Summer Olympics; in response to global economic crisis, government announces $586 billion government investment in economic infrastructure building

Notes

PREFACE

1. Jared Diamond, *Guns, Germs, and Steel: The Fates of Human Societies* (New York: Norton, 1999), 324.
2. Karl A. Wittfogel, *Oriental Despotism: A Comparative Study of Total Power* (New Haven, Conn.: Yale University Press, 1963).
3. Victor Mair, ed., *Contact and Exchange in the Ancient World* (Honolulu: University of Hawai'i Press, 2006), 3–5.

CHAPTER 1

1. Because only male descendants of a king could succeed him, it was important for a king to have many sons, and many consorts (i.e., secondary wives) helped make that possible.
2. I take this term from Valerie Hanson, *The Open Empire: A History of China to 1600* (New York: Norton, 2000), 35, 52.
3. Arthur Waley, trans., *The Book of Songs* (1937; reprint, New York: Grove Press, 1960), 34.
4. Sun Tzu, *Art of War*, trans. Ralph Sawyer (Boulder, Colo.: Westview Press, 1994), 167.
5. Confucius was born as Kong Qiu and came to be known to his disciples as Kongzi (Master Kong) or Kong Fuzi (Venerable Master Kong). When Jesuit missionaries from Europe went to China in the sixteenth century, they began to study and to translate the writings attributed to Kong Fuzi into European languages. To make these writings more accessible to their European readers, they Latinized Kong Fuzi into Confucius.
6. Simon Leys, trans., *The Analects of Confucius* (New York: Norton, 1997), ch. 15, verse 13, p. 76.
7. The ideograph for *ren* is 仁, combining an element on the left meaning person and the two lines on the right that indicate two. Thus, the ideograph carries the built-in implication of people in relationship.
8. Mencius is the Latin-sounding name Jesuit missionaries in China assigned to Mengzi in the sixteenth century. These are the only two Chinese philosophers who have come to be known in the West by their Latinized names.
9. *Mencius*, rev. ed., trans. D. C. Lau (London: Penguin Books, 2003), 106.
10. *Tao Te Ching*, trans. D. C. Lau (Harmondsworth, England: Penguin Books, 1963), 57.
11. *The Book of Chuang Tzu*, trans. Martin Palmer (London: Penguin Books, 2006), 78.

CHAPTER 2

1. These were walls of rammed earth, not to be confused with the later brick walls of the Ming dynasty that form the prototype of today's tourist sites.
2. Mark Edward Lewis, *The Early Chinese Empires: Qin and Han* (Cambridge, Mass.: Harvard University Press, 2007), 152–54.
3. Burton Watson, *Ssu-ma Ch'ien, Grand Historian of China* (New York: Columbia University Press, 1958), 67.

4. One other Han tomb deserves mention for the insight it sheds on Han life: the tomb of the Han imperial prince Liu Sheng, one of the brothers of Han Wudi. Liu Sheng and his wife, Princess Dou Wan, were buried in suits made of more than 2,000 small square or rectangular plaques of jade, each with four holes drilled in the corners so they could be tied together with fine wire made of gold. Small carved jade plugs were used to block all the apertures of their bodies. Whether these suits were intended to preserve the bodies of the prince and princess or to ward off evil spirits in the netherworld, these tombs confirmed what earlier texts had claimed, that members of the Han royal family were often buried in such jade funeral suits. The tomb was also filled with tables and utensils for eating and drinking, including beautiful bronze vessels for ancestral sacrifices, bronze lamps, and incense burners, all suggesting that the dead souls in the tomb were expected to carry on their daily activities just as the living.

5. Elfriede R. Knauer has recently amassed a great deal of evidence to support her thesis that this folk deity, Queen Mother of the West, was in fact inspired by the Greco-Roman deity Kybele or Cybele. Knauer's richly documented study provides striking evidence that Chinese civilization was never as isolated and self-contained as most modern scholars have long assumed. See Elfriede R. Knauer, "The Queen Mother of the West: A Study of the Influence of Western Prototypes on the Iconography of the Taoist Deity," in *Contact and Exchange in the Ancient World*, ed. Victor H. Mair (Honolulu: University of Hawai'i Press, 2006), 62–115.

6. Ban Zhao, "Precepts for My Daughter," in Wilt Idema and Beata Grant, *The Red Brush: Writing Women in Imperial China* (Cambridge, Mass.: Harvard University Asia Center, 2004), 37.

CHAPTER 3

1. John E. Wills, Jr., *Mountain of Fame: Portraits in Chinese History* (Princeton, N.J.: Princeton University Press, 1994), 101.

2. The commercial development of Jiankang is well described in Shufen Liu, "Jiankang and the Commercial Empire of the Southern Dynasties," in *Culture and Power in the Reconstitution of the Chinese Realm, 200–600*, ed. Scott Pearce, Audrey Spiro, and Patricia Ebrey (Cambridge, Mass.: Harvard University Asia Center, 2001), 35–52.

3. Quoted in Etienne Balazs, *Chinese Civilization and Bureaucracy*, trans. H. M. Wright (New Haven, Conn.: Yale University Press, 1964), 241.

4. Ibid., 238.

5. Ibid., 239.

6. About a century after the Seven Sages, another poet, Tao Qian, achieved unparalleled fame for resigning his government post to tend his fields and write poetry celebrating the beauties of nature and the joys of private life.

CHAPTER 4

1. Mark Edward Lewis, *China's Cosmopolitan Empire: The Tang Dynasty* (Cambridge, Mass.: Harvard University Press, 2009), see esp. 163–78.

2. S. A. M. Adshead, *T'ang China: The Rise of the East in World History* (Basingstoke, England: Palgrave Macmillan, 2004), 85–86.

3. Edward H. Schafer, *The Golden Peaches of Samarkand* (Berkeley: University of California Press, 1963), 15; Lewis, *China's Cosmopolitan Empire*, 169–70.

CHAPTER 5

1. "Jian zi mulanhua," trans. Eugene Eoyang, in *Women Writers of Traditional China*, ed. Kang-i Sun Chang and Haun Saussy (Stanford, Calif.: Stanford University Press, 1999), 93.

CHAPTER 6

1. Hongwu Emperor, "Dismissal of Excessive Local Staff Because of Their Crimes," trans. Lily Hwa, in *Chinese Civilization: A Sourcebook*, 2nd ed., ed. Patricia Ebrey (New York: Free Press, 1993), 207.

2. Robert B. Marks, *The Origins of the Modern World: A Global and Ecological Narrative from the Fifteenth to the Twenty-first Century*, 2nd ed. (Lanham, Md.: Rowman and Littlefield, 2007), 80; Dennis O. Flynn and Arturo Giráldez, "Spanish Profitability in the Pacific: The Philippines in the Sixteenth and Seventeenth Centuries," in *Pacific Centuries: Pacific and Pacific Rim History since the Sixteenth Century*, ed. Dennis O. Flynn, Lionel Frost, and A. J. H. Latham (London: Routledge, 1999), 23.

3. One recent estimate is that the population grew from 85 million in 1393 to 155 million in 1500, 231 million in 1600 and 268 million by 1650. Martin J. Heijdra, "The Socio-economic Development of Ming Rural China (1368–1644)" (Ph.D. diss., Princeton University, 1994), chap. 1, sec. 3, "Population." Heijdra's estimates are well summarized, and explained as relatively conservative, by F. W. Mote, *Imperial China: 900–1800* (Cambridge, Mass.: Harvard University Press, 1999), 745.

4. Wang Yangming, "A Record for Practice" (*Chuanxilu*), quoted and translated in Philip J. Ivanhoe, *Readings from the Lu-Wang School of Neo-Confucianism* (Indianapolis: Hackett Publishing, 2009), 142.

5. This name change helped justify the Manchu conquest of the Ming in terms of the ancient Chinese philosophy of change in the five-phase theory. Ming 明 (bright) signifies fire, and Jin 金 (gold), being a metal would succumb to fire. By contrast, Qing 清 (pure) has the water radical on its left side, and in five-phase theory, water quenches fire.

6. Art historians today feel considerable ambivalence toward the Qianlong Emperor. On the one hand, he did more than any other emperor to create the world's largest Chinese art collection, the Imperial Palace Collection (much of which was carried to Taiwan in 1949 but part of which remains in Beijing). On the other hand, he sometimes marred beautiful paintings with many of his red imperial seals and, in some cases, with his mediocre calligraphy.

CHAPTER 7

1. Qianlong edict to King George III, September, 1793, quoted in *The Search for Modern China: A Documentary Collection*, ed. Pei-kai Cheng and Michael Lestz (New York: Norton, 1999), 109.

2. Lord George Macartney, *An Embassy to China, Being the Journal Kept by Lord Macartney During his Embassy to the Emperor Ch'ien-lung, 1793–1794*, ed. J. L. Cramner-Byng (London, 1962), quoted in Raymond Dawson, *The Chinese Chameleon: An Analysis of European Conceptions of Chinese Civilization* (London: Oxford University Press, 1967), 205.

3. While the British were the main traders in opium, between 1800 and 1839 American merchants sold about 10,000 chests of opium in China as well.

4. He actually compensated the Western merchants with five pounds of tea for every pound of opium turned in.

5. Robert Hart, *These from the Land of Sinim: Essays on the Chinese Question* (London: Chapman and Hall, 1903), 54–55.

6. "Poem to Xu Xiaoshu in Contemplation of Death," quoted and translated in Mary Backus Rankin, *Early Chinese Revolutionaries: Radical Intellectuals in Shanghai and Chekiang, 1902–1911* (Cambridge, Mass.: Harvard University Press, 1971), 1.

CHAPTER 8

1. R. H. Tawney, *Land and Labor in China* (1932; reprint, Boston: Beacon Press, 1966), 74.

2. Red Army Slogan, quoted in Stuart Schram, *Mao Tse-tung* (Harmondsworth, England: Penguin Books, 1967), 159.

3. Zhang Xueliang threw himself on Chiang Kai-shek's mercy at the conclusion of this episode, and Chiang placed him under house arrest, where he remained (in Taiwan after 1949) until 1991, when for the first time he was allowed interviews with the press. Even then he refused to criticize his commander, saying only that they had differing views of the Japanese threat in 1936.

4. Mao Zedong, *In Memory of Dr. Norman Bethune* (December 21, 1939), in *Selected Works of Mao Tse-tung*, vol. 2 (Peking: Foreign Languages Press, 1967), 337–38.

5. Selections from Mao Zedong, *Talks at the Yan'an Forum on Literature and Art, May, 1942*, in *Selected Works of Mao Tse-tung*, 3:82.

CHAPTER 9

1. Mao Zedong, "The Chinese People Have Stood Up!" Opening Address at the First Plenary Session of the Chinese People's Political Consultative Conference, September 21, 1949, in *Selected Works of Mao Tse-tung* (Peking: Foreign Languages Press, 1977), 5:15, 17.

2. Mao never recognized his first "wife" because she was chosen by his parents, and his second wife was killed by Chiang Kai-shek's Nationalist army in 1930.

3. Hand-written posters with large characters and sometimes with drawings were pasted on walls and hung from wires as a common means of public protests in China at least from late imperial times if not earlier. They became a major means of communication and political infighting during the Cultural Revolution.

4. The term "capitalist-roader" was used to castigate people Mao charged with secretly wanting to restore capitalism in China. It came to be loosely applied in the Cultural Revolution to anyone who believed in using economic incentives to motivate people or anyone who was insufficiently worshipful toward Mao himself.

5. Jiang Qing eventually hanged herself in her prison cell in 1991.

6. Mao himself behaved almost as a Chinese emperor, keeping a whole group of young girls who attended to his needs and were also expected to go to bed with him upon demand. Of course, the Chinese people knew nothing of this hypocrisy of Mao; it became known only through a candid memoir by Mao's personal physician, Dr. Li Zhisui, *The Private Life of Chairman Mao*, trans. Tai Hung-chao (New York: Random House, 1994).

7. Wei Jingsheng, "The Fifth Modernization," trans. And quoted in *Seeds of Fire: Chinese Voices of Conscience*, ed. Geremie Barmé and John Minford (New York: Noonday Press, 1989), 277.

8. Fang Lizhi, Speech at Tongji University, November 18, 1986, quoted in Richard Baum, *Burying Mao: Chinese Politics in the Age of Deng Xiaoping* (Princeton, N.J.: Princeton University Press, 1994), 201.

9. In China, 1989 was also a highly symbolic year; it marked the fortieth anniversary of the People's Republic, the seventieth anniversary of the May Fourth Movement, and the 200th anniversary of the French Revolution.

10. Citing unidentified research by Gary Clyde Hufbauer, Ted Fishman argues that the average American family saves at least $500 a year from the impact of China's

manufacturing prowess on the price of the world's consumer goods. Ted Fishman, *China Inc.* (New York: Scribner, 2005), 253–54.

11. In an ironic reversal of the Opium War days, by propping up the value of the U.S. dollar and keeping China's currency artificially low relative to the dollar, China now purposely enables America's addiction to cheap credit, deficit spending, and consumerism in order to keep Americans buying Chinese products.

Further Reading

GENERAL AND TOPICAL HISTORIES

Barfield, Thomas J. *The Perilous Frontier: Nomadic Empires and China, 221 BC to AD 1757*. Cambridge, Mass.: Blackwell, 1989.

Berthrong, John H. *Transformations of the Confucian Way*. Boulder, Colo.: Westview Press, 1998.

Clunas, Craig. *Art in China*. New York: Oxford University Press, 1997.

Cohen, Warren I. *East Asia at the Center: Four Thousand Years of Engagement with the World*. New York: Columbia University Press, 2000.

Ebrey, Patricia. *China: Cambridge Illustrated History*. 2nd ed. Cambridge: Cambridge University Press, 2010.

Elvin, Mark. *The Retreat of the Elephants: An Environmental History of China*. New Haven, Conn.: Yale University Press, 2004.

Hansen, Valerie. *The Open Empire: A History of China to 1600*. New York: Norton, 2000.

Mote, F. W. *Imperial China, 900–1800*. Cambridge, Mass.: Harvard University Press, 1999.

Schoppa, R. Keith. *Revolution and Its Past: Identities and Change in Modern Chinese History*. Upper Saddle River, N.J.: Prentice Hall, 2002.

Shaughnessy, Edward L. *China: Empire and Civilization*. New York: Oxford University Press, 2000.

Spence, Jonathan D. *The Search for Modern China*. 2nd ed. New York: Norton, 1999.

Spence, Jonathan D., and Annping Chin. *The Chinese Century: A Photographic History of the Last Hundred Years*. New York: Random House, 1996.

Wills, John E., Jr. *Mountain of Fame: Portraits in Chinese History*. New York: Norton, 1994.

Wood, Frances. *The Silk Road: Two Thousand Years in the Heart of Asia*. Berkeley: University of California Press, 2002.

Wright, Arthur F. *Buddhism in Chinese History*. Stanford, Calif.: Stanford University Press, 1959.

Yang Xin, Richard M. Barnhart, Nie Chongzheng, James Cahill, Lang Shaojun, and Wu Hung. *Three Thousand Years of Chinese Painting*. New Haven, Conn.: Yale University Press, 1997.

ANTHOLOGIES

De Bary, William Theodore, and Irene Bloom. *Sources of Chinese Tradition*. Vol. 1. 2nd ed. New York: Columbia University Press, 1999.

De Bary, William Theodore, and Richard Lufrano. *Sources of Chinese Tradition*. Vol. 2. 2nd ed. New York: Columbia University Press, 2000.

Ebrey, Patricia. *Chinese Civilization: A Sourcebook*. 2nd ed. New York: Free Press, 1993.

Hammond, Kenneth J., ed. *The Human Tradition in Premodern China*. Wilmington, Del.: Scholarly Resources, 2002.

Hammond, Kenneth J., and Kristen Stapleton, eds. *The Human Tradition in Modern China*. Lanham, Md.: Rowman and Littlefield, 2008.

Idema, Wilt, and Beata Grant. *The Red Brush: Writing Women of Imperial China*. Cambridge, Mass.: Harvard University Asia Center, 2004.

Kang-i Sun Chang, and Haun Saussy, eds. *Women Writers of Traditional China: An Anthology of Poetry and Criticism*. Stanford, Calif.: Stanford University Press, 1999.

Lau, Joseph S. M., and Howard Goldblatt. *The Columbia Anthology of Modern Chinese Literature*. 2nd ed. New York: Columbia University Press, 2007.

Mair, Victor H., ed. *The Columbia Anthology of Traditional Chinese Literature*. New York: Columbia University Press, 1996.

Mair, Victor H., Nancy S. Steinhardt, and Paul R. Goldin, eds. *Hawai'i Reader in Traditional Chinese Culture*. Honolulu: University of Hawai'i Press, 2005.

Mann, Susan, and Yu-yin Cheng, eds. *Under Confucian Eyes: Writings on Gender in Chinese History*. Berkeley: University of California Press, 2001.

Ropp, Paul S., ed. *Heritage of China: Contemporary Perspectives on Chinese Civilization*. Berkeley: University of California Press, 1990.

EARLY CHINA: BEGINNINGS TO 221 BCE

Di Cosmo, Nicola. *Ancient China and Its Enemies: the Rise of Nomadic Power in East Asian History*. Cambridge: Cambridge University Press, 2002.

Loewe, Michael, and Edward L. Shaughnessy, eds. *The Cambridge History of Ancient China: From the Origins of Civilization to 221 B.C.* New York: Cambridge University Press, 1999.

Raphals, Lisa. *Sharing the Light: Representations of Women and Virtue in Early China*. Albany: State University of New York Press, 1998.

Thorpe, Robert L. *China in the Early Bronze Age: Shang Civilization*. Philadelphia: University of Pennsylvania Press, 2006.

EARLY IMPERIAL CHINA: QIN AND HAN DYNASTIES, 221 BCE–220 CE

Csikszentmihalyi, Mark, ed. and trans. *Readings in Han Chinese Thought*. Indianapolis, Ind.: Hackett, 2006.

Lewis, Mark Edward. *The Early Chinese Empires: Qin and Han*. Cambridge, Mass.: Harvard University Press, 2007.

Loewe, Michael. *Faith, Myth and Reason in Han China*. Indianapolis, Ind.: Hackett, 1994.

Scheidel, Walter, ed. *Rome and China: Comparative Perspectives on Ancient World Empires*. New York: Oxford University Press, 2009.

Twitchett, Denis, and Michael Loewe, eds. *The Cambridge History of China*. Vol. 1. *The Ch'in and Han Empires, 221 B.C.–A.D. 220*. Cambridge: Cambridge University Press, 1986.

Wang Zhongshu. *Han Civilization*. Trans. K. C. Chang. New Haven, Conn.: Yale University Press, 1982.

PERIOD OF NORTH-SOUTH DIVISION, 220–589 CE

Lewis, Mark Edward. *China between Empires: The Northern and Southern Dynasties*. Cambridge, Mass.: Harvard University Press, 2009.

Pearce, Scott, Audrey Spiro, and Patricia Ebrey. *Culture and Power in the Reconstitution of the Chinese Realm, 200–600*. Cambridge, Mass.: Harvard University Asia Center, 2001.

Watt, James C. Y., An Jiayao, Angela F. Howard, Boris I. Marshak, Su Bai, and Zhao Feng, with contributions by Prudence Oliver Harper, Maxwell K. Hearn, Denise Patry Leidy, Chao-Hui Jenny Liu, Valentina Raspopova, and Zhixin Sun. *China: Dawn of a Golden Age, 200–750 AD*. New York: Metropolitan Museum of Art, 2004.

MIDDLE IMPERIAL CHINA: SUI (581–618), TANG (618–906), SONG (960–1279), YUAN (1279–1368)

Adshead, S. A. M. *T'ang China: The Rise of the East in World History*. Hampshire, England: Palgrave Macmillan, 2004.

Benn, Charles S. *China's Golden Age: Everyday Life in the Tang Dynasty*. New York: Oxford University Press, 2002.

Ebrey, Patricia. *The Inner Quarters: Marriage and the Lives of Women in the Song Period*. Berkeley: University of California Press, 1993.

Franke, Herbert, and Denis Twitchett. *The Cambridge History of China*. Vol. 6. *Alien Regimes and Border States, 907–1368*. Cambridge: Cambridge University Press, 1994.

Gernet, Jacques. *Buddhism in Chinese Society: An Economic History from the Fifth to the Tenth Centuries*. Trans. Franciscus Verellen. New York: Columbia University Press, 1995.

Gernet, Jacques. *Daily Life in China on the Eve of the Mongol Invasion, 1250–76*. Trans. H. M. Wright. Stanford, Calif.: Stanford University Press, 1962.

Johnson, Wallace, ed. *The T'ang Code*. 2 vols. Princeton, N.J.: Princeton University Press, 1979 (vol. 1), 1997 (vol. 2).

Kuhn, Dieter. *The Age of Confucian Rule: The Song Transformation of China*. Cambridge, Mass.: Harvard University Press, 2009.

Lewis, Mark Edward. *China's Cosmopolitan Empire: The Tang Dynasty*. Cambridge, Mass.: Harvard University Press, 2009.

Rossabi, Morris. *Khubilai Khan: His Life and Times*. Berkeley: University of California Press, 1988.

Sen, Tansen. *Buddhism, Diplomacy and Trade: The Realignment of Sino-Indian Relations, 600–1400*. Honolulu: University of Hawai'i Press, 2003.

Smith, Paul Jakov, and Richard von Glahn, eds. *The Song-Yuan-Ming Transition in Chinese History*. Cambridge, Mass.: Harvard University Asia Center, 2003.

Standen, Naomi. *Unbounded Loyalty: Frontier Crossings in Liao China*. Honolulu: University of Hawai'i Press, 2007.

Twitchett, Denis, ed. *The Cambridge History of China*. Vol. 3. *Sui and T'ang China, 589–906*. Pt. 1. Cambridge: Cambridge University Press, 1979.

Twitchett, Denis, and Paul Jakov Smith, eds. *The Cambridge History of China*. Vol. 5. *The Five Dynasties and Sung China, 960–1279 AD*. Pt. 2. Cambridge: Cambridge University Press, 2009.

Weatherford, Jack. *Genghis Khan and the Making of the Modern World*. New York: Three Rivers Press, 2004.

Wright, Arthur F. *The Sui Dynasty*. New York: Knopf, 1978.

LATE IMPERIAL (EARLY MODERN) CHINA: MING (1368–1644) AND QING (1644–1911)

Brook, Timothy. *The Confusions of Pleasure: Commerce and Culture in Ming China*. Berkeley: University of California Press, 1999.

Fairbank, John K., ed. *The Cambridge History of China.* Vol. 10. *Late Ch'ing Empire 1800–1911.* Pt. 1. Cambridge: Cambridge University Press, 1978.

Fairbank, John K., and Kwang-ching Liu, eds. *The Cambridge History of China.* Vol. 11. *Late Ch'ing Empire 1800–1911.* Pt. 2. Cambridge: Cambridge University Press, 1978.

Huang, Ray. *1587: A Year of No Significance, The Ming Dynasty in Decline.* New Haven, Conn.: Yale University Press, 1982.

Mote, Frederick W., and Denis Twitchett, eds. *The Cambridge History of China.* Vol. 7. *The Ming Dynasty, 1368–1644.* Pt. 1. Cambridge: Cambridge University Press, 1988.

Peterson, Willard J., ed. *The Cambridge History of China.* Vol. 9. *The Ch'ing Empire to 1800.* Pt. 1. Cambridge: Cambridge University Press, 2002.

Pomeranz, Kenneth. *The Great Divergence: China, Europe and the Making of the Modern World Economy.* Princeton, N.J.: Princeton University Press, 2000.

Rowe, William T. *China's Last Empire: The Great Qing.* Cambridge, Mass.: Harvard University Press, 2009.

Smith, Richard J. *China's Cultural Heritage: The Qing Dynasty, 1644–1912.* 2nd ed. Boulder, Colo.: Westview Press, 1994.

Schneewind, Sarah. *A Tale of Two Melons: Emperor and Subject in Ming China.* Indianapolis, Ind.: Hackett, 2006.

Spence, Jonathan. *Emperor of China: Self-portrait of K'ang-hsi.* New York: Vintage, 1988.

Spence, Jonathan. *God's Chinese Son: The Taiping Heavenly Kingdom of Hong Xiuquan.* Hammersmith, England: HarperCollins, 1996.

Wong, R. Bin. *China Transformed: Historical Change and the Limits of European Experience.* Ithaca, N.Y.: Cornell University Press, 1997.

TWENTIETH-CENTURY CHINA

Barme, Geremie, and John Minford. *Seeds of Fire: Chinese Voices of Conscience.* New York: Farrar, Straus and Giroux, 1989.

Becker, Jasper. *Hungry Ghosts: Mao's Secret Famine.* New York: Holt, 1998.

Bergere, Marie-Claire, and Janet Lloyd. *Sun Yat-sen.* Stanford, Calif.: Stanford University Press, 2000.

Fairbank, John K., and Albert Feuerwerker, eds. *The Cambridge History of China,* Vol. 13. *Republican China 1912–1949.* Pt. 2. Cambridge: Cambridge University Press, 1986.

Fairbank, John K., and Denis Twitchett, eds. *The Cambridge History of China.* Vol. 12. *Republican China, 1912–1949.* Pt. 1. Cambridge: Cambridge University Press, 1983.

Fenby, Jonathan. *Chiang Kai Shek: China's Generalissimo and the Nation He Lost.* New York: Carroll and Graf, 2004.

Hershatter, Gail. *Women in China's Long Twentieth Century.* Berkeley: University of California Press, 2007.

Hessler, Peter. *Oracle Bones: A Journey between China's Past and Present.* New York: HarperCollins, 2006.

Kang, David C. *China Rising: Peace, Power, and Order in East Asia.* New York: Columbia University Press, 2007.

MacFarquhar, Roderick, and John K. Fairbank, eds. *The Cambridge History of China*. Vol. 15. *The People's Republic*. Pt. 2. *Revolutions within the Chinese Revolution, 1966–1982*. Cambridge: Cambridge University Press, 1991.

MacFarquhar, Roderick, and Michael Schoenhals. *Mao's Last Revolution*. Cambridge, Mass.: Harvard University Press, 2006.

Pan, Philip P. *Out of Mao's Shadow: The Struggle for the Soul of a New China*. New York: Simon and Schuster, 2008.

Shirk, Susan L. *China: Fragile Superpower*. New York: Oxford University Press, 2007.

Snow, Edgar. *Red Star over China*. 1938. Reprint, New York: Grove Press, 1994.

Spence, Jonathan. *The Gate of Heavenly Peace: The Chinese and Their Revolution, 1895–1980*. New York: Viking, 1981.

Terrill, Ross. *Mao: A Biography*. Rev. and expanded ed. Stanford, Calif.: Stanford University Press, 1999.

Wakeman, Frederic, and Richard Louis Edmonds, eds. *Reappraising Republican China*. New York: Oxford University Press, 2000.

Westad, Odd. *Decisive Encounters: The Chinese Civil War, 1946–1950*. Stanford, Calif.: Stanford University Press, 2003.

White, Theodore H., and Annalee Jacoby. *Thunder out of China*. 1946. Reprint, New York: Da Capo, 1980.

Websites

Asian Studies World Wide Web Virtual Library
*http://coombs.anu.edu.au/
WWWVL-AsianStudies.html*
  Maintained by the Australian
  National Library, this site contains
  comprehensive Asian studies listings of
  online journals, information systems,
  databases, study abroad programs,
  and bookstores.

Association for Asian Studies
www.aasianst.org
  Official site for the Association for Asian
  Studies, the main U.S.–based scholarly
  organization for Asian specialists in
  all disciplines. Contains information
  on the association's publications and
  conferences and a comprehensive page
  of Asian studies links.

China the Beautiful
www.chinapage.com/main2.html
  Many pages devoted to Chinese
  culture, including art, poetry,
  calligraphy, and current events.

China Daily
www.chinadaily.com.cn/
  English-language daily newspaper
  from the People's Republic of China.

China Historical Geographic Information Systems
www.fas.harvard.edu/~chgis/
  A remarkable collection of digitized
  historical maps of all kinds, from 222
  BCE to 1911 CE, combining historical,
  social, economic, and geographic
  data using contemporary Geographic
  Information Systems technology.
  Hosted by Harvard University.

China-related Web Sites
*http://orpheus.ucsd.edu/chinesehistory/
othersites.html*
  An annotated list of sites on China
  and Chinese history, from the
  University of California at San Diego.

Classical Historiography for Chinese History
www.princeton.edu/~classbib/
  Authored by Professor Benjamin
  Elman of Princeton University.
  This site includes comprehensive
  bibliographies in addition to exercises
  in utilizing classical Chinese sources.

The Complete Reference to China-Chinese Related Web Sites
http://chinasite.com/
  Contains more than 8,500
  China-related sites and is updated
  daily; supports a general index that
  runs the gamut from Chinese history
  to Chinese restaurants.

East Asian Studies Center, Indiana University: Outreach Page
*www.indiana.edu/~easc/outreach/
educators/index.shtml*
  Provides resources for K–12 teachers
  and students of Chinese and East
  Asian history and culture.

A Visual Sourcebook of Chinese Civilization
http://depts.washington.edu/chinaciv/
  Designed by Patricia Buckley
  Ebrey, this site provides maps, a
  timeline, and a wide range of visual
  material to supplement the study of
  China at any level. Includes pages
  on geography, ancient tombs,
  Buddhism, military technology,
  painting, homes, gardens, clothing,
  and graphic arts.

Warring States Project (University of Massachusetts at Amherst)
www.umass.edu/wsp/
  Innovative research of Bruce and
  Taeko Brooks on the Warring States
  period, tracking the formative
  intellectual developments of the fifth
  through the third centuries BCE,
  leading up to the unification of the
  Qin Empire in 221 BCE.

Acknowledgments

I am deeply indebted to the editors of this series, Bonnie Smith and Anand Yang, and to Nancy Toff of Oxford University Press, for inviting me to attempt such an overview of Chinese history. I greatly appreciate their confidence and their constructive criticisms. Three excellent outside readers gave me more helpfully sharp criticisms of my first draft than I wanted. I also want to thank Sonia Tycko for her expert help in locating and securing the illustrations for this volume, Joellyn Ausanka for managing the production process so cheerfully and efficiently, and Martha Ramsey for her expert copyediting. Brad Stern graciously contributed two photos, and the generosity of Andrea and Peter Klein greatly facilitated my research and helped make possible the illustrations in this volume. My intellectual debts are far too many to summarize here. I especially thank Thomas Massey of Clark University for being my sounding board and for his many suggestions on the overall thrust of this book. Bruce and Taeko Brooks have helped maintain my interest in, and shape my views of, early Chinese history. I'm extremely grateful to my wife, Marjorie, my most important source of support and inspiration. The oversights and errors that remain are entirely my own.

Index

Money, paper, 78, 82, 84
Moneylending, 69
Mongol Empires, 68, 73, 79–82
Mozi and Mohists, 15, 19
Music, 55, 64–65, 84
Musicians, 55

Nanjing, 38, 85, 86, 87; civil war and, 121,
    122; as Jiankang, 38; Rape of (1937),
    129–30; Taiping Rebellion and, 106, 107
Nanjing, Treaty of (1842), 105
Nationalist (Guomindang) Party, 115–16,
    124, 129, 130; Communists and, 120,
    121–22, 134; in Taiwan, 134, 137, 153.
    See also Chiang Kai-shek
National Revolutionary Army, 121
Naval expeditions, 88, 90; British, 105
Neo-Confucianism, 73, 84
Neolithic cultures, 1–2
Nestorian Christians, 55
New Life Movement, 123
New Marriage Law, 136
Nirvana, 43. See also Enlightenment
Nixon, Richard, 144
Nobility. See Aristocracy
Nomadic groups, 38, 61, 65, 72–73, 79;
    cultural hybridization and, 38, 48;
    Jurchen, 71, 95; Khitan, 53, 68, 71;
    Tangut, 68–69; Tibetan, 61, 97, 99;
    Tuoba (Xianbei), 45, 46, 48, 55; Turk,
    53; Xiongnu, 25, 26, 28, 37–38, 50
Northern Expedition, 121
Northern Qi dynasty, 48
Northern Song dynasty, 71
Northern Wei dynasty, 45–46, 47, 48
Northern Zhou dynasty, 48, 50–51
North Korea, 136, 138

Ögödei, Khan, 80
One-child policy, 151–52
"Open Door Notes" (John Hay), 110
Opera (zaju), 84
Opium trade, 103–5, 106, 107, 111
Opium War, 105–6, 117, 150
Oracle bones, 3, 6, 7, 8, 10

Painting. See Art and artisans
Paper, invention of, 31
Paper money, 78, 82, 84
Parthia, 28
Patriarchy, xv
Peasants, 12, 13, 20, 40, 77, 124–26;
    collectivization and, 135–36, 140–41;
    Communist Party and, 126, 131, 132,
    135; parasitic disease and, 124–25;
    poverty of, 124; rebellion by, 95, 97, 101,
    106–7; "responsibility system" and, 146
Peking Man, 1
Peng Dehuai, 126, 127, 132, 141, 142

People's Liberation Army, 133, 134, 135,
    138, 149; Red Guard and, 142, 143;
    Tibet and, 141
People's Republic of China, 133–55;
    agriculture in, 135–36, 140–41, 146;
    Cultural Revolution in, 142–46, 147;
    Great Leap Forward in, 140–41; Korean
    War and, 136, 138; student protests in,
    148, 149–50. See also Communist Party;
    Mao Zedong
Philosophers, 12–13, 16, 17
Plum in the Golden Vase (Jin Ping Mei), 92
Poetry, 49, 63–64, 70; by women, 75
Political systems: Bronze Age, 10; Buddhism
    and, 45; Mandate of Heaven and, 14
Polo, Marco, 82
Population growth, xiv, 78, 101, 155; Han
    dynasty, 32, 36; Ming dynasty, 90, 91;
    one-child policy and, 151–52; Tang
    dynasty, 62
Porcelain, 79, 88, 90–91
Portuguese traders, 91, 102
Precepts for My Daughters (Ban Zhao),
    34–35
Price inflation, 134
Printing, 73
Publishing, 92. See also Books; specific title
Pure Land Buddhism, 56
Puyi, Henry (Xuantong Emperor, Qing),
    114, 128

Qi, state of, 21
Qianlong Emperor (Qing), 99–100, 101,
    102–3
Qian Qianyi, 94
Qin dynasty, 11, 13, 18, 20–25; rebellion
    ending, 24
Qin Shi Huangdi, 21–24
Qing dynasty, 89, 95–106; Boxer Rebellion
    in, 111, 112, 113; British trade mission
    and, 102–3; imperial style, 97–100,
    101; Japanese aggression and, 108, 109;
    literature of, 100–101; Opium War,
    105–6; reform attempts in, 108, 110,
    111, 112, 113; Taiping Rebellion and,
    106–7
"Qingming Festival Along the River," 76–77
Qin Gui, 71, 72
Qiu Jin, 114
Quanzhou, 78
Quotations of Chairman Mao, 142

Rebellion and revolt, 30, 48, 60, 61, 62;
    Boxer, 111, 112; peasant, 95, 97, 101;
    Taiping, 106–7; Wuchang, 114–15; Yuan
    dynasty, 85
Rebirth (reincarnation), 42, 43, 56, 81
Records of the Grand Historian (Sima
    Qian), 29–30

Red Army, 126–28, 131. *See also* People's Liberation Army
Red Guards, 142–44
Red Turban movement, 85–86
Reforms, 47–48, 110–11, 112–13; of Deng Xiaoping, 146, 148; Ming dynasty, 94–95; Qing dynasty, 97, 99, 108; of Wang Anshi, 69–70, 73
Revolts. *See* Rebellion and revolt
Rice cultivation, 1, xiv–xv, 38–39, 70, 75–76
Roads and highways, 22
The Romance of the Three Kingdoms, 37, 92, 127
Roman Empire, 36
Romantic love, 147
Ruan Ji, 41
Ruizong Emperor (Tang), 59
Russian revolution, 119–20. *See also* Soviet Union

Sacrifice. *See* Human sacrifice
Sage-kings, 2, 100
Scholar-officials, 18, 29, 40, 41; courtesans and, 93, 94; Han dynasty, 31; Manchu rule and, 97, 98, 100; Ming dynasty, 86–87, 90, 91, 92, 94, 95; purge of, 35, 87, 95; rivalry with palace eunuchs, 90, 95; Song dynasty, 6, 70, 73, 75, 80; Yuan dynasty, 83. *See also* Bureaucracy
Seven Sages of the Bamboo Grove, 40–41
Shang, Lord, 20
Shang dynasty, 2–9; bronze technology of, xi, 3, 4, 5, 8; oracle bones, 3, 6, 8, 10; writing in, 7–8
Shanghai, 121, 142, 151
Shenzong Emperor (Song), 69, 70
Shi Huangdi, Emperor of Qin, 21, 22–23, 24
Shizu Emperor (Yuan), 81. *See also* Khubilai Khan.
Shu Han dynasty, 37
Shun, "sage-king," 2
Silk production, 39
Silk Roads, 66; Central Asia and, 28–29, 31, 53, 55, 56, 61, 66
Silver, as medium of exchange, 90–91, 94, 95; opium trade and, 102, 103
Sima Qian, 18, 29–30, 31, 33
Sino-Indian trade. *See* Indian trade
Slaves, sacrifice of, 6–7
Social hierarchy, 38, 50, 54, 120; Bronze Age, 8, 10; Confucianism and, 13–14, 31; Han dynasty, 30–31. *See also* Aristocracy
Song dynasty, 67–82; economy of, 75–78, 79; iron industry in, 76–78, 82; Mongol threat to, 80–81; Neo-Confucianism in, 73; nomadic groups and, 68; scholar-officials of, 68, 70, 71, 73, 80; Southern Song, 71, 78, 79, 81, 84

Song Huizong Emperor, 70–71
Song Jiaoren, 115, 116
Song Taizu Emperor, 67, 68
Son of Heaven, emperor as, 83, 86, 102. *See also* Mandate of Heaven; *specific emperor*
Soong, T. V., 123
Soong family, 122–23
Soong Meiling, 122–23
Southeast Asia, 62, 78, 91
Southern Song dynasty, 71, 78, 79, 81–82, 84
Soviet Union, 133, 136, 139, 140, 144
Spain, 91, 102, 109–10
Spice trade, 61
The Spring and Autumn Annals, 11
Stalin, Joseph, 122, 138, 140
Standardization, by Qin empire, 22
Stilwell, George, 133
Stirrups, for horses, 37, 80
The Story of the Stone (Cao Xueqin), 100–101
Student protests, in Beijing, 117–18, 148, 149–50
Su Dongpo (Su Shi), 70, 73
Suffering *(dukkha),* 42
Sui, Duke of, 50
Sui dynasty, 48, 49, 50–51, 53
Sui Wendi Emperor, 49, 51, 53
Sun Quan, 37
Sun Yat-sen, 113–15, 116, 119, 120, 121
Sunzi, 16; *The Art of War,* 12, 127
Suzong, Emperor (Tang), 61

Taiping Rebellion, 106–7
Taiwan, 40, 91, 97, 108; Nationalists in, 134, 136, 153
Tang dynasty, 52–66; art of, 64; Buddhism in, 45, 46, 54–57, 65; legal code, 54; philosopher-kings of, 59; poetry of, 63–64; powerful women in, 57–59, 75; rebellions ending, 59–61, 62, 67
Tang Gaozong, Emperor, 57, 58
Tang Taizong, Emperor, 53–54, 57
Tanguts, 68–69
Tan Sitong, 110
Tantric Buddhism, 43
Tarim Basin, 9
Tawney, R. H., 126
Taxation, 20, 45, 48, 69, 123; Ming era reform, 94–95; Qing era reform, 97, 99; Song dynasty, 75; Sui dynasty, 51, 52; Tang dynasty, 54, 61
Tea trade, 62, 103
Temuchin (Genghis Khan), 79–80
Theravada Buddhism, 42–43, 44
Three Hundred Tang Poems, 63
Three Kingdoms era, 37–38
Tiananmen Square demonstrations, 144, 149–50

The
New
Oxford
World
History